CATERING MANAGEMENT PRACTICES

Edited by

Jyoti S. Sharma

AKANSHA PUBLISHING HOUSE

NEW DELHI - 110 002 (INDIA)

AKANSHA PUBLISHING HOUSE
4649/21-B, Ansari Road
Daryaganj, New Delhi - 110 002
Phones: 23263193, 9811582579
E-mail: ektabooks@yahoo.com

Catering Management Practices

First Published, 2006
ISBN 81-8370-067-5

PRINTED IN INDIA
Published by M.P. Misra for Akansha Publishing House, New Delhi
and Printed at Aryan Enterprises, Delhi

Contents

Preface

> Be unselfish. That is the first and final commandment for those who would be useful, and happy in their usefulness. If you think of yourself only, you cannot develop because you are choking the sources of development, which is spiritual expansion through thought for others.
>
> —*Dr. Charles W. Eliot*

Food is the most basic necessity of every living being besides air and water. As such the tradition of catering (i.e. cooking) is as old as the history of man. With the passage of time, out from home it became significant part of hotel, hospitality and tourism industries. There is no exaggeration in saying that catering is the heart of hospitality and social life of man.

As an academic discipline, catering is taught in different courses of home science, food science and technology and hotel and tourism management. Catering is a perfect art and science. The success of many modern commercial ventures, social life and events at regional, national or international level rests upon efficient catering management. Even the very survival of man and a happy and healthy life heavily depend on catering. Hence, it is a multidisciplinary subject encompassing, business and management, health and nutrition, medicine etc. within its fold.

The present volume is a modest attempt in the direction of presenting valuable information on catering management, which is flourishing industry. Only most relevant aspects are taken for elaborate discussion.

The main topics included herein are—Cooking Technology: An Introduction; Food Stuff: Selection & Preparation; Kitchen Management; Spices: Types and Utility; The World of Delicacies; Kitchen Equipments; Preparing Some Popular Foods; and The Beverages. A glossary of most relevant terms is also appended. Definitely, the learner, i.e. trainees, trainers and all professionals in the field will find this most useful and informative.

In fact, the information contained herein is gathered from various sources—all secondary, e.g. books, abstracts, magazines and newspapers, contributed by leading practitioners in India and abroad. We owe a deep sense of gratitude to them all for borrowing the results of their empirical works. All credit for this ought go to the original contributors. We are equally grateful to those also who made available the requisite information. We express our thankfulness to many friends, colleagues and well wishers for their inspiration, encouragement and assistance. We are thankful to our publishers also for materializing this venture elegantly in the present shape.

Comments suggestions, and constructive criticism from different quarters are welcome which will help us enhance the quality and utility of the work.

—Editor

1

Cooking Technology: An Introduction

"Unless your cask is perfectly clean, whatever you pour in it turns sour."

—*Horace*

Basically, to prepare food by the action of heat, as by boiling, baking; or (of food) to be come ready for eating through such a process is called cooking. In fact, this is application of physical and chemical methods of processing foods from the time of harvest, slaughter or catch, during storage and till the time of consumption.

The main objectives of such processing (i.e. cooking) are: (1) Improving aesthetic quality leading to better acceptability. (2) Enhancing nutritive value. (3) Avoiding deteriorative changes.

Why Cooking Needed?

1. Practically, cooking partly sterilizes food. Above 40°C (104°F) the growth of bacteria falls off rapidly and in general it ceases above 45°C (113°F). Non-sporing bacteria are killed at item apertures above 60°C (140°F) for varying periods of time, e.g., to make milk safe, it is pasteurized at 63°C (145°F) for 30 minutes or at 72°C (161°F) for 15 seconds. Boiling kills living cells, with the exception of spores, in a few seconds. Spore- bearing bacteria take about 4 to 5 hours of boiling to be destroyed. To destroy them in a shorter period of time higher temperatures must be used.

2. Also, Cooking helps make food more digestible. Complex foods are often split into simpler substances during cooking. This helps the body to absorb and utilize the food more readily.
3. Cooking enhances palatability.
4. Cooking makes food more attractive in appearance and, therefore, more appetizing.
5. Cooking introduces variety. Various types of dishes can be prepared using the same ingredient.
6. Cooking helps provide a balanced meal. Different ingredients combined together in one dish make it easier to provide a balanced and nutritious food.

Materials Needed

Different raw materials are used in cooking to produce a complete dish. Each ingredient in a dish has a special part to play and a knowledge of what each food does is necessary to understand cooking thoroughly. Grouping the foods according to their use, makes it possible to remember the facts better. The materials are thus classified according to the part they play in making up a dish. The following is a classification of raw materials.

1. Foundation ingredient;
2. Raising agents;
3. Fats and oils;
4. Eggs;
5. Salt;
6. Liquid;
7. Flavourings and seasonings;
8. Sweetening agents; and
9. Thickening agents;
10. Preservatives etc.

Foundation Ingredient: Almost every dish has a foundation ingredient on which the other ingredients are based. The foundation ingredient can be a liquid or a solid, e.g., flour in bread, meat in roast, milk or stock in soups. When examining a recipe for proportions, all foods which serve the same purpose should be reckoned together. It is not only necessary to know the proportions of various ingredients but also the composition of the different ingredients and the action of heat on these. Heat may not affect the whole material but only certain constituents.

Basically Food is composed of the following major constituents:

(i) Carbohydrates; (ii) Fats and oils; (iii) Proteins; (iv) Minerals and (v) Vitamins.

Effect of Heat on Protein: Protein coagulates or sets when heated. The white of an egg is a good example. The coagulation process helps in keeping the nourishment within the food; it is sealed in by the formation of a coat on the outside. Hence, when boiling protein foods such as meat and fish, put them in hot water. When roasting meat, put it in an oven which is at a fairly high temperature, and then reduce the heat. Another action of heat on meat is the softening of the muscle fibres. Normal cooking methods cause the elastin in the connective tissue to shrink, and the collagen is converted into gelatin by heat in the presence of water, and as a result the muscle fibres separate and meat becomes tender. This is done more satisfactorily at a medium temperature than at a high temperature. Meat also shrinks during cooking. The higher the temperature the greater the shrinkage. Cooking at medium temperatures renders protein foods more digestible. The myoglobin in the muscle tissues and haemoglobin in the capillaries give meat its red colour. Both these decompose on heating causing the brown colour which is generally found in cooked meat. The change takes place at a temperature of 65°C (149°F). At high temperatures the protein itself gets denatured thus making it less nutritive.

Action of Heat on Carbohydrates: Generally starch swells up and becomes softer. Starch is enclosed within granules. These starch granules cannot be easily digested but heating makes them swell up and then burst and release the starch. Starch itself becomes gelatinized. Sugar is changed into invert sugar (by a process where sucrose is broken down into glucose and fructose) when heated with fruit juices or other weak acids. In the presence of invert sugar, the solubility of sucrose is increased, and it tends to recrystallize more slowly. Inversion raises the boiling point and lowers the freezing point of a sugar solution. Invert sugar is slightly more easily digested and absorbed.

When sugar is boiled it passes through regular stages till it becomes caramelized at 163°C (325°F).

The following are the stages thorough which it passes:

	°C	°F
Small thread	102°C	216°F
Large thread	103°C	218°F
Pearl	106°C	222°F
Soft ball	114°C	237°F
Hard ball	120°C	247°F
Soft crack	143°C	290°F
Hard crack	156°C	312°F
Caramel	163°C to 177°C	325°F to 350°F

Action of Heat on Fats: Fat melts when it comes in contact with heat. At high temperatures fats decompose into fatty acids and acrolein. Darkening of fat is caused by cooking at high temperatures and also by the presence of carbonized bread crumbs and small particles of cooked food. The temperature at which decomposition sets in, when an amount of fat is heated, is known as its smoke point. The specific temperature at which this takes place varies with different fats and is lowered by repeated heating.

With repeated use, fat deteriorates, because of excessive temperature, moisture, air and the presence of carbonized crumbs and small pieces of food, to a point where it will just bubble in the pan, too weak to perform the function of frying. Abnormal absorption caused by frying for too long at too low a temperature also contributes to the breakdown. Fat also begins to thicken and become gummy.

Action of Heat on Vitamins: Vitamin C is the only vitamin which becomes unstable when heated, although careful cooking helps to retain some of it. Vitamin A and D are not destroyed by ordinary methods of cooking. Vitamin B may be destroyed during cooking if cooked at high temperatures, e.g., baking of biscuits and manufacture of breakfast cereals, by the addition of baking soda, or away.

Action of Heat on Minerals: There is no appreciable loss of minerals due to cooking, excepting when cooking liquor is thrown out. Some minerals are made readily available by cooking.

Fats and Oils: Normally, fats are solid at normal temperatures and melt when heated. Those used in cooking are butter, margarine, lard, suet, dripping and hydrogenated fat. Oils are liquid at normal temperatures but solidify at lower temperatures. The commonly used cooking oils are coconut oil, sesame oil, cotton-seed oil, olive oil, peanut oil, mustard oil, corn oil, and sunflower oil.

Hydrogenation of Oils: Whale oil, cottonseed oil, soya bean oil, peanut oil, etc., are sold as shortenings of varying consistencies. The conversion of oil into fat is brought about by a process known as hydrogenation. This consists of treating oil under pressure and at a suitable temperature with hydrogen, in the presence of a catalyst, usually nickel.

Under these conditions the unsaturated fatty acids present in the oil combine with the hydrogen. This chemical process brings about a physical change, the liquid oil becoming a solid fat. The unsaturated fatty acids are chiefly those of the oleic type but when hydrogenated, are converted into stearic acid which is solid. The varying consistencies are due to the process of hydrogenation being stopped at different stages.

Fats are used in cooking either as shortening agents or as frying media. Fats are used in confectionery to enrich the food and to impart to them shortening qualities. Collectively they are referred to as shortening agents. Their effect is to break down or destroy the toughness of gluten, so that instead of being hard and tough to eat, foods containing fat break off short and readily melt in the mouth.

The factors to look for in shortenings are:

(i) *Shortening Value:* The shortness or shortening power it gives to the result. Shortness is necessary for the baking of biscuits, cookies, wafers and pastries.

(ii) *Creaming Value:* This affects the cake volume.

(iii) *Stability:* Its keeping quality. If the stability is not good, the keeping quality of the product will be decreased.

(iv) *Water Absorption Power:* Correlated to emulsification value of shortening.

(v) *Consistency:* Hardness or softness depending on the purpose, e.g. hardness is needed for puff pastry, softness for cake-making.

Fats as shortening agents add to the nutritional and satiety values of flour mixtures and contribute to their characteristic flavour and texture. The type of fat and the way in which fat is incorporated affect the texture, as in short crust pastry, flaky pastry and puff pastry. As heat melts fat, cooking must be done at the correct temperatures so that the flour can absorb the fat as it melts. If the heat is insufficient, the fat runs out of the mixture and is wasted, besides leaving the food tough and dry. Fat which has been broken up into very fine particles, as in creaming, is more easily absorbed than fat left in large pieces. In general, the richer the pastry the hotter the over, and the richer the cake the cooler the over.

Generally, the richer the pastry the hotter the oven, and the richer the cake the cooler the oven. Fat as a frying medium functions in three ways. It serves to transfer heat to the articles to be fried, it adds to the nutritive value of the food and it contributes to the flavour of the food. Fat used as a frying medium should have a high smoke point, low congealing point, low moisture content, high stability and acceptable flavour.

Rendering of Fat: Rendering of fat is the process of melting to extract fat from fatty tissues. A good supply of dripping can be obtained by rendering down suet (fat surrounding the kidney of a cow or sheep) and pieces of fat from meat. This can be done in two ways:

1. Cut the fat into small pieces and place in a baking tin in a slow oven until the fat has melted and there are only crisp brown pieces of tissue left. Strain through a fine cloth into a clean basin pressing the tissues to squeeze out all fat.
2. Cut the pieces of fat as for above method. Place in a pan without a lid and with very little water. Boil until the water has evaporated and then heat very gently until the fat melts and leaves only crisp brown pieces of tissue. Strain as before.

Clarification: This is a method of cleaning used fat. For this process, put fat in a pan with enough water to cover it. Bring to boil without covering. Strain and cool. Lift off the cake of fat floating on top, turn it upside down and scrape off any foreign particles sticking to the bottom.

Some Major Types of Fats and Oils

Fat/Oil	**Margarine**
Source	Groundnuts; palm, coconut and fish oils, milk whey.
Properties	Not easy to spread when chilled. Distinctive flavour not to everyone's taste.
Uses	As above but not used for its flavour. Economical for baking.
Fat/Oil	**Butter**
Source	Cream
Properties	Salted or unsalted. Difficult to handle when chilled, unique flavour and enriching qualities.
Uses	Not suitable for deep frying. For shallow frying, add 1 table spoon oil to raise smoking point.
Fat/Oil	**Soft-blend margarine**
Source	As above
Properties	Will spread when chilled.
Uses	Excellent for all-in-one cake and pastry making.
Fat/Oil	**Low-fat spread**
Source	Blended vegetable oils.
Properties	Half the calories of butter, less fattening than margarine.
Uses	Can be used for most baking, but not for pastry.
Fat/Oil	**Cholesterol-free spread**
Source	Vegetable oils.
Properties	Spreads when chilled.
Uses	As above.
Fat/Oil	**Aerated white vegetable fat**
Source	Blended vegetable oils.
Properties	More flavour than lard. Easy-to-mix, creamy texture.
Uses	Can be used for most purposes, but rather expensive for deep frying. Excellent for fork-mix pastry.
Fat/Oil	**Lard**
Source	Pork
Properties	White solid fat, very economical.
Uses	Good for short-crust pastry when combined with margarine. Does not cream with sugar. Good for shallow frying.

Fat/Oil	**Corn oil**
Source	Corn.
Uses	Suitable for all purposes, especially deep frying.
Fat/Oil	**Sunflower oil**
Source	Sunflower seeds.
Uses	As above.
Fat/Oil	**Sesame and almond oils**
Source	Sesame seeds, bitter almonds All purposes.
Properties	Delicate flavour.
Uses	All purposes.
Fat/Oil	**Suet**
Source	Lamb or beef.
Properties	Hard white fat. Available shredded or solid.
Uses	Best used for suet pastry, pudding and stuffing.
Fat/Oil	**Spreading blend**
Source	Buttermilk, butter oil, vegetable oil.
Properties	A mixture of butter and margarine. Low fat content. Just over half the calories of butter. Slight butter flavour. Spreads when chilled.
Uses	Suitable for all cooking, except frying. Baking results acceptable. Do not use for pastry.
Fat/Oil	**Olive oil**
Source	Olives.
Properties	Distinctive flavour.
Uses	Suitable for most purposes, but not for deep frying.
Fat/Oil	**Solid vegetable oil**
Source	Palms.
Properties	Suitable for all purposes, except dressings because it solidifies when cold.
Fat/Oil	**Soya bean oil**
Source	Soya beans.
Properties	Distinctive flavour.
Uses	Suitable for all purposes, but not ideal for dressings. Low shelf life.
Fat/Oil	**Coconut oil**

Source	Coconuts.
Properties	Strong aroma and flavour.
Uses	Used mainly in Kerala.
Fat/Oil	**Soft-blend margarine oil**
Source	Groundnuts.
Properties	Distinctive flavour.
Uses	Suitable for all purposes.
Fat/Oil	**Blended oil**
Source	Vegetable and animal oils.
Uses	Can be used for the same purposes as corn oil but needs straining after use if it is to be refused for deep frying.

Raising Agents: Generally, a raising agent is used to puff up the food so that it spreads and rises, thus making it light instead of close and heavy. The tiny air spaces caused by the raising agents are retained during the process of cooking. The leavening of the flour mixture is accomplished by the expansion of incorporated air and by the internal production and expansion of water vapour and carbon dioxide.

When the product is heated, the air expands and part of the water vapourizes. The formation of carbon dioxide requires the presence of suitable micro-organisms or chemical agents. During the first part of heating, gas production is accelerated and the gas formed expands as the temperature rises. Gluten, a substance found in flour, develops when moisture is added, and helps to keep the raising agent within until the food sets, thus helping to make the food light. Gluten is a sticky, elastic substance which stretches as the air or gas expands and prevents these from escaping. The air or gas trapped in the mixture expands further when heated and makes the cooked food light. Too much raising agent raises the food too rapidly, breaks the surface and allows the gas produced to escape.

Baking powders are mixtures of sodium bicarbonate

with some suitable acid such as cream of tartar, diluted with corn-flour to give a product the desired strength. The cornflour also serves to separate the acid and the base, thereby increasing the stability of the mixture during shelf life. General proportions used are 1-2 tsp baking powder per 450 gm of foundation. The richer the mixture, the less the baking powder required. When the mixture is of an acidic nature, (as when sour milk, buttermilk, treacle, vinegar or jams made from acid fruits are used) the addition of cream of tartar or tartaric acid is not necessary, since the soda will act upon these other foods and cause the required gas to be given off. Four tsp baking powder is equal to approximately one tsp of soda in a carbon dioxide yield. In certain flour mixtures variations from neutrality are deliberately sought by including a reaction with either soda or cream of tartar, e.g., to get the dark, rich colour in chocolate cakes which many people prefer, sodium bicarbonate is used.

(i) Chemicals: Chemicals such as sodium bicarbonate, cream of tartar, baking powder, ammonium carbonate, etc., are added to mixtures to make food light. In each case the result is the production of carbon dioxide.

(ii) Air: Air is incorporated by sifting flour, by creaming shortening, by beating eggs or by beating the mixture itself.

(iii) Water Vapour: Water vapour is formed in quantities sufficient to raise the mixture when liquid and flour are in equal volumes.

(iv) Addition of Yeast: Carbon dioxide is produced either from sugar by yeast, or from a carbonate, usually sodium bicarbonate, by action of an acid. Yeast also produces enzymes which are able to split disaccharide sugars. Yeast consists of microscopic, unicellular plants which are capable of rapid multiplication when conditions are favourable

and which obtain energy by breaking down sugars to carbon dioxide and alcohol. This process is known as fermentation, and is brought about by the enzyme zymase found in yeast.

Activated Dry Yeast: This develops more rapidly than dried yeast and is the type now available. It can be used in straight dough mixing. It is less perishable than compressed yeast. The shelf life of both dried yeast and activated dried yeast is longer at refrigerated temperatures than at room temperature.

Dried Yeast: This is a mixture of yeast and corn-flour or cornmeal pressed into cakes and dried. The yeast continues to live but in an inactive state. When furnished with warmth and moisture, it begins to develop and multiply, but this process is slow. Dried yeast has to be soaked in lukewarm water and mixed with very soft dough (sponge) for a preliminary period of development before all the other ingredients are added.

Compressed Yeast: This is a moist mixture of yeast plants and starch. The yeast remains active and will grow and multiply rapidly when added to dough. It has to be kept at refrigerated temperatures and keeps well for only a few days. If held in the freezing compartment, it retains its activity for a longer period.

Eggs: Although hens' eggs are the most popular, eggs of turkeys, guinea fowls, ducks and geese are also used. Eggs are used in various forms in cooking:

1. As a leavening by foam formation to make the dish light, as in souffles or meringues.
2. For binding, as in egg croquettes.
3. To improve flavour and colour, as in cakes.
4. To add to the nutritive value:
   (a) The protein of eggs is unexcelled in quality,

and is used as a standard against which other food proteins are measured.

(b) *Eggs* make a substantial contribution of vitamins A and D and also contain a small amount of B complex vitamins and minerals.

(c) The essential fatty acids are more finely emulsified in eggs than in any other food thus assuring easy, complete digestibility and ready utilisation.

5. To decorate and garnish dishes.
6. To enrich a mixture as in the case of rich cakes.
7. As a thickening, as in custards and cooked salad dressings.
8. For emulsification, as in mayonnaise sauce.
9. As a nourishing and easily digestible food for invalids.
10. For coating, as in fried foods.
11. As a quick-cooking and nourishing dish for breakfast or main meals.
12. As the first semisolid food taken by infants.

Both yolks and whites of eggs coagulate when heated. The temperature at which coagulation begins, the rate of coagulation and the firmness of the gel will depend on:

(a) Intensity of heat,

(b) Length of heating period,

(c) The presence of added material such as water, milk, sugar and salt.

Practically, Acid and salt speed up the process of coagulation, e.g., to prevent disintegration of eggs when poaching, vinegar and salt are added.

Notably, sugar increases the temperature at which coagulation takes place. When eggs are diluted by adding milk or water, the coagulation temperature is raised. If water is added instead of milk, coagulation results in a flocculent rather than a gelled structure.

An undiluted whole egg begins to coagulate at 57°-66°C (135°-150°F) and to gel at 70°-74°C (158°-165°F). The white of the egg alone starts coagulating at 58°-62°C (136°-144°F) and begins to gel at 62°-70°C (144°-158°F). In all cases, the higher the cooking temperature, the more rapid the coagulation and the firmer the gel. Changes associated with the cooking of eggs can however, be produced at temperatures much below boiling, by a longer heating period.

The egg that is cooked for a longer period at a lower temperature is superior in nutritive value, as well as in flavour, to an egg cooked at a higher temperature for a shorter period. The blue ring round the yolk of an egg, sometimes found in a hard-boiled egg, is due to the formation of ferrous sulphide. This is brought about by the union of iron released from the yolk of the egg and hydrogen sulphide from the white, which in turn is released from sulphur found in the white. The amount of such discolouration depends on time and temperature of cooking, and the age of the egg. Cooking for 30 minutes in water at 85°C (185°F) followed by rapid cooling, gives very little discolouration. Eggs which are six weeks or more old discolour rapidly. In any case, boiled eggs used for stuffing, garnishing etc., should be cooled quickly after boiling, after cracking or without cracking.

Fresh Eggs: The shell of an egg may be either brown or white depending upon the breed of hen producing it. But, irrespective of colour, the shell of a fresh egg always has a delicate velvety appearance, called "bloom", that is due to the protective mucous coating which the shell has when the egg is laid. The inner air cell of a fresh egg is small. The contents when broken out from the shell show an upstanding, well-rounded yolk covered with a clinging layer of thick egg white, which, in turn is surrounded by a relatively smaller amount of thin egg white. The yolk may be either golden or light yellow, depending upon the amount of carotenoid pigments contained in it, and the white is practically colourless or possibly slightly opalescent. There is no adore other than that characteristic of eggs, and when cooked, the flavour will be excellent.

Deterioration of Eggs: As soon as the egg is laid, changes begin to take place which, if not checked by suitable storage conditions, result in undesirable deterioration. The following are the identification marks of deterioration.

Shell: With deterioration, the mucous protective covering of the shell soon disappears, leaving the shell shiny and more porous, so that moisture and carbon dioxide can pass more easily through it from the egg contents. This causes a loss in weight of the egg, a contraction of egg contents, and a resulting enlargement of the air space between the two membranous linings of the shell.

Egg White: Accompanying the loss of carbon dioxide through the shell, the reaction of the egg contents, especially of the egg white, changes from nearly neutral in the fresh white, to alkaline, becoming progressively more alkaline as the egg ages. It should be said, however, that factors other than the loss of carbon dioxide may be responsible for the increase in this alkalinity. As egg deterioration progresses, the thick white gradually loses its firm, jelly-like consistency and decreases in volume, while the volume of thin egg white increases. These changes continue until the entire white portion becomes watery and drains away from the yolk when the egg is broken out of the shell. The cause of this change in thick egg white is not, at the present time, entirely clear, although various reasons have been advanced to account for it.

Egg Yolk: Upon aging, the yolk of the egg also becomes

more liquid and enlarges as water passes into it from the white through the enveloping vitellin membrane. As a result, the increasing volume of the yolk stretches the surrounding membrane and weakens it so that, in the broken-out egg, the yolk is no longer upstanding and well-rounded, but instead becomes wide and flat. Indeed, with continued aging, the membrane which encloses the yolk may become so weakened that it breaks when the egg is opened, and, as a consequence, the white and yolk cannot be separated from each other.

Substances with Off-odours: Finally, in aging eggs certain chemical reactions occur among the various egg components which yield compounds that impart characteristic and familiar off-odours and flavours; and if these reactions continue long enough, such eggs become inedible.

Among the compounds that are made from these reactions is the foul-smelling, gaseous substance, hydrogen sulphide. When eggs are heated for some time, as when hard-boiling them in the shell, this gas, formed chiefly in egg white, passes through the vitellin membrane and reacts with iron compounds in outer yolk areas to form ferrous sulphide which can be seen as a black, film-like deposit enveloping the yellow, hard-boiled yolk. Although this film can be encountered to a certain extent in a fresh egg, its formation can be largely avoided--if the aging of the egg has not been carried too far-- by taking care not to prolong the cooking period unnecessarily, and by being careful to use the hard-boiled egg immediately.

Boiling Eggs: Put enough water into a pan to cover the egg and bring it to the boil. Lower the egg into the water with a metal spoon.

(i) Duck's eggs must be boiled for not less than 14 minutes.

(ii) Reduce the heat and cook gently for 3-4 minutes for a lightly cooked egg. For a moderately soft egg, allow 4-5 minutes. For a hard-boiled egg, allow 10 minutes.

(iii) Put the hard-boiled egg into cold water and leave to cool to prevent the formation of dark rings round the yolk.

Salt: Salt, although used in small quantities, is an essential ingredient for both sweet and savoury dishes. Salt helps to bring out the flavour of other ingredients. If too much is added, food becomes inedible, and too little makes food insipid. Gauging the right amount to be added is learned by experience.

Salt adds to the nutritive value of food by providing an essential mineral, sodium chloride. Salt has physical effects on the gluten of flour. In reasonable quantities it strengthens gluten and increases its resistance to the softening effects of fermentation. Too much salt on the other hand will remove the power of gluten to hold gas. Salt also acts as a preservative; it speeds up coagulation of eggs and lowers the freezing point of food.

Liquid: Liquid is necessary to bind dry ingredients together, to dilute food, to act as a cooking medium and to thin down a gravy or sauce. Milk, water, stock and fruit juices are the most commonly used liquids. Eggs may be used for binding. When too little liquid is added, the food does not get cooked, or as in the case of cakes, it retards the action of raising agents, resulting in a hard, heavy cake. Gravies or soup containing insufficient liquid are 'stodgy'. Too much liquid results in a watery product, or, as in the case of cakes and puddings, makes them soggy.

Flavourings and Seasonings: The taste and acceptability of food depends to a very great extent on the correct amounts of flavourings and seasonings. These are variable ingredients and the types and amounts necessary for different dishes must be carefully studied. To add just enough and no more should be the aim of every cook.

Those which combine taste and smell such as essences, cardamom, nutmeg, basil, thyme, etc., are called flavourings. Those which only enhance taste are seasonings, e.g., red chillies, mustard, pepper, etc.

Sweetening Agents: These are not as necessary as salt. Their lack will not affect the texture of the food or the lightness of a dish. A bad cook generally adds too much sweetening to cover other faults.

The following are the major types of sweetenings generally used:

(i) Sugar,
(ii) Treacle,
(iii) Syrups such as golden syrup, etc.
(iv) Molasses or Jaggery,
(v) Jams,
(vi) Honey,
(vii) Fruit juices.

If too much sweetening is used, food becomes cloying and if too little is used, sweet dishes become tasteless.

Sugar	
Type	Granulated sugar (white)
Description	Refined sugar medium-size.
Uses	All-purpose but for many tasks another type may be better or quicker.
Type	Castor sugar
Description	Refined white sugar with the smallest crystals.
Uses	Because it dissolves quickly it is especially good for cake-making, whisked sponges and sauces. Best for caramels and syrups.

Type	Icing sugar
Description	Made from sugar--relatively large crystals ground to a fine powder. Contains a small percentage of calcium phosphate to prevent clogging.
Uses	Finest and smoothest of all sugars. Best for icing for cake decorations, for meringues and for sprinkling and coating. Sometimes takes on a slight greyish tinge if sieved through a metal sieve or if a metal spoon is used.
Type	Preserving sugar
Description	Refined white sugar--relatively large crystals, makes it ideal for preserving.
Uses	Dissolves slowly and does not clog bottom of pan or form as much scum as granulated sugar when used for preserving. Can also be used (coloured) to decorate cakes and breads.

Thickening Agents: Thin foods such as milk, soups, gravies, curries, etc., are often improved by the addition of a thickening agent. The thickening used also increases the nutritive value.

Starchy foods and eggs are commonly used as thickening but sugar will thicken a syrup, and gelatin will set a thin liquid if chilled. Ground onion, coconut and poppy-seeds are used for thickening curries in Indian cookery.

Role of Weighing and Measuring

This is a very important aspect of cookery, particularly for bulk of food production. To obtain a standard product with a standard yield, as is essential for commercial foods, weighing and measuring must be done accurately. A set of scales, measuring jugs, and standard measuring cups and spoons must be provided in every kitchen. The scales should denote both grams and ounces and the measuring jug both liters and pints. Weighing is more accurate than measuring but for expediency, measuring can be used. When measuring, it is better to use level measurements, as this is less subject to error. Spoons and cups vary greatly in size.

Ingredients Preparation

Solid foods which are to be mixed have to be reduced into sizes which will allow them to combine readily. A certain amount of preparation is thus necessary.

Washing: This is done to remove superficial dirt. Wash vegetables, meat and fish in cold water before any preparation is done. If they are soaked for a long period or washed after cutting there is greater loss of water soluble minerals and vitamins.

Peeling and scraping: Spoilt, soiled and inedible portions are removed. Skins of vegetables like potatoes, carrots, etc., or of fruits, are removed by either peeling or scraping. When peeling, remove as little of the fleshy part as possible.

Paring: Remove surface layers by cutting as in paring an apple. A circular motion is used.

Cutting: Reducing to small parts by means of a knife or scissors. When the reduction is done by a chopping knife or a food chopper it is known as chopping. Cutting into even-sized cubes is called dicing. Cutting into very fine pieces is mincing. Shredding is cutting into fine long pieces with a knife or shredder. Slicing is also cutting into thin long pieces, but these are not as fine as in shredding.

Grating: Reducing to fine particles by rubbing over a rough, sharp surface.

Grinding: Reducing to small fragments by crushing in a mill, a grinding stone or an osterizer.

Mashing: This is a method of breaking up soft foods such as cooked potatoes or vegetables.

Milling: used for cereals, to remove husks, etc.

Sieving: Passing through a mesh to remove impurities, to break down to even portions, or to enclose air.

Steeping: Extracting colouring and flavouring by allowing ingredients to stand in water generally at a temperature just below boiling point.

Centrifuging: Promotion of separation through the application of a whirling force, e.g., separating cream from milk.

Emulsification: Blending one liquid with another in which it is insoluble, e.g., oil and egg yolk in mayonnaise.

Evaporation: Removal of excess moisture by heating.

Homogenization: Subdivision of large drops into smaller ones by forcing them through a small opening under great pressure, e.g., fat in cream.

Mixing Procedure

Beating: This method can be used with thin mixtures or liquids. This should be done carefully with the aim of enclosing air. This term is used synonymously with whipping, e.g., beating of eggs.

Blending: Mixing two or more ingredients thoroughly.

Cutting: In Usually the incorporation of fat in flour and other sifted ingredients with a knife. This method produces a relatively coarse division of the fat and does not result in blending, e.g., cutting fat into pastry mixture.

Folding: Mixing by a careful lifting and dropping motion. The edge of the spoon is used and the mixture is lifted, turned completely and gently replaced. All the movements in this method, though deft, should be so gentle that the different ingredients are almost coaxed together,

Kneading: Manipulating by alternating pressure with folding and stretching. The food is pressed with the knuckles.

The dough is brought from the outside of the bowl or basin to the centre and at the same time the bowl is moved so that a different section is kneaded each time. This ensures a thorough distribution of ingredients, e.g., bread dough, chapati dough, etc.

Creaming: Softening of fat by friction with a wooden spoon, generally followed by the gradual incorporation of sugar as in cake making.

Pressing: This is done to shape foods like cutlets and sometimes as a method of subdivision to separate liquids from solids by weights or mechanical pressure, as for paneer.

Rolling: In Rolling butter or fat in a soft dough, e.g., puff pastry.

Stirring: Mixing foods with a suitable tool such as a spoon by a circular motion in contact with the pan. Generally this is a gentle movement but is changed to suit different dishes, as when used to prevent sticking or burning in hallways and toffees. If used too vigorously, it tends to drive out air or other gas previously enclosed as raising agent.

Rubbing: In Rubbing fat into flour using the tips of the fingers and thumb and lifting the hand out of the basin as in the case of short crust pastry. Rub until the mixture looks like bread crumbs.

Texture: Texture is the term used to describe the characteristics of a finished food product. The order in which the ingredients are added, the way of mixing and the method of cooking affect the resulting product. A good cook should not only be able to distinguish between one texture and another but also be able to produce what he or she wants. Only by observation, experience and perseverance will a person be able to know what the correct texture of a particular product should be. A brief description of some commonly found textures and their correct occurrence is given below, but it must also be borne in mind that the difference between one texture and another is very fine.

Firm and Close: The air bubbles made by the raising agents are many but small, and the mixture is not in the least spongy. The fat included prevents the mixture from being too hard, e.g., in biscuits or plain short pastry.

Short and Crumbly: This is similar to firm and close, but more fat is added, e.g., in shortbread or nankhatais.

Spongy: A soft and elastic texture showing inclusion of air, e.g., Swiss rolls, sponge cakes and idlis.

Light and Even: Holes are plentiful and of a fair size. The food is firm but not hard or tough. It is neither as short as pastry nor as spongy as sponge cakes, e.g., Madeira cake, Queen cake.

Flaky: This is caused by the method of adding fat. Thin crisp layers are formed, separated by air pockets. The flakes themselves should not be tough, e.g. flaky and puff pastry, chiroti, etc.

It must be remembered that the following textures should be avoided in any dish:

Coarse: Holes are large and uneven, and the food is sunken in the centre. This is brought about by the addition of too much raising agent or too little liquid.

Tough: Coarse mixtures are also tough. Toughness is caused by too much liquid or through incorrect mixing. This will also result if too little fat is added.

Hard: A bad fault brought about by the addition of too much liquid or too much pressure while mixing. Hard mixtures are usually heavy since the air enclosed is removed.

Various Methods of Cooking

While the correct preparation of ingredients and correct mixing are necessary, greater skill is needed in the actual cooking of the food.

1. Roasting

Spit Roasting: The food to be cooked is brought into direct contact with the flame of a clear, bright fire. The food is basted with fat and also turned regularly to ensure even cooking and browning. This method, now known as spit roasting, is not often used as only good quality meats are suitable for it. Roast meats, however, have a very good flavour, and are still served in large hotels and in special restaurants and hotels, e.g., as barbecued meat.

Pot Roasting: This method is used to cook small joints and birds if no oven is available, but a thick heavy pan is essential. Enough fat is melted to cover the bottom of the pan. When the fat is hot the joint is browned. It is then lifted out and 2 or 3 skewers are put into the pan, on which the joint is placed. This is to prevent the joint from sticking to the pan. The joint should just touch the fat. The pan is then covered tightly with a well-fitting lid and cooked over a very slow fire. The joint could be basted if lean and turned occasionally to ensure even cooking. Prepared root vegetables and potatoes can also be cooked around the meat.

Oven Roasting: This has now taken the place of spit roasting, because of its convenience, although only first class meat, poultry and vegetables are thus cooked. It is done in a closed oven with the aid of fat. The joint is raised out of the fat by means of bones or a trivet to prevent the meat from frying and becoming hard. Frequent basting, however, is essential. The food is put into a fairly hot oven for 5 to 10 minutes and the temperature is lowered to allow the joint to be cooked through. Cooking in a moderate oven for a longer time produces a better cooked joint than cooking at high temperature for a shorter period. There is also less shrinkage. Therefore, more portions can be obtained. Aluminium foil is now used in oven roasting. The joint is larded or browned in fat. A matignon [finely minced 2 medium carrots, 2 onions, 2 sticks of celery (heart), 1 tbsp ham, 1 sprig thyme, 1/2 a bay leaf crushed and stewed in butter] may or may not be used to cover the joint which is then wrapped tightly in aluminium foil and cooked in the oven till done. This method is an improvement on oven roasting as the meat retains its moisture and flavour.

2. Baking

The food to be cooked is surrounded by hot air in a closed oven. The action of dry heat is modified by the steam which arises from the food whilst cooking. Bread, cakes, pastry, puddings, vegetables and potatoes may be cooked by this method.

4. Boiling

Food is cooked by surrounding it with boiling or simmering liquid (stock or water). Only just sufficient liquid should be used to cover the food to be cooked. To retain nourishment and flavour in food, plunge into boiling liquid. Allow to reboil and then to simmer. The liquid thus obtained is known as Tot Liquor and contains some nourishment and flavour. This should not be wasted. It can be used as a substitute for stock when stock is not available or cooled and used to prepare stock. If a well-flavoured stock is required, vegetables and meat should be put into cold water and allowed to cook gently. Salted or pickled meats should always be started in cold water.

Vegetables grown above the ground are cooked in boiling salted water and vegetables grown below the ground are started in cold salted water with the exception of new potatoes and new carrots. Dry vegetables are started in cold water. Salt is added only after the vegetables are tender.

Fish should be put into hot liquid and allowed to just simmer.

4. Frying

Frying is a method of cooking whereby the food to be cooked is brought into contact with hot fat. Food cooked in this way is said to be indigestible, but if the method is correctly and carefully carried out, the food is quite suitable for normal people. The frying has the following advantages:

(i) It is a quick method of cooking,

(ii) Fried food is very appetizing,

(iii) The keeping quality of fried food is strengthened. It is however, an expensive method of cooking meat as only the best parts are suitable (chops, liver, etc.). For other foods and for reheating of food, frying is a good means of providing variety.

There are two types of frying:

(a) Deep Fat Frying: The food is completely immersed in hot fat and, therefore, a large quantity of fat is required. The quantity of fat requires some time to heat. Special care must be taken to prevent overheating of fat, as this spoils both the food and the fat. The fat decomposes at high temperatures.

(b) Shallow Fat Frying: Only a little fat is used and the food is turned over in order that both sides may be browned. Generally this method is applied to pre-cooked food unless the food takes very little time to cook (omelette, liver, etc.). Some foods contain sufficient fat in themselves (e.g., bacon, sausages, etc.) and additional fat is not necessary although some cooks prefer to use a little fat. Fat absorption is greater when food is shallow fried then deep fried. If the fat is not hot enough the food breaks up and absorbs extra fat thus making the product unfit for consumption. Use a frying basket wherever possible to remove fried foods easily.

Practically, all foods require coating before frying, since not only are the juices and flavour of the food to be kept in, but the fat must be kept out.

The following methods are used for:

(i) eggs and bread crumbs;
(ii) flour and milk (not suitable for deep fat frying);
(iii) batter (flour, milk and eggs);
(iv) thinly rolled pastry;
(v) oatmeal or vermicelli;
(vi) lamb or pig's caul;
(vii) began (gram flour or chick pea flour) batter.

Sweets and savouries both may be cooked by this method without the flavour affecting the fat or the food, provided correct principles are applied. Food cooked by deep fat frying has a much better appearance than that cooked by shallow fat frying as it is evenly browned.

Frying Procedures

(i) Have the fire clear and hot.
(ii) Apply coating evenly. The bread crumbs used should not be coarse. Remove any excess and firmly press on loose crumbs.
(iii) Fry to a golden brown on both sides turning over the food if necessary,
(iv) When frying chicken dry off all moisture before dipping in flour.
(v) Use fat with a high smoke point. The fat must be quite still and at the right temperature required, before the food is put in.
(vi) Do not put in too many pieces of food at the same time as this will lower the temperature.
(vii) See that the temperature is not increased for increased output,

(viii) Follow a time and temperature chart.

(ix) Once fat has been used for frying, strain and store in cans in a refrigerator,

(x) Drain well on absorbent paper and serve attractively,

(xi) Cover fats left in the fryer between frying periods and maintain at a temperature not higher than 200°F.

(xii) Make the food into suitable sizes and shapes and see that it is free from cracks.

(xiii) Replenish the original volume with fresh fat after each frying period.

(xiv) Fat begins to thicken, getting to be what is known as gummy or syrupy, with continuous use. This condition is known as polymerization and such fats are more viscous than fresh fat. Since there are no known food additives for inhibiting this condition, fat that has reached this stage is no longer fit for use.

(xv) Darkening of the fat is caused by cooking at too high a temperature which carbonizes loose bread crumbs and small particles of fried food. Such fat should be strained and replenished with fresh fat before being used again.

(xvi) Fats that are used for frying should have high stability. Normally fats themselves do not get rancid during the frying process but rancidity in the finished product affects the keeping quality and acceptability of the product. For commercial purposes fat of over 100 hours stability is desired for continuous trouble-free frying.

5. Steaming

The food to be cooked is surrounded by plenty of steam from fast boiling water directly or by having the food in a basin or other dish placed in steam or boiling water. This is a slow process of cooking and only easily cooked food can be prepared by this method.

Advantages of Steaming

(i) Food cooked by this method is easily digested,

(ii) All nourishment and flavour are kept in the food,

(iii) Food cannot be easily overcooked.

(iv) Pudding basins and other containers need not be filled to the top, thus allowing room for food to rise and so making food light.

Steaming Process

(i) Prepare the vessel and have the water boiling fast.

(ii) If a basin is to be used as a container inside the steamer, see that it is greased and covered with a well-fitting lid or with greaseproof paper. This is to prevent condensed moisture from falling on the food.

(iii) Keep a kettle of boiling water handy so that the water in the steamer can be replaced as it boils away. Frequent refilling however, should be avoided as this causes a draught on food.

(iv) Never allow the water in the steamer to go off the boil, except when preparing dishes with eggs as the main ingredients, such as custard. For this, water must be kept at the simmering point otherwise the custard will curdle.

(v) Dish food quickly and serve hot. An appropriate sauce must accompany steamed food to make it appetizing, as steamed food is generally bland.

6. Poaching

Poaching is cooking slowly in a minimum amount of liquid which should never be allowed to boil but should be just off boil. Fish, fruits and eggs are poached. When poaching eggs, a little vinegar and salt are added to the liquid to help in quicker coagulation and thus prevent disintegration.

7. Stewing

This is a very gentle method of cooking in a closed pan using only a small quantity of liquid. The food should never be more than half covered with the liquid and the food above this level is thus really cooked by steam. As the liquid is not allowed to boil during cooking the process is a slow one.

Advantages of Stewing

(i) Cheap cuts of meat, old fowls and tough or under-ripe fruits may be prepared by this method as the slow, moist method of cooking softens fibres, rendering the food tender.

(ii) Meat and vegetables may be cooked and served together, making an appetizing dish, while saving fuel and labour.

(iii) Stewed food may be cooked in the oven after other food is cooked, or it may be cooked on the side of the fire or on a very small gas or oil flame, thus again saving fuel.

(iv) All nourishment and flavour are retained so the food is very appetizing.

Stewing Practices

(i) Have a pan with a well-fitting lid ready,

(ii) Prepare the food and cut into pieces convenient for serving,

(iii) Use tepid liquid, which is just sufficient to half cover the food.

(iv) Bring just to boiling point and then simmer very gently until the food is perfectly tender. Never allow a stew to boil for "a stew boiled is a stew spoilt".

8. Broiling

Broiling is cooking by direct heat and is synonymous with grilling. In pan broiling, the food is cooked uncovered on hot metal such as a grill or a frying pan. The pan or grill is oiled slightly to prevent sticking. Excess fat accumulated while cooking should be poured off.

9. Grilling

This is sed synonymously with broiling. This is cooking by dry heat. The food is supported on a grid iron over the fire, or on a grid placed in a tin under a gas or electric grill, or between electrically heated grill bars.

Grilling over the Heat: This is cooking on greased grill bars with the help of fat over direct heat. Only first class cuts of meat, poultry and certain fish can be prepared this way. The grill bars are brushed' with oil to prevent food from sticking, and can be heated by charcoal, coke, gas or electricity. The bars should char the food on both sides to give the distinctive flavour of grilling. The thickness of the food and the heat of the grill determine the cooking time. Grills are typical a la carte dishes and are ordered by the customer to the degree of cooking required, such as rare, medium rare, medium or well done.

Grilling under the Heat-salamander: Cooking on grill bars or on trays under direct heat. Steaks, chops, etc., are cooked on the bars but fish, tomato, bacon and mushrooms are usually cooked on trays. This method can also be used in the preparation of foods au gratin and when glazing is required.

Grilling between Heat: Food is cooked between electrically heated grill bars.

Infrared grilling This is cooking by inferred radiation. This method reduces cooking time considerably, e.g., a steak can be grilled in one minute.

10. Braising

This is a combined method of roasting and stewing in a pan with a tight-fitting lid. To be strictly correct this method requires a special pan but a casserole dish or stew pan makes a good substitute. The meat should be sealed by browning on all sides and then placed on a lightly fried bed of vegetables (generally root). Stock or gravy is added which should cover two- thirds of the meat. The flavourings and seasonings are then added. The lid is put on and the food is allowed to cook gently on the stove or in the oven. When nearly done the lid is removed and the joint is frequently basted to glaze it. This latter process is always done in the oven.

Soups

Aim of Soup Making: To prepare an appetizing, economical and easily digestible dish by extracting nourishment and flavour from the solid to the liquid.

Stock is the foundation of all good soups. Stock is made by putting solid food into cold water and by a long slow process of cooking extracting the nourishment into the liquid. The best stocks are made from meat and bones together, e.g., white consomme. Since this is expensive for household purposes as well as for institutional feeding, bones and leftovers are used. The following stocks are adequate as well as economical.

Bone Stock: Use any kind of bones, cooked or uncooked. Place in a pan. Cover with cold water, add a little salt and bring to the boil. Simmer gently to allow the scum to form on the surface then gently remove it. A little cold water could be added occasionally to accelerate the process. Skim well and for each 600 ml of liquid add one onion, one carrot and a bouquet garni. Put the lid on and simmer very slowly for at least 2 to 3 hours. Strain. Cool quickly and use. Meat and bones not only contribute flavour but body. Body is largely made up of gelatine and other soluble products extracted from meat and bones. Depending on the size of the bones and the way they are cut, stock from meat bones is simmered from 4 to 10 hours and poultry from 2 to 6 hours.

The best bones to use for stock are those from young animals. These contain more gelatine and the marrow contains more flavouring ingredients. Shin and knuckle bones are best with neck bones next. The bones are best cut into 4 lengths and split.

To make 5 litres of good stock use 2 kg. of meat bones, 6 litres water, 12 kg. of flavouring vegetables (mirepoix).

In a brown stock, the meat, bones and vegetables are first browned.

In a white stock, they are not browned. Also avoid using highly coloured vegetables such as carrots, beans etc.

Vegetable stock: Use any mixture of vegetables, the outside leaves of cabbage, cauliflower stalks, celery stalks and leaves, shells of peas, etc. All these must be washed thoroughly to free them of grit, sand and worms. Shred vegetables and add to cold water. Cover and boil for 20 to 30 minutes. Strain and use.

Fish Stock: Cover the fish bones, skin, head and other trimmings with water or milk and water. Add 1 small onion, 2 cloves, 1/2 a bay leaf and a sprig of parsley. Bring to boil. Cover and simmer for 20 minutes. Strain and use.

Emergency Stock: Dissolve meat or yeast extract in boiling water or in pot liquor.

Pot liquor is the water in which meat, poultry, fish, vegetables, macaroni, etc., have been boiled for the table where the purpose is to retain as much nourishment and flavour in the solids as possible. This is done by putting the solids into hot water but still some nourishment and flavour escape into the liquid. This liquid (pot liquor) can be used as a substitute for stock. No stock will keep for very long. Because stock is a good medium for bacterial growth, great care must be taken in its preparation and storage. In hot climates stock should be stored in a refrigerator and boiled to prevent spoilage. Cool quickly by emptying into shallow and clean bowls. Stock which contains starchy foods should not be used after 12 hours.

Consomme: A clear soup prepared from beef, chicken or game stock, garnished with a variety of ingredients. This can be served hot or chilled. Consomme takes its name generally from the garnish, e.g. Consomme Julienne-- consomme garnished with boiled matchstick-like strips of vegetables such as carrots, beans, turnips, etc. Consomme Royale consomme garnished with savoury custard cubes.

Broth: A good stock (beef, mutton or chicken) cooked with diced meat, vegetables and rice or barley and served with the solids. Some of the nourishment is retained in the solids by putting them into tepid liquid. Broths are also different from ordinary soups in having the thickening (rice, barley, macaroni, etc.) put in at the beginning and cooked with the other ingredients.

Puree: A soup thickened by its main ingredient and passed through a sieve. Milk or a little flour blended with milk is added to prevent the puree from separating, but not as a thickening. The consistency of the soup should be like thick cream. Generally served with croutons (fried cubes of bread). Examples: puree-de lentils, puree de haricot blanc, puree Parmentier, puree de tomatoes, puree de pois frais.

Potage or Soupe: These terms cover a wide variety of soups, e.g., potage bortsch, potage minestrone, potage mulligatawny, soupe au gumbo, soupe aux rognons, etc.

Cream: A soup of cream consistency which is generally made with vegetable puree mixed with bechamel or white sauce. It can be finished with cream if desired, e.g., creme de celeii, creme de tomato.

Veloute: A thick soup made from white stock and roux, finished with a liaison of yolks and cream.

Chowder: An American soup resembling a stew made of meat, fish or vegetable with milk, salt pork and various seasonings. Crackers are generally added just before serving. Examples: prawn chowder, oyster chowder, pork chowder, vegetable chowder.

Gumbo: A regional dish that originated from the American South. Contains okra, rice and a seasoning called fille, which is powdered young sassafras leaves.

Bisques: These are thickened fish soups generally made from shellfish and fish stock and thickened with cream. Diced fish is served in it. Example: bisque de homard. The value of any soup will depend on the ingredients used. Clear soups are of value only to stimulate the appetite at the beginning of a meal while thick soups such as cream, veloute and puree, chowders, broths, etc., are nourishing as well as appetizing.

Coulis: A term often used for thick soups made with a puree of shellfish, e.g. coulis d'ecrevisses, coulis de crabes. Sometimes the term is also used for liquid purees such as chicken, game or vegetables.

2

Food Stuff : Selection & Preparation

"The world's most effective diet consists of exactly four words: "No more, thank you."

—*Kate Smith*

Here in this chapter we will discuss about main raw food ingredients, i.e. food stuff. Each one stuff is being given an elaborate treatment.

Seafood is much palatable and most popular all over the globe. Fish is the most commonly used seafood. A number of varieties are there of fishes with different taste etc.

FISHES

Fin fish are vertebrates and have skin and scales which cover the body. They move with the help of fins. They are subdivided into:

1. *Oily fish* which are mainly round fish and contain fat all over the body. The amount of fat varies from 1.5% to 20% in different varieties. These fish are often pigmented and tend to be surface fish. Example: mackerels, sardines etc.
2. *White fish* which are mainly flat fish, and contain oil only in the liver. Most of these are deep sea fish. Common local examples are pomfret, sole etc.

Shellfish, are invertebrates. They are subdivided into:

1. *Molluscs:* (a) Bivalves (e.g. oysters, scallops, mussels, clams and cockles) which have two distinctly separate shells joined by a hinge-like membrane. The movements of the shell are controlled by a strong muscle. When the muscle relaxes, the two halves of the shell fall open. The shell also opens when the organism dies, thus exposing the contents of the shell to contamination from outside, resulting in quick putrefaction, (b) *Univalves:* (e.g. whelks and winkles). These are recognized by the characteristic spiral formation of their shells, which unlike those of bivalves are not divided into halves.

   The shells of molluscs increase at the rate of one ring per year to allow for the growth of the organism. The age of the mollusc can thus be roughly estimated by the number of rings on the shell.

2. Crustaceans have a segmented, crust-like shell (e.g. lobsters, crabs, prawns, shrimps). The shells of crustaceans do not grow with the fish, unlike those of the molluscs, but are shed every year, with a new one forming to suit their new size.

How to Select Fish? The following points must be borne in mind while selecting fish:

(i) Eyes should be bright and not sunken.

(ii) Gills should be red.

(iii) The tail should be stiff,

(iv) The flesh should be firm and not flabby.

(v) The scales if any should be plentiful,

(vi) There should be no unpleasant odour.

(vii) To test a cut piece, press down with a finger, and if an impression is left then the fish is stale.

(viii) Any tendency for the raw flesh to come away from the bones is a dangerous sign.

Scaling and Cleaning

(i) To scale, use the blunt side of the knife. Holding the fish by the tail, scrape firmly from the tail towards the head. Wash well to remove any loose scales,

(ii) Remove fins and trim tail,

(iii) To clean fish such as herrings, mackerel, etc., slit the belly, using a pair of kitchen scissors, from the head to almost half way down. Remove the head if desired,

(iv) In the case of flat fish such as pomfret, etc., cut away the gills, and make a small opening in the belly. Remove the entrails and wash well. If the head is to be removed, do this with a semicircular cut at the base of the head.

To bone herrings After slitting and cleaning, open gently. Turn over and place the inside on hard board. Press firmly along the backbone to loosen the bone. Turn over and starting at the head raise the backbone with the thumb and forefinger. Pull the bone steadily away from the fish. After pulling out the bone, rinse the fish well and drain.

To fillet the fish: Slit the fish down the backbone with a sharp knife and separate the flesh from the backbone on each side with short sharp strokes. Then slit from the side and take out each fillet.

Cooking of Fish: The flesh of fish is very delicate and, therefore, great care must be taken to prevent the flesh from breaking during cooking. When boiling or cooking fish, the liquid should be at simmering point before fish is added as the connective tissue in fish is softer and the quantity is less than in meat. When preparing fish stew or fish curry, fish is put into cold liquid to flavour the gravy as well. Whole fish may also be covered with a cold liquid and brought to boil. This is done to prevent shrinkage of the skin. Steaming is a better method of cooking fish as it is a gentle method. Fish cookery is not a special method of cooking. All methods of cooking can be applied bearing in mind that the delicacy of the flesh of the fish and the fat content of the fish determine the cooking method. The time taken is always much less than for cooking meat. An average timetable is as follows, but much depends on the size and shape of the fish.

Boiling and baking		10 minutes per 500 gm and 10 minutes over
Steaming		15 minutes per 500 gm and 15 minutes over.
Stewing		Half to three quarter of an hour formes time the stew begins to simmer.
Frying (for small fish or thin pieces)		5 minutes
Grilling		5 to 7 minute's
Lean fish	Steamed or	Poached, deep-fried or baked in a
Oily fish	Baked	Sauce. Baked, grilled or pan-fried.

Boiling of fish: Fish is generally boiled in a court bouillon. This is made of salt, water, milk and lemon juice for sea fish with white flesh. For salmon, trout and shellfish and various types of river fish the following court bouillon is used.

Court Bouillon

Water	1 litre
Salt	15 gm
Vinegar	75 ml
Carrots (sliced)	60 gm
Onion (sliced)	60 gm
Bay leaf	1

Parsley stalks	2 to 3
Peppercorns	6
Thyme	1

Simmer all ingredients for 30 to 40 minutes.

Strain and use as required.

Notably, the stock after fish is boiled can be used as a base for different types of sauces. Fish is cooked when the flesh separates easily from the bone. Test at the thickest part nearer the bone. It there is no bone then the fish is considered done when a creamy substance begins to run from the fish.

Grilling of Fish: Heat the grill and grease the rack. Clean fish. Sprinkle over with salt, pepper and lime juice. Gashes should be made on the fish to allow heat to penetrate, otherwise the outside becomes dry before the inside is cooked. For large fish, baste frequently with melted fat. For oily fish such as herrings and sardines, no extra fat is required.

Steaming of Fish: Place the fish in a steamer. Sprinkle with salt and pepper. The water in the steamer must be fast boiling all the time the fish is cooking, if large, the fish can be turned once. Test as for boiling.

Baking of Fish: This method is most suitable for medium sized fish or the middle portion of a large fish. Scale and clean, but leave the head and tail on. Stuff the belly with a savoury forcemeat (11 gm fresh bread crumbs, 60 gm fat, grated rind of half a lime, 2 tsp chopped parsley, $^1/_2$ tsp mixed herbs, salt and pepper and egg or milk to bind). Sew up with a needle and coarse thread. Do not fill the fish too tightly or it will burst, since the stuffing swells when it is cooked. Place the fish in a baking tray with a little fat, in a moderately hot oven, and cook till the flesh leaves the bones. To serve, remove the thread. Garnish with parsley and lemon. Serve with a sharp sauce.

Frying of Fish: Fish can be fried whole, if small, or cut into steaks or fillets or pieces if large. For cut pieces, it is preferable to coat the fish with egg and bread crumbs or seasoned flour *and milk.**Frying of Fish:* Fish can be fried whole, if small, or cut into steaks or fillets or pieces if large. For cut pieces, it is preferable to coat the fish with egg and bread crumbs or seasoned flour *and milk.*

Soused Herring or Mackerel: Soused herrings and mackerel are served as an hors d'oeuvre or for breakfast. Scale and clean the fish. Cut off the head and tail. Remove entrails. Wash well. Put back roe if any. Place on a plate. Sprinkle over with a little salt and leave for a couple of hours. Drain the fish. Roll up and place in a casserole dish. To 500 gm of fish add 12 peppercorns, 1 bay leaf and a large onion thinly sliced. Pour over equal proportions of vinegar and water, the liquid being just sufficient to cover the fish. Bring quickly to boil and simmer for a few minutes before removing from the casserole. Serve garnished with parsley.

Shellfish

Selection: They should be bought in season as far as possible. They should be medium- sized and of good weight. It is best to buy them alive, particularly oysters, crabs, and lobsters. If they are dead, the following precautions must be taken: (a) The claws of crabs should be springy and not hanging down, (b) The eyes should be bright, (c) The tail of lobsters should spring back when stretched out. (d) Shrimps and prawns must be crisp, (e) Oyster shells should be tightly closed.

Preparing and Serving Shellfish: Shellfish can be served in a variety of ways. Lobsters and crabs are boiled alive. The meat is removed after cooking, flaked and replaced in their own shells with sauces or served in salads or other cold dishes. The meat is mixed with sauce and served in patties, or in scallop shells or on toast and canapes. Smaller shellfish such as prawns and shrimps must be shelled first, the intestines (the black thread- like substance found at the back) removed, then washed and cooked. They are served whole, boiled or steamed, stewed or in curries, fried with masala or in batter, devilled and in soups. Shrimps and oysters can be covered with sauces. Lemon and vinegar are served with shellfish to aid in digestion.

When fish is served as a main dish, it is usually served with potatoes, a salad or a cooked vegetable and a sauce.

MEAT

The term meat is generally applied only to butcher's meat--beef, mutton, lamb, pork etc. The tenderness of the meat depends on the age and feeding of the animal, on the hanging and preparation after killing. Muscle structures have an effect on the tenderness and the texture of the meat. The skeletal muscles are made up of fibres which are composed of proteins, salts and nitrogenous extractives. The fibres are grouped parallel to each other in bundles held together by connective tissue and surrounded by a sheath of heavier connective tissue. The size of the bundles varies with different muscles and determines to some extent the texture of the meat.

There are two kinds of connective tissue, collagenous or white connective tissue and elastic or yellow connective tissue. The flavour of meat is determined by various factors such as feeding, age, sex and maturity. The older the flesh the greater the flavour in most cases; young flesh is not so highly flavoured but is sweeter and more tender. Flesh of male animals is stronger in flavour than that of females unless the animal has been castrated. Well developed muscles are usually more strongly flavoured, e.g., chicken leg as compared with breast.

The longer the meat is hung the stronger the flavour, owing to certain chemical changes. Meat should not be eaten immediately after killing. It has to be hung till tender. Shortly after death rigor mortis sets in and the muscles stiffen. Meat must be hung at 1° to 3°C (about 34° to 38°F) at least, till this passes off and until the acids which then develop have had a chance to soften the connective tissue. The enzyme present in the tissues also helps to make the meat render and more juicy. In cold countries this process takes at least 3 days but it is much quicker in warmer temperatures, varying between 12 to 24 hours. If so desired meat can be hung for a longer period. Not all meats should be hung like this and veal and pork particularly should be eaten fresh. They should also be thoroughly cooked before use.

Old meat and meat with considerable muscular development will be darker in colour and stronger in flavour. The flavour of the meat varies depending on the saltiness and sweetness of the blood, the species, the age and sex of the animal and the degree of maturity when eaten. Another factor is fat. Pork and mutton for example, have individual flavours depending on the fat. The third factor is the amount of sugar in the meat which on cooking tends to caramelize. Wherever possible select meat which is marbled. This is meat where the fat is interspersed between the muscle fibres and connective tissue. This shows good feeding. Marbling helps to keep the meat moist when cooked by dry methods. Marbled meat is also more nutritious. There are no special methods of cooking meat and the fundamental methods of cooking can be deftly adapted to suit the particular joint.

The amount of connective tissue present in the meat determines to a great extent the method of cooking. When connective tissue is present in large amounts, the meat, being tough, is cooked by moist methods. For those cuts which have only a small amount of connective tissue, dry heat cooking may be used. Long-fired cuts of meat require longer cooking than short-fired ones. They should be stewed or braised to make them tender. Shorter-fired meat is cooked by dry heat. The most developed muscle fibres are usually the longest and these coarser fibres are found in the legs, neck and tail.

The shorter fibres are found in the fillet, rump and loin. Dry heat cooking (roasting, frying and grilling or broiling) develops the characteristic meat flavour, coagulates the proteins, thus making fibres firm, hardens the connective tissue, and changes the colour. This change in colour is caused by a change in the composition of haemoglobin. Shrinkage is observed in meat cooked by the dry heat method.

Moist cooking (braising, boiling, stewing, etc.) besides developing flavour and coagulating the meat, softens the collagenous tissue, thus rendering meat tender. Elastic connective tissue is softened only slightly by moist heat. There is no shrinking in meat cooked by moist methods.

It should be noted that when cooking-meat it is desirable to retain the juices in the fibres. Steaks, roasts, etc., are cooked either at a constant temperature of 149°C (about 300°F) for beef, veal and lamb and 177°C (about 350°F) for pork, or by the searing method, where the meat is cooked at a high temperature for the first 10 minutes and then cooked at a lowered temperature. This method was supposed to help in retention of juices but this has been disproved although the aroma, flavour and colour that accompany searing are preferred by some. Steaks are usually grilled at 204.5°C (about 400°F). Studies have illustrated that a lower oven temperature 171°-177°C (about 300°-350°F) as compared to a higher temperature 218.3°-232.2°C (about 425°-450°F) results in less drip loss, less shrinkage, increased juiciness and more uniform colour throughout a cut. Overcooking or extended cooking at high temperature denatures the protein of meat, eggs, fish and birds or they toughen or become stringy or all three. If a roast is cooked at a high temperature, the time of cooking is decreased, but dripping and evaporation losses are higher, and the meat is not so evenly cooked. The degree of 'doneness' also affects this loss, the steak done 'rare' or 'underdone' showing' less than that done 'medium' or Veil done'.

A meat thermometer helps in determining the degree of 'doneness'. The thermometer should be inserted so that the bulb is at the centre of the cut but not in contact with the bone. For thin cuts the thermometer is not very satisfactory.

Meat meant for boiling should be dipped into salted boiling water and then allowed to simmer till tender. A pressure saucepan may be used to save time when cooking less tender cuts of meat. Care should be taken to prevent cooking of meat in a pressure cooker or at a high temperature longer than necessary, otherwise it becomes hard, dry and flavorless. Frozen meat may be prepared by the same methods as fresh meat. It need not be thawed before cooking. If it is not thawed, however, the cooking time is considerably increased, to as much as two to three times the time required for cooking thawed or fresh meat. Thawing can be done in the refrigerator or at room temperature. When meat is not thawed, it does not retain a coating such as egg and bread crumbs. Tenderisers such as papain (taken from raw papaya) may be used to soften the fibres before cooking. These must be applied to the meat, which should then be allowed to stand for one hour for a cut of 2.5 cm. (1") thickness. The acidity of vinegar, lemon juice, curd, cider and wine which can be added before or during cooking also helps tenderise meat.

Quality Determination: Mutton and lamb is meat from a lamb under one year old):

(i) A good quality animal should be compact and evenly fleshed,

(ii) The lean flesh should be firm, of a pleasing dull red colour and of a fine texture or grain,

(iii) There should be an even distribution of surface fat, which should be hard, brittle and flaky in structure, and of a clear white colour,

(iv) In a young animal the bone is pink and porous, so that when it is cut, a small amount of blood can be seen. With progressive aging the bones become hard, dense, white and inclined to splinter when chopped.

Dissection

(i) Remove the shoulders,

(ii) Remove the breasts,

(iii) Remove the middle neck and scrag end.

(iv) Remove the legs,

(v) Divide the saddle from the best end.

Approximate weight of the carcass of an Indian animal:

Lamb: 10 kg. (22 Ib.)

Mutton: 16.8 kg. (37 Ib.)

Whereas the approximate weight of an English animal is:

Lamb: 14 kg. (32 Ib.)

Mutton: 23 kg. (50 Ib.)

Pork

Fresh pork is at its best from September to April (the months with an 'r' in them). At 5 to 6 weeks it is known as suckling pig.

Quality Determination

(i) Lean flesh should be pale pink, firm and of a fine texture,

(ii) The fat should be white, firm, smooth and not excessive,

(iii) Bones should be small, fine and pinkish,

(iv) The skin or rind should be smooth.

Joints and Their Uses

	JOINTS		*USES*	*APPROX. WEIGHT*	
		French		(Lamb)	Mutton)
(i)	Shoulder	(L'epaule)	Roasting Stewing	2.00 kg	3.5 kg.
(ii)	Leg	(Le gigot)	Roasting Boiling	2.75 kg.	3.75 kg.
(iii)	Breast	(La poitrine)	Roasting Stewing	0.9 kg	1.75 kg.
(iv)	Middle neck	(Le collet)	Stewing	1.15 kg.	1.7 kg.
(v)	Scrag end	(Le cote decourverte)	Stewing Broths	450 gm.	0.9 kg.
(vi)	Best end	(Le carre)	Roasting Grilling Frying	575 gm.	20 kg.
(vii)	Saddle	(La selle)	Roasting Grilling Frying	1 kg.	3.5 kg.
(viii)	Kidney	(Le rognon)	Grilling Saute Braising	1.5 kg.	2.25 kg.
(ix)	Heart	(Le coeur)	Braising	115 gm	60 gm.
(x)	Liver	(Le foie)	Frying		350 gm,
(xi)	Sweetbread	(Le ris de veau)	Braising Frying		
(xii)	Tongue	(La langue)	Boiling Braising		

Pork

Fresh pork is at its best from September to April (the months with an 'r' in them). At 5 to 6 weeks it is known as suckling pig.

Quality Determination

(i) Lean flesh should be pale pink, firm and of a fine texture,

(ii) The fat should be white, firm, smooth and not excessive.
(iii) Bones should be small, fine and pinkish,
(iv) The skin or rind should be smooth.

	Order of dissection
1. Leg	
2. Loin	(i) Remove the head
3. Spare-rib	(ii) Remove the trotters,
4. Belly	(iii) Remove the leg.
5. Shoulder	(iv) Remove the shoulder.
6. Head (whole)	(v) Remove spare ribs.
	(vi) Divide loin from the belly

Joints and Their Uses

		Joints French	*Uses*	*Approx Weight*
(i)	Thigh	(La cuisse)	Roasting Boiling	4.55 Kg.
(ii)	Loin	(La longe)	Roasting Frying Grilling	5.45 Kg
(iii)	Spare rib	(Le cote decou -verte de pore)	Roasting Pies	1.35. Kg.
(iv)	Belly (Breast)	(La poitrine)	Pickling	1.8 Kg.
(v)	Shoulder	(L'epaule)	Boiling	
(vi)	Head (whole)	(La tete)	Roasting Sausages Pies	2.7. Kg.
			Brawn	3.6
(vii)	Trotters	(Le pied)	Grilling Boiling	
(viii)	Kidney	(Le rognon)	Saute Grilling	
(ix)	Liver	(Le foie)	Pate	

Bacon and Ham: Bacon is made by preserving the meat of carefully bred pigs. The preservative used is salt. This can be applied in two ways:

(i) by covering the meat with dry salt and allowing at least 4 weeks penetration;

(ii) by using a salt solution (brine).

This is injected into the flesh and then the meat is immersed in a salt solution for days. Sometimes a combination of the two methods is used-- brine is injected into the meat and the sides are then stacked and covered with dry salt for 2 to 3 weeks. It is then matured for about 3 weeks under controlled temperature. Desirable bacteria acting on the meat juices and salt produce the characteristics associated with well matured bacon.

This bacon is now ready for sale as 'green' or 'pale' bacon. In certain parts of the world the bacon is preferred smoked. So it is then hung over smouldering wood dust for 2 days. This extracts excessive moisture and gives the bacon a distinctive flavour. Smoking also improves the preservation as it acts as an antiseptic. This is particularly suitable in hot climates.

Good quality, well cured bacon should have a pleasant smell; the rind should be thin and smooth, the fat firm and free from any yellow marks, the lean part a good deep pink] colour and the flavour mild and mellow,

1. End Collar
2. Prime Collar
3. Fore Hock
4. Top Back
5. Top Streaky
6. Back and Ribs
7. Prime Streaky
8. Short Back
9. Thin Streaky
10. Long Back
11. Flank

12. Corner Gammon
13. Slipper
14. Middle Gammon
15. Gammon Flock

Ham and Gammon: Ham and gammon come from the hind leg of a pig Gammon is cut off the side of a cured porker. Ham, on the other hand is cue off at the fresh pork stage and includes a substantial part of the loin. It is cured after cutting, usually by the long process of dry salting.

Beef

Signs of Good Quality

(i) The lean meat should be bright red with small flecks of white fat.
(ii) The fat should be firm, brittle in texture, creamy white in colour and odourless. Older animals and dairy breeds have fat which is usually deeper yellow in colour,
(iii) Beef in good condition should have streaks of fat running through the lean section and the flesh should rise again quickly after being pressed with the fingers. Any cut surface should present a slightly moist appearance to the touch.

Order of Dissection: A whole side is divided into the forequarter and hindquarter, the division being between the wing ribs and fore ribs.

Hindquarter

(i) Remove the rump, suet and kidney,
(ii) Remove the thin flank.
(iii) Divide the loin and rump from the leg. (The leg will consist of topside, silverside, thick flank and shin)

(iv) Remove the fillet,

(v) Divide the rump from the sirloin,

(vi) Remove the wing ribs,

(vii) Remove the shin,

(viii) Bone out the aitchbone.

(ix) Divide the leg into topside, silverside and thick flank.

Forequarter

(i) Remove the shank,

(ii) Divide in half down the centres.

(iii) Take off the fore ribs,

(iv) Divide into joints.

Minute Steak: Sirloin cut into 1.25 cm. ($^1/_2$")thick slices, flattened with a cutlet bat dipped in water to make the steak as thin as possible, trimmed and grilled or fried.

Sirloin Steaks: Sirloin cut into 1.25 cm. ($^1/_2$") thick slices, trimmed and fried or grilled. *Double Sirloin Steaks:* Sirloin cut into 2.5 cm. (1") slices, trimmed and fried or grilled *Porterhouse and T-bone steak:* Complete slices of sirloin including the bone and fillet.

Chateaubriand: This is a double fillet steak taken from the head of a fillet of beef, 3.5 to 10 cm. (1½"-4) thick, with an average weight of 340 gm. to 1 kg. It is generally served grilled at a temperature of 204.5°C (about 400°F), done to the taste of the customer.

Fillet Steak: These are approximately 115 gm. to 170 gm. in weight cut into 2.5 cm. (1") thick slices trimmed and grilled or fried.

Tournedos: Taken from the middle portion of the fillet. Remove all fat.

Fillet Mignon: Taken from the tail end of the fillet. All fat and sinews are removed and it is minced or sliced as required.

Entrecote Steak: A slice of steak cut between two bones of a rib of beef, or cut from 1 contrefilet (bone sirloin or undercut), and weighing about 650 gm.; sufficient for four persons.

Poultry

Choosing Poultry: Only young birds are suitable for roasting; older birds may be boiled, steamed, braised or stewed. A roasting chicken should be about nine months to a year old; geese and other birds for roasting should not also be older than one year.

Signs of a Young Bird

(i) The feathers, especially the quills on the wings, should be easy to pull out.

(ii) There should be down all over the body, but especially under the wings,

(iii) No long hair on the body,

(iv) The skin should be white or clear and smooth,

(v) The feet should be supple, with smooth, even, overlapping scales,

(vi) The comb and wattle should be small and not well developed.

Points which Denote Good Condition in Ducks: The breast should be plump. The bill and feet are yellow in young birds, but they darken with age. The webbing of the feet should be smooth, tender and easily broken, and the underbill soft and pliable.

Preparation

Storing poultry: Fowls and ducks are best used fresh

and should not be stored longer than 1 or 2 days before cooking. Protect them from flies and hang by the feet in a dry airy place.

Plucking: If poultry is plucked while still warm the feathers are easier to remove.

(i) When plucking, do not sit in a draught or the feathers will blow about,

(ii) Put the bird on a large sheet of strong paper.

(iii) Take care not to tear the skin, especially when plucking game birds,

(iv) Hold the bird firmly with the left hand and pluck with the right.

(v) Pluck out small handfuls at a time, starting from under one wing then continue plucking until one side is completely clear.

(vi) Remove all the pin feathers with a knife.

Singeing: A bird can be singed in either of the two following ways. Care should be taken not to scorch or blacken the skin.

(i) Hold the bird by its head and feet, and quickly and carefully singe off the hairs over a small gas jet.

(ii) Hold the bird in the left hand and singe with a lighted taper or paper spill.

The Giblets: These can be used for making stock for gravy to serve with the roast bird, for enriching the stock when the bird is boiled, or for making giblet pie or giblet stew. The liver and kidneys are not boiled with the fowl, as they tend to darken the meat. They may be half-cooked, chopped and used as part of the stuffing or cooked in other ways. Instructions for cleaning giblets are given below.

Liver: Carefully cut away the gall bladder, taking

great care not to break it. *Stomach:* Remove any fat and reserve it. Scrape the gizzard lining well.

Heart: Cut free of tubes, cut open, and scrape away all congealed blood.

Kidney: With a large bird, such as a turkey or goose, these are large enough to be used. Cut them open and cut out the core.

Neck: Scrape away all congealed blood.

Wash the liver, *gizzard,* heart, kidney and neck in salt water and rinse well.

Drawing the Tendons: If a bird is not young and tender, it is advisable to draw the tendons from the legs before roasting.

(i) Carefully cut through the skin of the leg at the knee joint, taking care not to cut the tendons at the same time,
(ii) Break the joint and swing the leg free to expose the tendons,
(iii) Pull out the tendons one at a time with a strong metal skewer. There will be 7 of them in each leg.

Stuffing: Birds can be roasted, stuffed or unstuffed, but they are usually stuffed. Stuffing can be put inside the bird only, or both inside and at the crop, covered by the skin of the neck.

Veal forcemeat may be used for the inside and sausage meat for the crop or vice versa. Pack the veal forcemeat, or any similar stuffing, fairly loosely to allow for swelling.

Trussing

Method

A trussing needle and some thin, clean string will be

necessary. A trussing needle is a strong steel needle about 23 cm. (9") long with a large eye.

(i) Fold the skin of the neck over the back of the bird, and cross the tips of the wings over, to keep it securely in position.

(ii) Turn the bird breast upwards and put the tail through the vent.

(iii) Thread the trussing needle and pass it just under the top joint of the right wing through the bird and out through the same joint in the left wing. Run the needle back through the bird so that it enters and comes out just above the bottom joint of the wings.

(iv) Tie the ends of the string securely in a bow, taking care not to drag the flesh.

(v) Re-thread the needle, press the legs well into the sides towards the wings, plumping out the breast, and run the needle through the back of the bird, just under the thigh joint, and return through a point near the ends of the legs. Tie both ends of the string firmly together.

Second Method

(i) Fold the skin of the neck over the stuffing and secure firmly with a small skewer,

(ii) Turn the bird breast upwards and put the tail through the vent,

(iii) Pass a large skewer through the wing pinions to hold them securely in position,

(iv) Tuck the legs well into the sides of the bird to plump out the breast, then tie the legs firmly together with a string; pass the string underneath the bird, cross it, then bring it up again and twist it round the wing. Skewer and tie firmly.

Trussing a Fowl for Boiling

(i) Cut the skin of the legs all round at the knee joint, crack the joints and pull the shanks off with as many of the sinews as possible.

(ii) Thread the trussing needle and secure the wings in the same way as for the roasting bird, or fix them securely with a skewer,

(iii) Carefully loosen the skin round the legs, and slip them into the body of the bird. Secure in position with the trussing needle and string or with a skewer.

VEGETABLES

All vegetables, particularly green ones, are best when taken straight from the garden. But this is not always possible so it is essential that one should know how to judge a well-grown vegetable. A well-grown vegetable is usually tender and free from pests.

Vegetables are classified into three divisions:

(i) Leafy Vegetables: These should be crisp and give a crunchy sound when squeezed. Break the vein of a leaf; it should give a sharp snap. It the leaves are limp, then the vegetable is not fresh.

(ii) Root Vegetables: These should be firm and heavy for their size. They should be free from earth and grubs. Carrots should be heavy, smooth skinned and orange in colour.

(iii) Other Vegetables: Cabbage and cauliflower should be free from greenfly. The cabbage should have a firm heart and the outer leaves should stand the same test for freshness as green leafy vegetables. Cauliflower should have a close, white flower. Tomatoes should be of a rusty red colour and should not be soft. Runner beams and French beans should not be stringy. Peas should be full in the pod, and green. Ladies fingers should snap if the ends

are broken. Brinjals should have a smooth skin and should not be heavy for their size.

Vegetable and Diet

Vegetables play an important role in the human diet. Properly chosen and eaten, cooked or raw, they make an invaluable contribution toward the supply of vitamins and minerals. Root vegetables are good sources of carbohydrates, and pulses (peas, beans, lentils, etc.) of vegetable proteins. A good balance of ingredients essential for growth and maintenance in human beings is more easily attained by a diet made up of both plant and animal life.

Vegetables also provide variety in a meal, help to make a meal attractive by introducing colour, and furnish roughage. Mushrooms have been found to contain one or more antibiotics, one of which is effective against tuberculosis and germs which cause boils. Mushrooms which have always been a food favourite are rich in vitamins and low in calories. Seven average sized mushrooms have only 1-2 calories.

Whenever possible at least two vegetables should be served in addition to potatoes. Salads should be made popular and should be served at both meals.

Salads are dishes made up of meat, poultry, game, fish, shellfish, eggs, vegetables, fruits and milk products--normally served cold but can be served hot or frozen. They can be made out of a single ingredient or a combination of ingredients. Salads are normally served as an accompaniment to the main course, a meal by itself or a sweet course (dessert). There should be special stress on hygiene as most of the ingredients are served raw. The ingredients used and the colour, flavour, texture and presentation may be varied according to the purpose.

There are four basic parts in a salad:

The Underliner: These are generally greens either shredded or in large pieces. Tear the greens instead of cutting with *a* knife. The greens must be crisp and chilled. To keep the greens crisp, it is necessary to store them in a manner that retains the maximum amount of water in the cells. This could be achieved by storing them at refrigeration temperature in the hydrator drawer wrapped in a moist cloth or in a covered container. The loss of water in cells can be reversed. To do this reduce the temperature to 2-3°C (about 34°F), and moisten the greens. When the cells are once again filled with water the greens will be crisp.

Salad: This will form the major component and can be made of one ingredient or a combination of ingredients. Ingredients should look sparkling fresh with each individual piece intact. Fruits are particularly fragile and should be handled as little as possible. Dressings These make the salad more appetising although diet conscious people today eat their salads without a dressing.

Garnish: The garnish should be the focal point and should be carefully selected for its simplicity and to enhance eye appeal and flavour. Edible garnish is more appropriate than inedible ones. Sometimes the dressing is also used as a garnish by piping it in a decorative form on the salad.

Dressings: Dressing must be carefully selected. Depending upon the salad, the dressing could be either basic French or an emulsion. Pleasing flavours can be added to and variations made in the dressings by adding ingredients like cayenne pepper, tabasco sauce, diced hard boiled eggs, assorted herbs, a variety of cheeses, chutney, etc. Dressings should enhance the salad and not obscure it.

Special emphasic should be given to the quality of

ingredients, eye appeal, simplicity, neatness and contrast or harmony in colour and in texture. All ingredients should be edible, clean, fresh and free from defects, such as bruises, rotten spots, insects, dirt, sand and insecticide. Raw fruits and vegetables should be at their optimum stage of maturity. All inedible Portions should be removed. Remove any excess moisture from ingredients as it thins the dressing, making it less effective.

The aesthetic qualities are determined by the form and shape of the food as well as by the colour. Skilfulness and artistic cutting and arranging of salad ingredients can create an appealing effect.

Vegetables Preparation

They should be washed before peeling. A knife or a peeler may be used. The purpose of cutting is to ensure uniformity of size and even cooking. The types of cutting used for vegetables are dicing, chopping, grating, slicing, shredding, cutting into rings, mincing, etc. The object of preparation is to remove spoilt, soiled and indigestible parts.

Cooking: Fruits and vegetables are cooked for many reasons:

(i) To preserve them,
(ii) To soften the product,
(iii) To improve the flavour,
(iv) To increase the digestibility.

Whatever the methods of cooking applied, the objective is to lose as little as possible of the natural flavours, colour and nutrients. Cooking affects the palatability of the vegetables, i.e., their texture, flavour and colour. While palatability may not affect the nutritive value of vegetables, it affects their desirability.

All the different methods of cooking can be effectively employed in the preparation of vegetables. The effect of cooking on starch, protein and cellulose brings about the change in texture observed in vegetables when they are cooked.

The predominant cause for change in texture will depend upon the composition of the vegetable. For example, with leafy vegetables which contain a high percentage of fibre, the change in texture is primarily due to the effect of cooking on the hemicellulose, whereas in potatoes the gelatinization of starch is the chief factor. While this is true, it has also been noted that the change in any one ingredient is not the only cause that makes vegetables tender.

As the amount of protein in vegetables is small, the effect of coagulation during cooking is not of great significance. Alkalies such as baking soda aid in softening of vegetables as they speed up the solution of pectic substances and dissolve the hemicellulose. Acids, on the contrary, harden the vegetables, as acid precipitates pectin.

The texture of the cooked vegetables can be controlled to a great extent by the length of the cooking time. The longer the cooking period, the softer the product.

Flavour: The flavour of vegetables depends upon many substances--sugar, acids, tannings and a variety of volatile substances. There is a predominance of sweetness in beetroot, peas, corn and carrots, but each vegetable has other ingredients which contribute to its characteristic flavour and aroma. The pronounced bitterness or astringency of certain vegetables is due to the presence of tannin. The characteristic odour of the onion family-- chives, shallots, onions, garlic and leek--is due to a readily volatile substance--allyl propyl disulfide. As this substance is soluble in water the longer the vegetables are cooked in water, the milder is the flavour. The colour of the cooked product will depend on the kind and amount of colour pigment, the method of cooking and the acidity of the cooking medium. The colour pigments of fruits and vegetables are chlorophyll, carotenoids, flavones and anthocyanins. Tannings, though not colour pigments, undergo chemical changes during cooking and thus affect the colour of many cooked vegetables.

Chlorophyll: Chlorophyll is made up of two compounds, chlorophyll 'a' and chlorophyll 'b'. Both are organic esters and both contain magnesium. The reactions taking place during cooking affect these radicals. Chlorophyll is slightly soluble in water but dissolves easily in many organic solvents. Like other esters it is subject to hydrolysis, the reaction taking place in the presence of alkali, forming chlorophyll liens--salts of chlorophyll which are intensely green in colour. In the presence of acids, chlorophyll undergoes another type of decomposition with the loss of magnesium from the molecule. The resulting compounds are called phaeophytins. They are yellow to brown in colour.

Both reactions, with acids and with alkalis, are irreversible in the sense that chlorophyll cannot be formed again by treating the decomposed products with a neutralizing agent. Any cooking process which involves the use of acids or alkalies will affect the colour of green vegetables. During the life of the plant the chlorophyll is held in the cytoplasm of the plant cells in such a way that it is protected from the regions of changing acidity. When cell life is destroyed, the constituents of the cells intermingle and the green colour fades, becoming yellow and brown.

When a green vegetable is cooked the cell structure gets slowly destroyed and the acid of the cells gradually comes in contact with the chlorophyll. Hence green vegetables cooked for long periods lose their greenness. If the cooking pan is kept open during cooking, some of the acids of the vegetables may evaporate, preserving some of the green colour. When soda is added to the water in which green vegetables are cooked there is no loss in colour. The alkali neutralizes the acidity of thé vegetable and also speeds up the cooking process. Loss of colour also depends on the temperature of cooking. At high temperatures there is greater hydrolysis and, therefore, greater loss of colour.

Carotenoids: Carotenoids include two types of colour pigments--the hydrocarbons, e.g. carotene as in carrots, and the oxygenated hydrocarbons, e.g. lutein, the colouring matter in egg yolk. These pigments like all other hydrocarbons do not dissolve readily in water. They are also not affected by acids or alkalies. The oxygenated Carotenoids are also chemically resistant to acids and alkalies as well as insoluble in water. Other Carotenoids are xanthophyll, associated with carotene, lycopene (the red pigment in tomatoes and watermelon), zeaxanthin (the yellow pigment in egg yolks and corn), capsanthin and fucoxanthin.

Anthocyanins: Anthocyanins are colour pigments which are found more in fruits and flowers than in vegetables. The colour varies from red to blue. Red or purple cabbage, purple broccoli, beets and skins of aubergine and radish contain large amounts of anthocyanins. There are 28 known anthocyanins. They differ in their degree of solubility and sensitiveness to conditions which produce colour changes. They are inclined to be red in acidic and blue in basic solutions. The colour changes of anthocyanins, unlike those of chlorophyll, are reversible.

While cooking vegetables containing anthocyanins, the loss of colour as well as change of colour must be considered. Beets lose their colour or 'bleed' during the preparation.

This is due to the great solubility of anthocyanins. High temperatures bleach this pigment, the colour returning partly when it is cooled.

Natural acids in fruits increase the redness of the cooked fruit. The colour of cooked red cabbage depends on the acidity of the cooking water. Tap water gives it a purple colour. Red cabbage is produced by adding acid to the water. The addition of cooking soda gives a bluish product.

Flavones occur in all plants, but particularly in white onions, white cabbage, cauliflower, etc. In an acid medium, they are colourless, while in a basic medium they are yellow. The reaction like that of arithocyanin, is reversible. Vegetables such as cauliflower can be made to change colour from white to yellow and back by holding them in fumes of acid or ammonia. Flavones are readily soluble in water as can be observed from the colour of the alkaline vegetable water, which is yellow. During cooking it is important to see that white vegetables do not turn yellow. The addition of acids such as lime juice or vinegar will keep them white.

Boiling: To prevent the nourishment escaping into the liquid and also to curtail the action of plant enzymes which have harmful effects on vitamins vegetables are usually put into boiling liquid. The exceptions to this are dried vegetables and root vegetables which should be started in cold water. Salt is generally added to the water, except when cooking dry vegetables, which do not cook well if salt is added at the commencement. The lid is kept on generally, except when cooking green vegetables, where the volatile acids present in chlorophyll must be allowed to escape or else they will discolour the vegetables. Lime juice brings out the whiteness of cabbage and cauliflower if added before cooking.

Potatoes: Scrub and scrape new potatoes, peel and eye old ones. Keep under water to avoid discolouration. To boil, put in salted water and cook till tender, drain and use as required.

Roast *potatoes:* Parboil, drain and cook in dripping around the meat for at least 45 minutes.

Saute potatoes: Slice cold boiled potatoes and fry in very little fat till brown.

Potato chips: Two methods are used:

(i) Peel and cut them in to finger lengths. Parboil, drain and put into hot fat. Remove when half done. Put into smoking fat or boiling fat and brown just before serving.

(ii) Cut the peeled potatoes into finger lengths. Dry on a towel. Deep fry in a pan till a faint blue smoke rises. Fry chips until golden brown. Drain on absorbent paper, add salt.

Spinach: Remove the stalk and damaged leaves. Wash very thoroughly in several batches of water to remove grit and mud. Put into a pan. Add salt. Place over gentle heat, when the juice begins to run over spinach, raise temperature and boil for 15 minutes. Drain and chop or sieve as required. Add pepper and a small knob of butter to taste. Before cooking spinach and other leafy vegetables, soak them for some time in water to which a little sugar has been added. This improves the flavour.

Green peas: Shell peas and place in boiling water with ½ teaspoon of sugar, salt and a sprig of mint. Boil till tender. Drain. Take out the mint and add a little butter.

French beans: String the beans. Slice them diagonally and cook in boiling salted water till tender (approx. 20 minutes). Cook with the lid off. Drain well and add a knob of butter.

Brussels sprouts: Found in a temperate climate. Cooked the same way as cabbage but kept whole. Slit stalk end into four before cooking.

Cauliflower: Wash thoroughly, remove outermost leaves if necessary but leave some on. Turn over and cut across the stalk. Put the cauliflower into boiling salted water and cook for 20 to 30 minutes.

Cabbage: Wash well, remove coarse leaves but use dark outer leaves. Cut in half. Remove the hard centre stalk, shred. Cook in a little boiling and salted water till tender (10 to 15 minutes approx.). Drain well. A few bacon rinds can be added to the water. Serve plain or tossed in melted butter.

Broccoli: Three types--white, green and purple.

Purple and green: To prepare, remove coarse stalks and wash the leaves and sprigs. Boil. Serve same way as cabbage or cauliflower. Particularly good with white saxice.

White: Prepare and cook as for cauliflower.

Turnips: Peel rather thickly. Cook in boiling salted water till tender this takes 20 minutes to one hour. Drain, add white pepper and salt and butter. The cooked turnips can also be mashed up.

Vegetable Marrow: Very young vegetable marrow may be boiled whole and unpeeled. Cook in salted water for 15 minutes. Drain and serve with melted butter. Large marrows must be peeled and the seeds removed. Drain well and serve sprinkled with brown bread crumbs or with cheese sauce. Marrow may also be baked whole, (peeled or not) and stuffed with any savoury filling. Bake in a moderate oven at 177°C (350°F) for one hour. Cover the marrow with greased grease-proof paper.

Tomatoes: Grilled, fried, stewed, baked or raw.

Onion: Remove the root and the outer skin. Apart from being used as a flavouring agent, onions can be boiled and served as a vegetable or used stuffed.

Carrots: Scrub and scrape lightly. Peel old ones. Cut into strips or into roundels. Add just enough water, salt and a little butter. Cook till the carrots are tender and the water has evaporated. Serve sprinkled with chopped parsley. Young carrots can be boiled whole.

Sweet Pepper: Capsicum, red or green. This can be served cooked or raw. To prepare the pepper, wash, cut out the stalks and remove the seeds. Red and green peppers may be cooked together to make a colourful vegetable dish. Slice and cook in a little salted water. Add a knob of butter. They may also be served stuffed, baked, boiled or stewed.

Corn on the Cob: Remove the sheath and silk threads. Cook in salted, boiling water till *tender. Serve with melted* butter.

Beetroot: Cut out the stalks about 2.5 cm. (1") from the root, taking care not to damage the skin. Wash and boil in salted water till tender (about 2 hours). Peel off the skin. Cut into cubes or slices and either serve hot, coated with white sauce, or cold in vinegar.

Celery: Wash celery thoroughly, using a brush to remove all soil. Separate the stalks. Tie into bundles. Cook in boiling salted water till tender. Drain and serve with white sauce.

Leeks: Remove the coarse outer leaves. Cut out the roots and green top. Split the leaf end so that it can be washed thoroughly. Tie in bundles and boil in salted water. Drain. They are usually served with white or cheese sauce.

Broad Beans: Shell the beans. Cook them in boiling salted water and drain. Serve with parsley sauce. Skin older beans before serving.

Asparagus: Cut the woody portion, scrape the white part lightly. Remove any coarse spine. Tie in bundles. Place upright in a pan of salted water and boil for 10 minutes. Then lay the asparagus flat and cook till tender. Drain well, remove the string and serve with melted butter.

Artichokes: Only the lower parts of the leaves and lower sections are edible; Wash well. Cut off the stems and trim lower leaves if necessary. Place head downwards in boiling salted water and boil gently until tender, for about 30 minutes with the lid off. When cooked, the leaves should be easy to pull off. They may also be dipped in a thin batter and fried. Serve hot with melted butter or margarine or hollandaise sauce. Do not pour the sauce over the artichokes. The lower sections without the leaves may also be used, either raw or cooked, in salads.

Artichokes (Jerusalem): Scrub well, peel, and to keep them white until ready to be cooked, place in a bowl of water to which a little vinegar has been added. Boil or bake. Serve plain boiled in the same way as potatoes or with white sauce. A very good augratin can be made with these artichokes. Can be served in soups, separately or with another vegetable such as celery.

Colour Reaction of Vegetable Pigments

Pigment	*Vegetable*	*Colour in acid*	*Colour reaction in alkali*	*Colour reaction to metals*
Flavone	Cauliflower	Colourless (white)	Yellow	All-yellow Iron-brown
Anthocyanins	Red cabbage Beetroot	red	blue to green	Iron-blue Tin-purple
Carotenoids	Carrots	orange	orange	
Chlorophyll	French beans Spinach	olive green	bright green	Copper-bright Iron-green

Pulses

Pulses are a good source of vegetable proteins and vitamin B complex. Being substances with very little taste, they should be combined with spicy and strong foods, e.g. bacon, ham, etc.

In Western preparations pulses are combined with onion, tomatoes, leeks, celery and bacon rind.

In Indian preparations pulses are combined with spices, coconut milk, tomatoes, leafy vegetables and herbs.

Cooking:

(i) If with skin, soak overnight in boiling water to soften skin, e.g. haricot beans, thick peas, etc.

(ii) Wash first before soaking so that the pulses can be cooked in the same liquid in which they are soaked. Those with no skins like lentils can be soaked in cold water. Bring to boil and cook with lid on;

(iii) Add salt after cooking, as salt inhibits the normal cooking process of lentils and pulses. Those with skins can be made into a puree, as it is the skin that causes indigestion.

In Western preparations these foods are rarely served plain boiled. They are generally mixed with other foods and browned by baking or frying. Use liquids for soups and gravies.

Cheese: Cheese, one of the oldest known food products, is universally popular. The chemistry involved in changing semifluid milk into semisolid cheese is complex and many factors enter into the final curing of cheese to produce the different varieties but they all begin with the action of rennet or lactic acid which performs the same basic function, that of coagulating the milk proteins. Simply defined, cheese is the solid or casein portion of milk separated from the whey. The curdling of the casein is brought about by the action of rennet or lactic acid. The many different cheeses are the result of variation in the making and curing of each variety after initial curdling has taken place.

Classification: Cheeses are classified into large general groups according to whether they are started by the rennet or lactic acid method. They may also be classified as unripened, mould ripened and bacteria ripened or as soft cheese, hard pressed cheese or blue veined cheese. Cheese is one of the most highly concentrated of all protein foods. It is also readily digested. Experiments have shown that from 90 to 99% of all cheese is digested. It is also a complete protein. Since approximately 10 litres of fluid milk are required to make 1 kg. of cheese, cheese contains many of the nutrients of milk in highly concentrated form--milk proteins, fat, fat-soluble vitamins and minerals.

Wholemilk cheese contains the same properties as milk. Certain cheeses such as blue veined are made out of skimmed milk and, therefore, are less nutritious. Normally cow's milk is used to make cheese, but certain well known cheeses are made from goat's milk. The texture of the cheese from goat's milk differs slightly from that of cow's milk. It is more crumbly. Sheep's milk can also be used.

The quality of the cheese depends to a great extent on the breed and the condition of the animal and the fodder given to it. Cheshire cheese is said to owe its fine flavour to the wild radish on which the cows feed, and its special nature is due to the mineral in ; the soil. Cheshire cheese, therefore, cannot be made in any other place as cheddar cheese can. Certain cheeses develop a blue vein in maturing. This is sometimes a purely natural development, often sporadic and unpredictable. Sometimes fresh cheese is inoculated with pieces of blue cheese to catch the mould by contact. In some cases special bacilli are introduced.

The mould is sometimes strengthened by brushing the cheese clean while the skin is soft, dipping it in whey and then rubbing it slightly with butter. This is done once a day for 10 to 20 days. Main types of cheese are:

(i) Unripened soft cheese, e.g. Cottage cheese, Cream cheese, Neufchatel.
(ii) Ripened in moulds by bacteria, e.g. Brie and Camembert.
(iii) Ripened by bacteria, e.g. Limbourger.
(iv) Semi-hard, ripened by bacteria, e.g. Brick cheese, Munster.
(v) Semi-hard, ripened by bacteria in moulds, e.g. Gorgonzola, Roquefort and Stilton,
(vi) Very hard cheese with gas holes, e.g. Gruyere, Swiss Cheese, Parmesan,
(vii) Very hard cheese without gas holes, e.g. Cheddar, Edam, Gouda and Cheshire.

Dishing and Garnishing: A good cook not only takes pride in preparing a dish correctly but also in presenting it properly to appeal to the different senses. This is done by suitable decoration and the way it is placed on the serving dish. One of the chief points that must be borne in mind when both dishing and garnishing is neatness. Decoration that is done without restraint or badly carried out is worse than no decoration at all. Decoration done on hot dishes must be done quickly to prevent cooling of a dish which should be served hot. The colours of the garnish and the flavour should blend with the main dish. Proper garnishing has a three-fold role in food service. It helps "dress" the plate, "style" the product and adds colour, flavour and eye appeal of its own.

Accompaniments: Accompaniments are dishes such as sauces, salads or vegetables which are used to make a dish complete. They provide variety and improve the nutritive value of the meal. What accompaniments should go with what, is usually determined by custom, based on a desire to enhance the flavour, to increase the digestibility and to improve a dish, e.g. roast beef with Yorkshire pudding, roast pork with apple sauce, roast duck with sage and onion stuffing and orange sauce, fried fish and chips with tartare sauce or tomato sauce, roast chicken with roast potatoes, buttered peas and bread sauce.

Forcemeat or stuffing are used to add flavour and piquancy to meat. They also help to increase bulk.

Sage and Onion Stuffing

Ingredients	*Quantity*
Onions	225 gm
Fresh bread crumbs	50 gm
Salt and Pepper	to taste
Butter	30 gm
Powdered sage or	
Fresh sage (chopped)	1 tsp
Method	

1. Boil chopped onions till tender, in just enough water.
2. Add butter and star till melted.
3. Add remaining ingredients, mix well and use as required.

Force Meat Stuffing

Ingredients	*Quantity*
Fresh bread crumbs	115 gm
Suet, mutton dripping or Butter	50 gm
Grated lemon	½ lime
Chopped parsley	2 tsp
Mixed herbs	½ tsp
Salt and Pepper	to taste
Egg or milk to bind	

Method

1. Mix dry ingredients.
2. Add binding.
3. Mixture should be crumbly should not be pressed heavily and not mixed too wet.

Bread Sauce

Ingredients	*Quantity*
Milk	300 ml
Onion	10 gm
Margarine	30 gm
Fresh bread crumbs	50 gm
Cloves	2
Mace	a pinch
Lemon rind or a strip of lemon	
Seasoning	

1. Boil the milk. Infuse the hot milk with onion, cloves, mace and lemon rind for 30 minutes.
2. Strain over fresh bread crumbs, add seasoning and margarine; stir well to a smooth consistency.
3. Stand in a warm place to thicken. Reheat and beat well; add one tablespoon cream if desired.

Sauces: Sauce is a liquid adjunct to a dish such as meat, poultry and vegetables used to moisten the food, to enhance the flavour, to provide contrast in taste or colour and sometimes to improve the digestibility (e.g. Roast pork with apple sauce); generally thickened by means of a liaison such as roux egg, blood, etc.

"A correct sauce is that wonderful production of the culinary art which forms a pleasant and exquisite accompaniment to all kinds of fish, meat, poultry, game and vegetables." The skill and knowledge of a cook is shown in no other part of culinary art so clearly and prominently as in the way the sauces are prepared. To make a perfect sauce is the height of the art of cooking. The most simple dishes can be made appetizing by the addition of a good plain sauce while the most recherche dishes can be improved and made still more palatable by a well-made sauce.

Sauces in cookery are the essence of elegance. Every sauce, whether plain or rich, must possess a decidedly distinct flavour and character. Plain sauces should be simple and pure so that they taste of the materials employed, from which they take their name.

Richer sauces always require a longer and slower process for their preparation. Sauces were hardly made use of in English cookery till the beginning of the nineteenth century. Today there are at least 650 different types of sauces and gravies. A clever cook can devise as many varieties as he needs in sauces as an artist can paint pictures. The art of sauce-making consists in preparing liquids from various materials by cleverly extracting and combining certain flavours into the liquid.

Besides this, a good plate as well as the experience and skill of the most accomplished cooks and a thorough knowledge ledge of the taste of those for whom the dish is being prepared, are necessary. Gravy is not a sauce. It is generally the juice of meat or vegetables seasoned but not thickened like a sauce. According to textbooks on cooking, a gravy may be called a sauce but a sauce cannot be called a gravy. Many of the more elaborate sauces have gravies as their foundation ingredient. It is easier to call a thinner liquid a gravy and a thicker one a sauce.

Liaison

The various processes of thickening sauces as well as

soups are called "Liaison'. There are six distinct methods known for thickening sauces:

(i) Liaison with roux
(ii) Liaison with egg.
(iii) Liaison with butter and cream.
(iv) Liaison with kneaded butter and flour (manied).
(v) Liaison with blood.
(vi) Liaison with farinaceous products.

Roux: The most popular and the most widely used thickening is roux. Roux is a mixture of flour and butter cooked to a definite degree - white, fawn or brown colour. Flour and butter are generally used in the same proportion. Roux can be prepared beforehand and stored, but it should be kept in airtight containers.

Approximately 60 gm of roux is required for 60 ml of liquid. If the roux is used cold, the Stock used can be hot or cold. If mixed hot, the liquid, which should also be hot, must be gradually added to the roux away from the fire. This is then stirred over the fire till it boils. Roux should be allowed to cool slightly before the liquid is added to prevent the formation of lumps. All roux must be stirred constantly during the process of cooking.

White roux or Roux Blanc': This is a mixture of flour and butter cooked in a pan over a moderate fire without allowing it to get discoloured.

Blond roux or 'Roux Blonde': This is prepared by melting a certain quantity of butter and stirring in the same quantity or a little less of flour and by cooking it over a slow fire or in the oven till it gets a fawn colour.

Brown roux or 'Roux Brun': This is generally known as stock roux and can be prepared in bulk and stored. It is prepared more or less in the same way as 'Roux Blonde' but is cooked for a longer period to get a deeper brown colour. It is better to finish a brown roux in a slow oven so as to make it more brown without burning. This will also improve the aroma. With brown and blond roux, a mirepoix is added to give the-necessary flavouring to the sauce. Mirepoix is an essence or extract of meat and vegetables. The following ingredients are used: 225 gm bacon, 1 carrot, 1 bay leaf, 1 sprig thyme, 2 small onions, and 2 cloves garlic. Chop all ingredients and fry without browning.

Egg Liaison: This is a thickening composed of egg yolks beaten up and diluted with a small quantity of cream, milk or cold white stock. Cream is used more often than stock. When the soup or sauce is boiling it is removed to the side of the fire and a spoonful of the boiling liquid is added to the egg mixture gradually and then the whole is poured slowly into the sauce and stirred over the fire without allowing it to boil. It is passed through a tummy before it is served. This liaison is used largely for banquettes, white ragouts (usually of vegetables) and white fricassees.

Butter *and Cream Liaison:* Butter and cream are incorporated in sauces and soups just before they are served. After the liaison has been added the sauce or soup is stirred vigorously without reheating. The flavour of the sauce alters if butter and cream are added too soon or if the sauce is allowed to boil after the addition of the liaison. The same applies to a plain butter liaison as well. Butter is added in small amounts the moment the sauce is taken off the fire. It is then stirred with a whisk and served without being reheated.

Kneaded Butter and Flour Liaison: Knead as much flour into the butter as it will absorb, to form a soft paste. Mix in small portions into a hot thin sauce. Stir constantly till the butter melts.

Blood Liaison: This is mostly used with hare or other game. It is made by preserving the blood of hare or game to which is added a little vinegar to prevent clotting. It is then strained through a fine sieve and generally added to the sauces.

3

Kitchen Management

> Knowledge without common sense is folly; without method it is waste; without kindness it is fanaticism; without religion it is death. But with common sense, it is wisdom; with method it is power; with character it is beneficence; with religion, it is virtue, life and peace.

Kitchen is the nerve centre of hotel and catering industry, similary as in a home. The objective of Kitchen Management is to lead, organize and control the means of production and service of food.

The catering establishments policy should be interpreted to the best of advantage, whether they are concerned by being an establishment of repute or to earn a good profit. To manage the kitchen, the Kitchen Manager/Chef de Cuisine should have a sound practical knowledge and should have the ability to organize labour, delegate the responsibility to appropriate staff who communicate well. The maintenance and cleaning of the machines is his responsibility. Labour saving, automatic machines are replacing the manually operated ones, the persons handling the machines should be able to follow the correct procedure for assembling, use and cleaning.

Safety precautions have to be observed such as:

(a) Gas pilot lights must be lit before turning on the main jet;

(b) The liquids should never be stored above eye level;

(c) The pot handles sticking out should never be placed over the edges of the stove or sides of the tables;

(d) Sprinkle flour on hot lids and pans;

(e) If fat or liquid is spilt on the floor, it should be cleaned and salt sprinkled on top immediately;

(f) Hot fritures should not be carried;

(g) Knives if carried should point downwards;

(h) Sharp instruments should never be left in sinks.

Techniques Employed

Controlling of labour needs great tact and ability, their comfort, skill, work and welfare has to be seen to. A strict disciplinarian is respected by many, provided he has a good judgement in dealing with matters and understands people.

An efficient management will see that food cost is controlled and the people working in the kitchen are content in their jobs and the work given is comparable with their ability. Staff should be trained on the job and if the performance is good, incentives, increments or promotions should be given, if need be.

Certain factors such as budgetary control, portion control, cost control, proper purchasing, control of production and service, control of waste, etc. play an important part in managing the kitchen. Proper layout of work areas in the kitchen contribute to a successful catering establishment which will not only satisfy customers but also the staff will be contented. Cramped and lack of proper kitchens delay food preparation and service.

Certain points have to kept in view before planning such as the types of meals to be served, number of persons to be served, forecast of peak period, ventilation, proper drainage, etc. It is important that the kitchen should be close to the restaurant to facilitate efficient service. A work plan identifies the precise steps for the task--type of food to be prepared and served, number and size of portions, time taken for food service, method of food service and presentation, location for food service, e.g. banquet room, dining-room.

Facilities in Kitchen: By law, no food business is allowed to be carried on in any insanitary premises.

A well-planned layout largely depends on:

1. Receiving quality supplies
2. Proper storing of food
3. Food preparation--Mise-en-place
4. Cooking
5. Servery
6. Scullery (Pan wash)
7. Scullery (Crockery, cutlery wash up).

Proper placing of machinery, sinks and work-tables are contributing factors to the total daily kitchen mileage of food and unnecessary travelling by the kitchen staff. A perfect planned kitchen is one, where raw and cooked materials need the minimum of movement and require only to cover the same route once. Attention must be given to lighting, wiring, ventilation, planning, hot and cold water service and appropriate specialists should be consulted.

Kitchen Area: Alongwith the restaurant, the kitchen determines the number of customers to be dealt with during service period. Kitchen areas vary according to the type and number of meals provided, and if allowance is to be made for special functions.

Generally, as the number of customers increases, the area of the kitchen relative to the seating capacity tends to be reduced. Knowledge of peak load is essential for intelligent forecasting. The area may be 40% of the restaurant area, kitchen space estimates have been as low as 2½ to 4 sq. ft. per catering unit for a kitchen catering for 1,000 to as much as 9 to 10 sq. ft. per head per meal served in small establishments. However, the modern school of thought favours small and more compact kitchen premises. 3 sq. ft. per head is now considered adequate. This is the space recommended for labour saving and is based on work studies.

The floor is subjected to much traffic, so durability must meet the demand of the particular premises. The floor should be impervious to moisture and should not be affected by grease, salt, vegetable or fruit acids and preferably non-slip even when wet. There must be no joints or crevices where dirt, pests and vermin may accumulate and live in. The walls should be tiled to the ceiling or at least to a height of one metre. Above the eye level, can be painted.

The ceiling should not harbour dirt and must be regularly cleaned to prevent dirt and condensation dropping on to the surfaces and food items below. The woodwork should be gloss painted as this is easy to wipe clean. Doors should be self-closing and they should have easily cleaned kick plates and finger plates.

Natural light should be used, if possible. The artificial lights when used should be properly fitted and shadows be prevented. The windows and mechanical inlets using ducts and fans should be carefully planned and sited. Canopy over cookery equipment and range should be connected by ducts to exhaust fans. The ducts should be sufficiently high and the exhaust fans should have a strong pull for maximum extraction.

Food Preparation

While food preparation is the term employed to denote

cookery, meal production follows a flow pattern which commences with the purchasing and selection of materials, their handling and processing and the ultimate presentation of the dishes to the customer where "food service" takes over. It is therefore obvious that we should start at the beginning and see that the purchasing of food is done properly.

The budget committee is formed for the purpose of preparation, coordination, review and revision of budgets. The various departmental budgets and master budget represent a coordinated effort. The budget is made periodwise or annually. The seasonal character of the business is taken into consideration. The first step in preparation is giving management objectives for the forthcoming year and giving a proforma to be used in preparation of budgets. The accounts' section prepares their budget in duplicate and sends one copy to the Head of the Unit who is responsible for the budget of the catering establishment and the budget committee reviews it.

Purchasing: Buying quality and freshness of supplies and portion control are of the utmost importance for the operation of a successful business. Large establishments will often employ a Purchase Manager, as he can concentrate and get the best supplies. Requisition for supplies are placed with the Stores/Kitchen Stewarding Department at a specified time in advance by the Chef de Cuisine for highly perishable supplies. The storekeeper will forward his requisitions for "Dry Stores" and cleaning materials in the same manner. Suppliers should be changed from time to time.

The buyer should have a reasonable technical knowledge in catering, as he will be able to follow the requisitions properly and understand the importance of delivery times, size, quality and specifications, etc. The purchaser should assimilate information, new ideas and techniques, gathered from trade journals, visits to exhibitions and food processing plants. The frequent comparison of competitive price lists from suppliers must be done.

Selection of the Suppliers

(a) The prices are competitive for the goods specified in relation to quality.

(b) The goods offered should meet specifications by looks and other related factors. Samples should be taken for checking.

(c) Financial terms offered relating to credit facilities and discount for settlement.

Selection will then be made of at least two suppliers for each "group" of supplies required in certain "groups" which include many commodities such as groceries. Three or even more suppliers may be selected. Where supplies are obtained by contract, obviously this will not apply.

Instructions to Suppliers: After the selection has been made of various suppliers, written instructions on the following points should be made:

(a) The person or persons authorized to accept and sign for supplies.

(b) Delivery times and any special requirements of delivery.

(c) The names of people authorised to order supplies.

(d) No alteration will be accepted between quoted and invoice prices.

(e) That goods supplied are as ordered, including special instructions relating to "brands and sizes".

In case of a contract, it will operate for a given period often for one year. The purpose of "Contract" buying is to obtain the best supplies possible at a fixed price over a stated period.

Ordering of Supplies: Orders for supplies, generally fall in 3 categories:

(a) Daily orders,

(b) Weekly orders,

(c) Standing orders. Daily orders are usually placed for perishable items such as meat, poultry, game, fish, fruit, vegetables, milk and cream, etc. The orders can be placed by telephone, confirmed by a written order.

Weekly orders consist mainly of dry stores, i.e. groceries, etc. Standing orders--Certain types of supplies such as milk, eggs, bacon, etc. are ordered for a specified quantity. The quantity stated is the minimum requirement. If more is needed, supplementary order is given.

Store Control

Food control begins when the orders are placed; it ends when the ultimate cash takings are banked. The stores should be close to the preparation area. Basic aim is a smooth flow from stores to preparation, to cooking, to servery and from the servery to the restaurant and then back to the wash up, so there is need to provide storage space appropriate to the size of the kitchen. The functions of the stores is to receive, check, store correctly, issue goods as required against requisition properly authorised. Strict control should be exercised as it provides cost figures and assists in future budgeting.

It is essential to check all incoming supplies for quality, weight and price. Supplies received should be promptly taken into stock, non-perishables should go into dry stores. Perishable items be stored in cold rooms, freezers, etc. The ideal dry store temperature range is 15°C to 18°C. Refrigerators for perishable foods are maintained at 1°C to 4°C.

Records should be kept to show the stock of each commodity received, issued and on hand with dates of receipt and issue, so that at any time the management can check the accuracy of the record. The stock should be taken at least once a month. The best system of accounting is a card index comprising a separate card for each commodity and all issues supported by relevant documents.

Preparation and Processing

From purchasing and the acquiring of the raw commodities, we come to the next stage in the catering cycle, the preparation and processing. Again, the operation must be planned and controlled and a knowledge of the menu together with a clear indication of quantities required are essential. Preparation means preparing food for cooking. It may require cleaning or washing and portioning or cutting up.

The chef decides how the food needs preparation for cooking and the process. Traditionally, cooking is considered an art. Technically, cooking is regarded as a chemical process, the mixing of ingredients and the application of heat. As we progress from the basic and simple operative tasks into the more advanced craft area of cuisine, a further element is included and this is creativity.

Cookery is a technical skill, knowledge is required to decide how to prepare the food and process it. These are decision-making factors. The practical aspect involves manual dexterity and manipulative skills such as knife drill, piping bag drill and other craft skill. Whilst it is recognised and appreciated that some have a greater aptitude than others, proficiency and the building up of speed do come with practice. This is particularly true with manipulative, decision-making and other skills together with the acquisition of knowledge.

Cooking Brings all the Senses into Play: Sight in the

recognition of commodities and the eye appeal in the presentation of dishes.

Smell in the testing of freshness of food and identifying the various cooking smells.

Taste an important field and one allied to smell, testing for flavour, the use of seasoning agents and the correcting of food for service.

Touch in the whole field of manual dexterity, the use of the hands, in sampling or testing of food for freshness, texture and other factors.

Hearing in communications and listening to food being cooked, recognising if the cooking process is too fast or slow.

Kinaesthesia is the sixth sense. A general term involving the coordination of sense in performing a task. The knowledge and the recognition on an unconscious level, this being achieved by proficiency.

Cookery brings all the senses into play. This is important to assist in developing skill and in training. Most chefs have highly developed senses particularly of smell, taste and touch with a built-in-sixth sense, that of kinaesthesia.

The different types of food should have their appropriate preparation point and space. Whatever raw materials are used, consideration must be given to the different cooking processes and once this is done, the cooking equipments can be selected and sited. The cooking and serving of high quality food, in large quantities and to a strict time schedule, is an exacting task even under favourable conditions. By the correct choice, disposition and use of kitchen equipment, the physical strain can be eased.

The preparation of dishes involves a mode of procedure which we know as a recipe. This is cooking to a formula. A recipe is defined as a statement of ingredients and procedure for a dish. To a recipe there are three operations, the list of ingredients, the method and the presentation of the dish for service. Recipes in professional cooking are basically standardized, more of a scientific formula.

Menu Planning

Traditionally, a menu is a list of prepared dishes which are available to a customer. There are many hard and fast rules in the gastronomic laws which must be observed if one is to obtain success, for a badly compiled menu will spoil the complete meal.

To be able to compose a lunch, dinner or supper, menu is an art in itself and the composing of an elaborate dinner needs care in selection of the various courses so that each dish harmonizes with the other. The chef should try to compile menus with new dishes from time to time and see the likes and taste of the customers visiting the catering establishment. The recipes should be standardised so that the exact costing of the dishes could be ascertained.

Cost Control

Whatever the size of the establishment that is operated, the basic management essential from the cost control point of view is to know first how much money has been received and second how much it has cost to take that money. The caterer must learn how to understand this and be able to interpret the results so that adjustments can be made where and when necessary. This is very important for the financial success of a catering establishment.

The major costs of meals fall naturally into three distinct sections, the first being the cost of the food and second the cost of the overheads, which include fuel, light, heat, water, staff uniforms and laundry, social security payments, superannuation contributions, printing and stationery, cleaning materials, advertising, telephones and postage, flowers, etc. licences, maintenance, contracts, replacement of crockery and cutlery, linen, utensils, repairs in general, insurance, and finally rent rates and interest on capital outlay. The third section is labour, the salaries and wages. The relationship between these classes of costs is always a matter of interest, which varies considerably from one type of catering establishment to another, the overheads, etc. usually being greater than the bare cost of food.

The problem of any management control system is to make sure that a pre-determined food and wage cost percentage has been decided. This figure will take in all aspects of expenses. The final trading results will show that a correct return has been made. To obtain this the following information should be studied:

1. Details of all merchandise received must be recorded, as and when issued.
2. All purchases must be controlled.
3. Any over-production of food must be checked and of course reused in the best and most economical way.
4. Production--ingredients and amounts.
5. Check of sales with direct numbers catered for.
6. An efficient system of cash control.
7. Sales of any kind checked with cash receipts.
8. A record of costs for each section (wine, cigars, flowers, meals, rooms) must be made and recorded. These must be compared.
9. Total daily wage costs must be recorded.
10. A weekly summary of all the relevant details must be prepared.
11. The trading profit and loss account should be prepared.

Methods of Cost Control: There are three basic methods of cost control:

(a) Quantity.
(b) Selling Price.
(c) Cost Price.

An effective system will disclose shortfalls in receipts which may be due to one or more of the following:

(a) Faulty buying.
(b) Inefficient storing.
(c) Bad and wasteful cooking.
(d) Petty theft and leakage.

Having known that the receipts from sales are less than could have been expected from the amount of food consumed, it becomes worthwhile to examine more closely where the loss is occurring and to take corrective action before it becomes disastrous. Costing and control must be regular and continuous.

Quantity Control: The control of quantity consumed ensures that everything consumed has been accounted for. It does not ensure profitability, but provides a useful supplementary check and is simple to operate. For simple dishes, this method is good but not for complex dishes. For small establishments when one storekeeper is responsible and issues one egg and two bacon rashers for breakfast, it controls consumption.

Control of Selling Price: This method is also most suitable for establishments with a limited range of items on the menu, especially when each item contains a small number of standardised ingredients. It can be used in conjunction with quantity control. When a comprehensive range of dishes is served and the composition in each is not rigidly standardised, it becomes necessary to adopt a different method based on cost.

Cost Price: This system is the most practical and best understood. It allows for a certain elasticity and provides the chief with a margin for artistic development. The kitchen percentage entails the application of the following simple formula.

When stock taking is done, there may be minor discrepancies in the percentage, but this has to be taken into account.

Sometimes there are variations in the percentage of profit over a short period. Such variations could be due to seasonal influences on price -- the menu price is not normally altered for each variation in cost -- or because some items are more profitable than others and the sales may vary. When a kitchen percentage drops below the normal figure, it should be presumed that something is wrong.

The decline could have been caused by the following factors:

(a) Incorrect billing (i.e. customers not paying correct price).
(b) Portions too large.
(c) Inefficiency and waste in the kitchen.
(d) Faulty purchasing.
(e) Dishonest practices.

Net Profit

All expenditure (costs) can be classified as material costs, labour costs and overheads. It follows that the difference between total revenue and the total of these costs is the net profit before tax.

In a business solely concerned with the sale of food, the gross profit would be the difference between total income and cost of materials and would therefore be equal to labour costs + overheads + net profit. A relatively simple control system providing basic information regarding profits, costs and trends should be communicated to the management promptly and regularly.

"Portion Control" means the amount of size of a portion of food to be served to a customer.

Food costing and portion control are complementary and the need for this form of control comes from both sides of the business--from the caterer and his customers. There is a natural tendency for clients to eye one another's portion when they are served and if one is thought to be slightly larger than the others, there is apt to be resentment and a reaction detrimental to the good name of the establishment.

Only exact portion control can eliminate this. It is not something that can be introduced at the service point, it must start when orders are placed for supplies. Monitoring portion control could be done by direct supervision by sales analysis and by comparing the requisitions of each department with issues.

Purpose

1. To ensure fair portions for each customer.
2. To see that each department utilizes purchases to the full.
3. To control waste.
4. To ensure that standard costing is as accurate as possible.

Methods

1. Ordering the right quantity and quality and supervising when receiving it.
2. Even preparing the food in the production area, under direct supervision.

3. By proper checking of the service of food.
4. Comparing the requisitions of each department with issues.
5. By sales analysis.

Aids to Portion Control: Portion control is done by using equipment and utensils as for example a scoop (ladle) used mainly for ice-cream, can also be used for mashed potatoes as a portioner for mixture.

(a) Automatic Portion Control Equipments Include--
tea dispensers
butter pat machines
bread slicing and buttering machines
gravity feed slicers
coffee-making, e.g. Cona machines
mini steak moulding machines
milk dispensers

Utensils Used in Portion Control Include--

ladles
serving spoons and scoops
woven wire servers
scales
measures
dariole moulds
pie dishes
baking tins

Serving Dishes that Help in Portion Control-

glasses
coupes
sundae glasses
souffle cases
cocottes
casseroles
tureens
sauce-boats
vegetable dishes
entree dishes

Various Sizes: As portion sizes vary from one establishment to another between table d'hote and a la carte service, it is difficult to give definite average portion sizes.

Losses in Preparation: The percentage of the waste of vegetables in preparation will be according to the kind and the quality used. To compute portion control and cost, the waste from peeling and trimming and also the shrinkage in cooking must be considered. If there are unskilled workers, there will be a tremendous waste and a high food cost. They should be trained to judge quality merchandise in order to be able to appreciate its value.

Visual Aid Sheets: A portion control sheet can be used for costing various items of food or complete dishes. The object is to ascertain the total yield of a given commodity after preparation and processing.

Such a sheet can be used in the experimental or research kitchen of a catering group or in the food preparation area when compiling standardised recipes.

Standardised Recipes: They assist in food costing and portion control by taking the guess work away and substituting more exact approach, by listing the ingredients and methods, in a readily-understood form as the results will be uniform everytime it its featured. The food cost can also be known in advance if a price column is introduced provided it is kept up to date with any price changes. The standard recipe will give a warning when the price charged becomes uneconomical and an increase becomes necessary.

Portion control in the catering industry is one of the greatest factors that contributes to a successful business. The general rule should be "a fair portion for a fair price".

Budgeting and Forecasting

Budgetary control and forecasting is not a substitute for the management. It is a discipline of action and policy-making administered by the management to ensure that short-term and further objectives are attained. It makes possible the maximum use of the assets, material and labour available and more importantly imposes on the management the obligation to specify its objectives. By highlighting the problems facing the management, it directs its energy into the areas most in need of management attention and improves the effectiveness.

The discipline of accepted norms of performance must be willingly accepted by the management and all personnel concerned with the attainment of the targets and objectives. The self-imposed discipline is a prerequisite of success of any budgetary or forecasting scheme.

Profit is the motive of all commercial enterprises. The intelligent application of forecasting and budgetary control will enable the management to tackle the problems in a positive and effective manner to this end, having first defined its target.

Advantages: The immediate gains of an efficient budgetary control and forecasting system to the long-term advantage, are--(a) Individual ability and skill can be demonstrated and acknowledged. Enthusiasm and confidence in the objectives of the enterprise can be inspired by encouraging individuals to set their own targets and for them to see their contribution, (b) Training and recruitment scheme to meet known needs can be more purposefully arranged. The redundancy risk reduced, expensive high labour turnover curtailed by planning expansion in operations. A projected personnel policy is then possible, with great advantage to all, (c) Efficient and equitable incentive scheme to encourage activists requiring stimulus can be introduced, (d) The development of continuous trained management aware of the necessity to keep up to data, (e) The confidence, that whatever difficulties the future may hold, the team will be able and willing to surmount them.

Some specific factors should be looked into such as:

(a) The forecasting of revenue.

(b) The conscious thought must be applied by the person responsible to the menu of earning the money and to the methods he will use to ensure that more is not spent than can be afforded.

Budgetary control can be carried out because of forecasting. Forecasting is a projection into the future of current trends or the basis of all the information currently available. Historic records are invaluable, but need subdivision for accuracy.

Avoiding Wastage: Essential elements in any form of control of waste up to data planning are effective supervision and maintaining records.

As in any business, the following three items must be kept under constant examination:

A ... Correct use of payroll.

B ... Correct use of materials.

C ... Correct use of services.

A. 1. Over or understaffed according to requirements.
   2. Job description, work schedules, job analysis.
   3. Communications from the management.
   4. Staff consultation.
   5. Departmental understanding.
   6. Labour saving appliances, cost and space involved, evaluation, full utilisation.

B. Essentials of purchasing
   1. Knowledge of purchasing.
   2. Standardised ordering.
   3. Quality purchases, specification ordering.
   4. Perishables when 'in season'.
   5. Purchase only requirements.

C. Store and Stock Control
   1. Records of goods in and out.
   2. Quality and quantity control
   3. Correct handling and storage
   4. Correct issues. Requisitions authorised.

Kitchen Control

1. Not to over order.
2. Correct and careful preparation, cooking and services. Standardised procedures, recipes, etc.
3. Correct yields from items.
4. Utilization of left-over foods.
5. Control of daily issue. Amounts consumed. Daily returns made of raw and cooked foods.
6. Actual meals number against issues.
7. Portion control chart and enforcement.

Equipment, Utensils and Cleaning Materials

1. Strict control of issues.
2. Supervision and instructions required.
3. Return on breakages and losses.
4. Correct use of items and materials.

Overheads have to be Paid for out of Sales

1. Cost comparison for particular periods of time.
2. Replacement of outdated equipment.

A workflow plan is necessary for the chef to perform the task in the minimum time possible with least effort.

CATERING STAFF

The organisation of kitchens will vary, mainly due to the size and the type of the establishment. Obviously, where a kitchen has hundred Chefs preparing for banquets for up to 1000 people and a lunch and dinner service for 300-400 customers with a lacarte menu, the organisation will be quite different from a small restaurant doing thirty table d'hote lunches or a hospital diet kitchen preparing diets.

Even when there are two kitchens of a similar nature, the internal organisation may vary as each Chef de Cuisine will have his own way of running his kitchen. It has been found most satisfactory in organising the work of a kitchen to divide it into "Parties' or "Corners". The parties system was perfected by Escoffier and it was the result of studying about the food production and the recipes allocating tasks to different specialists so as to help produce the more complex dishes regularly, efficiently and swiftly. The kitchen was divided into sections, each one of which was responsible for a particular contribution to the entire food production system. In the kind of kitchen Escoffier organised, the parties system reached the height of complexity because the end-products had to be of the highest finish and yet be completed to order in rapid sequence for a substantial number of customers. A set pattern was made. Basically the principles of kitchen organisation represent a standard practice though there are no set rules for deciding how many sections and how many staff a particular kitchen requires. Each catering establishment has different factors to be taken into consideration such as extent of menu, number of persons to be served and management policy.

A large kitchen, which caters for a large number, will have more sections than a smaller kitchen catering for lesser numbers. The number of staff in a section is determined by the amount of work to be done and importance of the contribution of the section to the menus and the skill of work. The base of different kitchen organisations is taken from the Traditional Kitchen Organisation that was pioneered by Auguste Escoffier, the instigator of the partie or corner system. He had many sections such as grill, roast, vegetable, fish, sauce, soup, larder patisseur, etc. As everything was done manually it was necessary but now the sections have become fewer, because of labour-saving machines, convenience foods and combined catering equipment (microwave cum convection ovens, etc.), and the changing of public taste, which seeks simpler menus and meals.

Recent trends are that the kitchen organisations vary with almost every establishment. In former times there were specialised large staffs called brigades. The various sections were being clubbed together to suit the establishments.

Many kitchens use fresh food, ready to cook and sometimes ready to serve. This speeds the preparation and cooking times. The kitchens have become smaller and cooks more versatile.

New establishments employ less cooks.

The team of cooks and their assistants under the partie system is commonly called the KITCHEN BRIGADE.

Specialists head the parties and with their assistants help produce complex dishes with great speed and efficiency. All the heads of the parties come under the control of the Chef de Cuisine (Head) aided by one or more sous chefs. In small establishments, head of the larder or sauce section acts as Sous Chef.

Various Functions

Larder: The word larder has in professional kitchens a much wider significance. The larder is not simply a place where food is stored but a place where the raw materials for cooking are prepared and dressed. In large establishments, the work is further broken into sections.

The larder is a room set aside for the storage of perishable foods, both raw and cooked, where food as meat, fish, poultry and game are prepared and made ready for cooking. In this department too, all cold items found on the menu, such as hors d'oeuvres, cold dish or meat dishes, cold salads, etc. are prepared and dressed. For these functions to be effective, it is essential that:

1. The room be separate from the kitchen situated in a cool place. At the same time, it must be close to the kitchen to avoid undue running about between the two departments which are closely interrelated.
2. It should be suitably lighted, well-ventilated and sufficiently open to allow the staff to perform their duties in a clean and efficient manner.
3. It must be equipped with the necessary fittings, plant, machinery and tools in accordance with the volume, and or quality of the trade of the catering establishment in which it is situated.

Breakdown: Work is broken down into various fields such as salads, poultry, cold buffet, hors d'oeuvres, mousses, cold cuts, sandwiches, etc.

The butcher receives directions from the larder chef according to the commitments of the business. The butchery prepares various joints in advance according to the menu requirements. Each day certain quantities of meat are trimmed to the first stage, (removal of excess fat, skin and other inedible parts). The butcher carries out further preparations to certain meat items, i.e. boning and trimming to bring it to the stage for final cutting and trimming.

Each day a pre-arranged amount of meat is cut and trimmed to the final stages against the menu requirements. Usually in catering establishments with an extensive banqueting service, it will mean that the butcher will have a considerable amount of preparations in the stages mentioned above. By this method the section at all times is able to meet the requirements of the kitchen.

In the larger kitchens, the larder section includes fishmonger, who will trim and prepare the dish ready for service and delivery. The chicken is dressed, trussed or cut according to requirements of the menu. Quenelle mixtures are also prepared here. Charcutiery (port section) pork products and sausages are prepared. Rendering of dripping is also done here. All cold buffets, including afternoon receptions are prepared in the larder. Chef de Froid controls the cold buffet section. An important part of the larder duties is the rapid supply of various prepared foods to the kitchen at all times especially during service periods. Salads are prepared and assembled in this section. Hors d'oeuvres are also made and trolley is replenished by the hors d'oeuvriere. Decorative cut vegetables are prepared and they are used for decorating reveries.

Larder Control: If this department is to be run efficiently and economically, it is essential that chef larder manager should exercise the strictest possible control over the foodstuff received and stored in the department. This involves:

1. Checking the quality and quantity of all goods delivered to the larder.
2. Ensuring that all foodstuffs are stored at the required temperature and they can be easily checked.
3. That the food is protected from contamination by vermin.
4. That portion control is rigidly carried out, e.g. given weight of meat, or fish or vegetables, etc. should always produce the required number of portions of steaks, fish fillets, salads or hors d'oeuvres.
5. That stocks of food are regularly turned over.
6. That food is not overstocked.
7. That daily stock sheet kept by each should be submitted to the chief larder manager at the end of the day to enable him to write out his orders for the following day.

The Larder Chef, at a set time each day, notifies the Chef, of stocks, of cooked or raw materials remaining.

Sauce Section: The sauce section is responsible for providing all meat, poultry, game and offal dishes with the exception of those that are plain roasted or grilled. All the meat dishes are cooked and garnished. The partie will also provide all basic and finished sauces served hot, that are normally required by the various parties in the kitchen. Normally, one first commences early duty to cover the preparations and cooking of dishes as "Plat de Jour" as these often require a cooking time of 3-4 hours. Braising, boiling, peeling is also done in this section.

Similar to the fish partie an extensive part of the dishes are cooked, and a variety of cooked garnishes are also prepared. Miseen-place for banquets is also done here. The Chef Saucier does important work as he assembles dishes which have an impact on the customers.

Roast Section: The roast section is responsible for providing all roast dishes of meat, poultry and game. It is responsible for all grilled dishes of meat, chicken, offals and fish, and this duty is often delegated to the grill cook. The section is also responsible for the preparation of a number of dishes and the deep frying of the food items. It also prepares and finishes any savouries that are required.

Fish Section: This section is responsible for the provision of all fish dishes with the exception of those that are plain grilled or deep fried. The cleaning, descaling, filleting, crumbling is done by the fishmonger in larder.

Generally as a larger selection of fish are offered, an extensive mise-en-place is required.

At each service period, the following basic sauces are made ready for service: bechamel, white wine sauce, fish veloute, hollandaise and melted butter. Further, a number of garnishes are prepared in advance to a part cooked stage. By this arrangement, a variety of fish dishes particularly the poached and meuniere types can be done. Grilling is done by the grill cook or commis.

Vegetable Section: An entrement course in France was the responsibility of the entrement of vegetables, who skilfully prepared and cooked vegetables, which could be served as a separate course. An entrement was originally something sent to the table between the courses in France.

During the period before service, each day various quantities of vegetables are prepared, cooked, refreshed and placed into refrigerator. Peeling, cleaning and trimming are done by semi-skilled workers. Limited quantities of certain potato dishes are cooked and finished to varying degrees, kept ready when service begins. Vegetable garnishes are prepared here and given to other sections.

The cooking of eggs forms an important part of the work in this section. Particularly omelettes of various types, e.g. plain, garnished, stuffed and flat round omelettes.

Italian pastas but not noodles are also prepared in this section. Items like spaghetti, macaroni, rice may be sent to other sections for garnishes. The mise-en-place is carried out according to menu requirements. By this method, the vegetable cook and senior commis are able to cope with the finishing and serving of a vast amount of different dishes.

Management of cooking vegetables well for large numbers calls for particular knowledge, skill and judgement and should never be entrusted to an unskilled and disinterested cook.

Soup Section: It is the responsibility of this section to prepare soups such as consommes, creams, veloutes, purees, broths, bisques and many special international soups. All basic stocks are also prepared here. The cold soups are prepared and passed to the larder for service. The garnishes come from the larder and vegetable section.

Indian Section: This section is responsible for the preparation of all Indian dishes. The work is sub-divided into subsections such as: Indian (bread and rice, pulaos, biryanis, chappaties, puries, bhaturas, etc.), vegetables, (bhajees, curries), meat, (including eggs and fish), tandoor (seekh kababs, tandoor chicken, boti kababs), Indian sweets (jalebis, rasgullas, rabri, etc.) Each day a variety of dishes are prepared according to menu requirements.

Pastry Section: The work of this section is normally separated from the main kitchen and is self-contained in the matter of cold storage. The function of this section is to prepare hot and cold sweets, for lunches, dinners and pastries for tea-time and other occasions. It also prepares pastes like short and puff pastry, frying batters for making noodles for supply to other corners of the kitchen.

Sorbets and water-ice like items are made In pastry section. The service of ices and those sweets which are based upon ice-cream are prepared and assembled in Patisserie. They also include the sweet omelette au surprise and souffle surprise, melbas, etc. The art of pastry includes work like coloured sugars to make flower baskets and similar decorative centre pieces, work with fondant and icing sugar, gum pastes, fashioning of praline into decorative objects. Where hotels operate a bakery section, the responsibility is carried out by the master baker. Normally one commis will commence early duty each day to provide the mise-en-place required by the various sections. The section needs workers with skill, imagination and experience.

Pastry Mise-en-place: In common with the Larder and Kitchen Departments, the successful running of the pastry department depends on adequate mise-en-place.

Mise-en-place must not be confused with stores, even though stores are, in fact, a form of mise-en-place in that they are ordered in advance and are, in fact, preparation department. To the production department, mise-en-place is the only method of preparing ahead, as the preparation of mincemeat and Christmas puddings is done in this manner, it is usual to make the pudding early in November.

Briefly the following is the mise-en-place for kitchen and larder; it is only mentioned to prove the importance of mise-en-place. (These departments will explain more fully in their own lectures on the subject,)

Kitchen: Stocks, sauces, bechamel, vegetables.

Larder: Joints of meat, poultry, fish, meat for pies, puddings, etc.

In common with the Larder, the pastry is also a supplying department and the mise-en-place for these other departments must be taken into account.

Tartlet cases, bouche'es, Nouilles, pie and pudding covering, etc.

The following is a list of the most essential pastry preparations:

Pastes: Short, sweet, puff (left at four turns), brioche, pate a' crepe.

Creams: Butter-cream, frangipane, creme patissier, creamed rice.

The above should always be available, and kept in the refrigerator but not a freezing point: 40° is cold enough. Pastes become very difficult to manipulate if they are frozen.

The butter-cream is used for various gateaux, creamed rice for Condes, baked rice pudding (a' la carte).

The pancake batter is also for a' la carte service.

Creme Patissier has many uses, being a quick source of sweet souffles and weakened down for trifles, sauces, etc.

It is an advantage to have a supply of creme caramels for they are in constant demand as a' la carte-sweets.

Coryotes of fruit are used in the main meals and the mise-en-place must include figs and prunes as they are in constant demand at breakfast. Naturally, tinned fruit should be used only when fruits are out of season.

Genoese, Swiss Rolls, finger biscuits, meringues, vacherins are essential mise-en-place for the easy preparation for gateaux, trifles, meringue, Chantilly or glace, Charlotte Russe, etc.

Pastries can either be partly prepared in the form of frangipane tartlets, barquettes, etc. or the tartlet cases lined with paste and finished the following day, in the same method as such things as vol-au-vent, bouche, fleurons, etc.

If ice creams in their many forms are made on the premises, they should be made in advance; this includes bombes, biscuit glace, souffles, glaces. Sorbets are not suitable as mise-en-place.

Dry petit fours in the form of macaroons, langues des chats, etc. as also pastilles de menthe, fudge, coconut kisses are easily stored, leaving only the fondant and sugar dipped varieties to be completed on the day of use.

Duty and Responsibility

Chef de Cuisine: The Chef carries the full responsibility for his kitchen. He must be both cook and administrator, i.e. as well as being able to cook, an authority on culinary matters, he needs to be capable of ensuring quick service and maintaining discipline. He must have a strict sense of economy and efficiency. He should be fully acquainted with the prices, market trends, commodities in season and customer requirements. His principal function is to plan, organise and supervise the work of the kitchen.

He prepares a pre-determined percentage of profit and works in accordance with the policy of the establishment.

He is responsible for staffing, selection and dismissal in consultation with the Personnel Department.

If need be, he should train the trainee cooks. Modern experts favour relieving the Chef from the details of purchasing so that he can concentrate on more important aspects of managing his kitchen and attending to the actual food production side.

Purchasing is becoming specialised and is vital to the economic structure of the undertaking. It is done in consultation and cooperation with the Chef. The Chef is responsible for the staffing of the kitchen and for the organisation of duty rosters. The Chef concents himself with the quality of food and its presentation. He is the departmental head and is responsible to the management.

Sous Chef: The assistant head chef understudies the Head Chef in all his duties. It is the Sous Chef who calls up the order from the kitchen and supervises the service. He is mainly responsible for the efficient day-to-day functioning of the kitchen.

The Sous Chef supervises the practical kitchen activities. When the Chef is busy he can make ad hoc staff changes during the working day to relieve pressure. In large establishments, there are a number of Sous Chefs, especially when there are separate kitchens like grill-room, restaurant, banquet service.

Chef de Partie: For the different sections in the kitchen, there is a "Chef de Partie", i.e. roast cook, larder cook, etc. Each Chef de Partie is assisted according to the production load, by one or more commis cooks; first, second, third commis and also trainees. It is sometimes the practice, where long operating hours apply, for the working period to be split up between the Chef de Partie and his first commis, though the Chef de Partie is entirely responsible for his partie throughout the working period. Alternatively, there may be two separate and complete "brigades" rotating upon an a.m. and p.m. basis. This system is very much favoured, since it does away with split duties. All the Chef de Parties may be regarded as supervisors or foremen of their sections as well as skilled craftsmen.

Chef Rottiseur (Roast Cook): He is responsible for the production of all roasts and grills of meat, poultry and game, grilled and deep fried fish, deep fried vegetables, potatoes and savouries. He prepares sauces, accompaniments and garnishes for roasts and grills. In large establishments, grilled items are the responsibility of the grillardin or grill cook. It is usual for the grill cook to work under the supervision of the roast cook.

Chef Saucier (Sauce Cook): The sauce cook is usually the "star" party because his job is most complex. The Chef Saucier will be Sous Chef in the making and will eventually rise to Chef de Cuisine. It is here that all the sauces, meat, poultry, entrees are prepared together with the necessary garnishes. He prepares his own mise-en-place, for many items he will receive like steaks prepared from larder, etc. The sauces prepared must be distinctive but not overpowering.

Chef poissonnier (Fish Cook): The fish cook prepares all the fish entrees and the roast cook deals with all roasts and deep fried foods. The fish prepared comes from the larder and the Chef does the cooking, garnishing, saucing and the dishing of fish. The repertoire of fish dishes and their accompanying sauces is very challenging and extensive training and judgement are required from this Chef.

Chef Potager (Soup Cook): The soup cook prepares all types of soups, and is responsible for the garnishes accompanying the soups. The Chef sometimes begins work early; the work of the potager is important as soup gives an impression of the meal to follow.

Chef Entremettier (Vegetable Cook): The vegetable cook is responsible for the production of vegetables and potatoes.

Chef Garde Manger (Larder Cook): The larder cook is the most spectacular and the busiest, because the work is never ending. Besides feeding the main kitchen with prepared foods for processing, he has to keep the cold buffet supplied. It is a cold section and is the storehouse of the kitchen where all perishable foods are kept. He has a wide-range of work to do, as the larder has various sub-sections such as hors d'oeuvre, a salad section and a butchery section. The cold buffet work, sandwiches, canapes are also his responsibility.

Chef Patissier (Pastry Cook): The pastry cook has different status but certainly not less than the sauce cook and the larder cook. His work is specialised, and he prepares hot and cold puddings, cakes, pastries, bread, etc. He is also responsible for special display work and the supply to the main kitchen of items of pastry.

Chef de Banquet (Banquet Cook): In many of the large hotels with extensive banquet commitments, the brigade will have a Banquet Chef and one or two commis. The Banquet Chef is responsible for organising the service, co-ordinating with the Chefs de Partie, the time and service, numbers for the arrival of various dishes to the service area. He further arranges, to what point the dishes are finished and make the necessary arrangements to carry out completion at the service point.

Sometimes this will mean his having to move his service staff from one service point to another, i.e. there may be an established banquet service point in the larder, another in the pastry section, apart from the main service area in the kitchen allocated for this purpose. The Banquet Chef will coordinate with the banqueting manager regarding times, service numbers, special dishes required, and special instructions to the waiters concerned.

Chef de Petit de Jeuner (Breakfast Cook): He commences his duty very early. He does not rank as a Chef de Partie but nevertheless needs to be of good skill, within his limited field. He is responsible for the complete breakfast service. Afterwards he has to complete his mise-en-place for the following morning. Sometimes he assists the soup or vegetable cook.

Chef Tourant (Relief Cook): He is relief Chef de Partie. He takes over a section when its Chef goes on leave or has an off day. Chef is usually a senior, capable commis as he has the knowledge of the various sections.

Chef Communar (Staff Cook): In small establishments, the staff food is prepared by different Chefs de Partie. In large establishments, a separate section or a separate kitchen prepares the meals. Staff ordinarily prepare meals for lower or supervisory staff as the executives eat their meals in restaurants. Wholesome food and inexpensive meals are prepared.

Kitchen Porters/Commis: The head porter controls the issue and collection of laundry to the kitchen personnel that is supplied by the establishment.

Though a lot of duties of the kitchen porter require little skill, by correct good training, they become most valuable members of the kitchen brigade.

4

Spices: Types and Utility

> Waste is worse than loss. The time is coming when every person who lays claim to ability will keep the question of waste before him constantly. The scope of thrift is limitless.
>
> —*Thomas A. Edison*

Spices add to taste, makes things appeasing, palatable appetizing, and vigorable. Though spcies are used in food everywhere, but are given special emphasis in the orient, especially in India. Down through the ages India has been known as the land of spices. Sweet or pungent, aromatic and seductive spices have played a special part in the life, legend and ritual of the country. With the march of time, although there have been several changes in the use of spices, their qualities for enhancing food still reign supreme.

The basic function of spices in Indian food is to improve the flavour of the dish. Many spices such as cloves, coriander, cumin seeds, cinnamon, etc., because of their volatile oil contents, impart various flavours to the food. These appeal to the sense of smell and render the food more palatable. The primary quality the common man looks for in a food product is its organoleptic quality (or the sense of taste), rather than its nutritive value.

As a result even highly nutritious food is not accepted unless it is adequately spiced. It is only where pleasure to the eye and palate meet that food becomes fully acceptable. The best chefs of the world consider flavourings and seasonings absolute necessities for achieving this objective. The success of cooking depends largely on their aid. However, spices must be used with skill and, above all, sparingly.

All palates do not crave highly spiced foods, yet most people demand that food should be adequately spiced, for the flavour of insipid food can be improved very much by the use of some suitable spice.

Even the people of the West, particularly the English and Americans who have a tradition of bland food, are now introducing a variety of spices into their dishes and appreciating the added piquancy of the food. Western palates, however, are sensitive, and therefore can appreciate the subtle flavours more readily than we do, as unfortunately, owing to the continuous consumption of over spiced foods, we have lost this power. Whenever possible, only such spices should be used as bring out the natural flavours of the main ingredient, rather than imparting a new one. Intelligence, carefulness, thorough, sound judgement, a steady hand and a keenly perceptive palate are qualifications every cook must possess in order to prepare food that is appetizing and pleasant to the taste.

Importance and Advantages

Apart from enhancing the flavour and aroma of food, spices have a physiological action beneficial to our system. They act as a stimulus to the digestive system and help digestion in many ways. Every spice used in the making of a curry is a preservative. All have some antiseptic value and many are carminatives, i.e. they tend to reduce flatulence as in the case of omum (ajwain) water given to babies.

The traditional combination of spices used for certain dishes must have been made with this factor in mind, e.g. the use of ginger or mint with peas. Peas are flatulence-forming and ginger or mint counteracts this effect. Asafoetida, commonly used with pulses (dais) of various types functions in a similar manner. Some spices are used to give colour to food, to improve eye appeal, e.g. turmeric in yellow rice, red chillies in vindaloo, rattanjog in roganjosh, etc. Spices also serve as a thickening agent in the preparation of curries, e.g. onion and poppy seeds.

Other Uses

The therapeutic value of spices is well known. Spices and herbs play a very important role in some of the simple but effective home remedies. Almost every spice has medicinal properties. Investigations are being conducted scientifically to elucidate the therapeutic properties of the various spices.

Many have already been accepted and are being used today, e.g. aniseed (saunf) which has been used from prehistoric times as a flavouring for cough mixtures and as a herb tea to soothe the nervous system and induce sleep. Scientists have recently probed the effect of cloves on the digestion. Studies of clove oil have shown that it stimulates the flow of gastric juices and is non- injurious to the lining of the stomach. Garlic has been accepted in both India and China as one of the treasured spices and medicinal agents. It has been indicated in the treatment of numerous diseases such as haemorrhoids, rheumatism, dermatitis, abdominal pains, coughs, loss of appetite, etc.

Although garlic is claimed to be useful in the treatment of such a variety of diseases, it is not popular because of its strong smell and pungency. Research has now made it possible to administer the active principle of garlic in a fairly concentrated form. Ginger tea is used commonly to ease an ailing stomach.

Nutmeg is used medicinally to cure biliousness, diarrhoea and headaches. The ancients prized the seeds of fenugreek because of its stimulating effect on the digestive system. To enhance the flavour and aroma of foods, spices may be used whole or in pieces, as in pulaos and biryanis, or in powdered or ground form. Indian cooks are artists in the use of spices.

Money may limit the variety of spices used by some, but others are limited only by their own creative imagination. While freshly ground masalas (mixed curry spices) are preferred to powdered masalas, owing to the shortage of domestic labour there is a definite trend today towards using spices mainly in powdered form. Many combinations of spices to suit different tastes are marketed today as various forms of curry powders. When using spices in powdered form it is essential that the powders be extremely fine. Coarse powders do not blend well with the rest of the ingredients; this causes a separation thus allowing the spices to float. The fine powders should be mixed into a paste with vinegar or water and then fried well before meat or vegetables are added. Besides curry powders, practically all the dry spices such as coriander, turmeric, cumin, fenugreek, cloves, cinnamon, mustard, etc., can be cleaned, dried and powdered.

Varieties

With the developemnt and introduction of modern techniques, moist spices such as onion, garlic and ginger are now obtainable in powdered form. This process, while retaining the original flavours, improves the keeping quality of spices, and makes transportation more economical and easy. Onion powder is used commercially in the manufacture of processed meats and sausages, and for flavouring vegetables and meat. Garlic powder has many commercial uses and is also now being used by the housewife who wants a clean and convenient method of using this popular flavour. Ground masalas are also available in the market today. They are packed in plastic bags and sold, but the keeping quality of these is poor as they are susceptible to spoilage. All powdered spices, however, must be kept in airtight containers to prevent spoilage and deterioration in aroma and flavour, caused by the evaporation of volatile oils.

Further liquid spices now available in the market as straight liquid spices, such as liquid red chillies, green chillies, ginger, coriander, cumin, garlic, nutmeg, cinnamon, cloves, cardamom, asafoetida, saffron, curry leaves, etc., or as ready-to-use compounds such as liquid masala for curries, pulao, mutton, fish, etc., have revolutionized the use of spices. These liquid spices are extracts of indigenous natural spices and are the result of years of research. By the separation of the active principles from the residual matter, concentrations are prepared.

These are easy to use and are being used widely in the commercial manufacture of sauces, fruit juices, ketchups, salad dressings, tinned pulaos, curries, etc. They have a better keeping quality than curry powders, and mix readily with the rest of the ingredients, thus bringing a uniformity of colour and flavour to the food. They are clean, "compact, suitable for transportation and storage and are available in glass bottles with droppers, ranging from 15 ml (½ oz) to 500 ml (1 Ib). They impart original flavours and colours. Thickening agents such as ground onion, poppy seeds, coconut and coconut milk should still be added to maintain the desired texture of the food. For those spices where flavour is the primary function as in cardamom, cloves, cinnamon, nutmeg, etc., the liquid form can be used most effectively.

It also makes it possible to be able to use out-of-season flavours. For example, when ginger or green chillies are not available, as in the summer months, the same flavours can be readily obtained by using liquid spices. Provided they are used carefully, liquid spices do not in any way increase costs, while at the same time they save labovir and time.

Allspice: This is the berry of 'Eugenia Pimenta', a small tree grown in the West Indies. The berries are gathered when green and unripe and dried in the sun. Then they turn black. Large quantities of these are used for the manufacture of sauces and pickles sold commercially. The berries combine the flavour of cloves, cinnamon and nutmeg. This spice is also known as 'Jamaica Pepper'.

Cloves: A very old and important spice, the clove was known before the time of the early Egyptians. The word is taken from the Latin 'Clavus' and the French 'Clou' both meaning nail, which describes its shape. The clove tree (of the order of the myrtle) grows to a height of 9 metres. The unopened flower buds are carefully harvested. Upon browning, they lose half their weight. Cloves are used in both Western and Indian dishes, both savoury and sweet, e.g. pulaos, cooked ham, sauces such as bechamel sauce and bread sauce, meat dishes, fruit salads, baked apple, etc. The oil of cloves is used in dentistry to soothe toothaches, and its antiseptic properties are well known. It is grown on the islands of Zanzibar, Pemba and the East Indies, West India and other tropical regions.

Mustard: A product of great antiquity and grown in most parts of the world, mustard is used in both Western and Indian preparations. It is used in the West in powdered form, as a table condiment and for flavouring sauces, etc. The pungency is more fully brought out when mustard is moistened with water (prepared mustard). In India it is used whole for tempering dishes, and in pickles. It is also an important ingredient in certain masala powders, e.g. vindaloo.

Nutmeg and Mace: These are the only known cases of two different spices from the same fruit. Nutmeg is grown in the Dutch East Indies and Grenade in the British West Indies. The tree begins bearing fruit at the age of 8 years and continues to yield for half a century or more. In its wild state the tree grows to a height of about 22 m. or 70 ft. The nutmeg fruit resembles an apricot in size and shape. What we call the nutmeg is the seed. It is protected by a thin shell; the shell has a coat of orangy flesh which dries into mace. Although the aroma of mace is similar to that of nutmeg, separate uses exist for each. Nutmeg is used in Western and Indian dishes in puddings, sweetmeats, for flavouring egg and milk and in some curries. Mace is also used to flavour sauces, stocks, sweet dishes such as halwas as well as in betel nut mixtures. Nutmeg is used grated fine and mace coarsely crushed. When buying nutmegs choose those which are round, compact, of oily appearance and heavy for their size.

Cinnamon: This is taken from the bark of an evergreen tree belonging to the 'laurel' family and is chiefly cultivated in Ceylon and the East Indies. First the outer bark is stripped of the three-year-old branches, and then the inner bark is loosened and dried. The best cinnamon should not be too dark in colour and should be as thin as paper. It has a fragrant odour and its taste is pleasant and aromatic. It is used in both Western and Indian cookery, in cakes, buns, ketchup, pickles, in pulaos with cardamom and cloves, etc. It is used in the preparation of garam masala for curries.

Pepper: This is obtained from the seeds or berries of the plant 'piper nigrum' which grows in Malabar and other parts of India. Black pepper is made from dried whole berries, and white pepper from the same berries with the husk dried and removed. Pepper is one of the most universally popular spices, and is used in every type of savoury dish to improve flavour and to add to its piquancy. It is also one of the table condiments.

Cardamom: This is the fruit of a reed-like plant, native of the mountains of the Malabar Coast, but cultivated in Jamaica as well. The fruit is a small pod and the seeds within the pods have a strong, sweetish flavour. The pods vary from 0.5-2 cm. 1/4-1") and more in length. The small-sized ones are considered the best. Rich curries like khorma include cardamom. Powdered cardamom is a big favourite in cakes, puddings, halwas, etc. Pulaos and biryanis also depend on this spice for their popular flavour. Tincture of cardamom is used in stomach medicines.

Mignonette Pepper: This is ordinary white pepper coarsely crushed.

Long Pepper: It is a spice similar in taste to ordinary pepper but not so pungent.

Cayenne Pepper: Dried fruits of the capsicum plant grown in the Cayenne Islands. This is red in colour, resembling the red chillies of India without being as pungent. This is used in Western cookery where pungency is required, e.g. for devilled prawns.

Krona Pepper: Bright red pepper from the Hungarian paprika. It is much milder than cayenne pepper and forms a palatable seasoning for Western savoury dishes.

Red Chillies: Chillies are grown in large quantities in India and are used extensively in Indian savoury preparations. They also form an important ingredient of curry powders. Apart from being used as a condiment, they are also used in several medicinal preparations for the treatment of lumbago, neuralgia, rheumatism, etc. Although there are several varieties they fall under two main groups: *Capsicum anum* and *Capsicum frutescens*. The variety acuminatum (Capsicum Anum) is the principle source of commercially used red chillies.

Coriander: The fruit of a plant called 'Corianderum Sativum' of the parsley family. It is extensively used in the preparation of Indian savoury dishes and forms an essential ingredient of curry powders. It is used in the preparation of frankfurters (sausages) and by confectioners and distillers. The leaves are used for flavouring curries, in salads and chutney and as a garnish.

Cumin seed: This is a herb of the caraway type, producing seeds of a pleasant smell and flavour which are very popular. It is most widely grown in several European countries, India and Mexico. The cumin plant is less than 30 cm high. The seeds come from the fruit and their slightly bitter taste is said to stimulate the appetite and digestive system. Cumin is added to curry powders and used whole in savouries, biscuits and fried rice. It is also used in the manufacture of liquors, pickles and sausages.

Turmeric: This is the aromatic root or rhizome of a plant grown in India and the West Indies. It is sold in root form and as powder. The hard resinous flesh of the dried root varies from a dark orange to deep reddish brown, but in the powdered form it exhibits a characteristic yellow colour. Turmeric is a member of the ginger family but has a different flavour. It is used in curry powder not only for imparting colour and flavour to curries but also because of its preservative qualities. Game and meats that are dried are soaked in liberal quantities of turmeric and salt. Turmeric is used freely in Indian medicines too. Plasters of it are applied in cases of bruises; as a dry dressing on open wounds; paste of turmeric and neem leaves is used to heal smallpox marks, and so on. Turmeric has sometimes been used to replace the more expensive saffron as a colouring agent.

Ginger: This is the tuberous root of a plant 61 cm. (2ft.) or more in height and is one of the few spices that grow underground. Ginger is mainly produced in Jamaica and to a less extent in Sierra Leone, China, Japan and India. Because of its stimulating and digestive properties it is employed medicinally for dyspepsia and colic. It is also frequently used to disguise nauseous tastes in medicines.

The most common use of ginger is in making masalas, soft drinks, pickles and preserves, and in confectionery such as ginger biscuits, gingerbread, snaps, etc. Crystallized ginger is made from the young roots and is a delicacy. The best grades selected are called 'stem ginger'. Instant pickle can be made by chopping fresh ginger and green chillies and adding lemon juice together with salt. It is delicious specially one day after preparation.

Fenugreek: These are the dried ripe fruits of an annual plant grown in many European countries and India. The fresh leaves and tender stalks are used widely as a vegetable. Because of their stimulating effect on the digestion they are administered medicinally even to horses and cattle. The seeds are used in making curry powders and fried whole for seasoning pickles and vegetables. When ground with water, fenugreek becomes a slimy paste and so is used to give batters smoothness.

Aniseed: The seed is small, oval in shape, somewhat similar to caraway and it grows in China, Mexico, Peru, Argentina, Spain, Malta, Syria, Lebanon, India, Pakistan, Hongkong and Egypt. The seed is small, oval in shape, somewhat similar to caraway and is usually a greenish brown in colour. It is used in Western preparations and in Indian dishes. It is identified with the licorice flavour. It is used in making licorice confections, in baking, in the cordial anisette and other liquors. Its digestive properties are well known and it can be eaten plain after a meal.

Fennel Seed: The dried fruit of a perennial herb of the parsley family, fennel is grown -in Europe, India, Lebanon and Argentina. The seed has a licorice-like flavour resembling anise. Fennel is used both whole and ground. Bakers use it whole in Italy to stud breads and rolls. It is also used in sweet pickles, in the seasoning of soups, fish dishes, sauces, and in South Indian meat curries. It is also attributed with medicinal properties.

Burnet: This is not used much in cookery now except for salads. When bruised it smells like cucumber.

Caraway Seed: Fruit of a perennial plant of the parsley family. It has a pleasant, slightly sharp flavour with a sweet undertone. It is a native of Europe. Caraway seed is mostly used whole and is the principal flavouring in rye bread, and is widely used in rolls, biscuit and cakes. It is also used in cheeses, sauerkraut, pickles, soups, meats and stews. It is the chief ingredient of 'Kummel Cordial'.

Aromatic Herbs and Plants: The ones commonly used are parsley, bay leaves, thyme, marjoram, sage, tarragon, chervil, chives, onions, shallots, garlic etc. The bouquet garni which is the mainstay of French cookery consists of sprigs of chervil, chives, thyme, bay leaves, tarragon and parsley.

Parsley: It possesses a wonderful quality of masking the taste of a stronger flavour; so do not use too much of it when flavouring a dish. It plays an important part in cookery. It not only gives a finishing touch to stews and soups and sauces, but it is also used a great deal for garnishing purposes. Powdered parsley is an excellent herb which imparts a delicate flavour. To make powdered parsley, infuse some parsley leaves in boiling water for a few seconds. Drain and put into a hot oven to dry. Put through a sieve and use as required.

Tarragon and Chervil: The leaves of chervil possess a flavour which is appreciated by many people. Tarragon belongs to the same family as wormwood and the botanical name is 'Artemisia Dracunculus'. Of all the pot-herbs, tarragon and chervil give the strongest smell. They are used a great deal in French cookery for entrees, sauces, soups, salads, chad-froids, etc. Tarragon leaves are also used for flavouring vinegar.

Thyme: It belongs to the same family as mint. The

leaves are used fresh or dry for stuffings, soups, etc. It possesses a highly aromatic flavour and should, therefore, be used sparingly. Lemon thyme is a smaller variety and has a strong perfume like the rind of lemon. Leaves of ajwain (omurn) can be used as a substitute for thyme.

Capsicum: There are many types of of capsicum cultivated in the East and West Indies and in America. The capsicum fruit is both pungent and stimulating. In Mexico the pods are called chili and they are used to make hot-pickle and chili-vinegar. It is the powder of the dried seeds and pods that goes to make cayenne pepper. Capsicums are considered to be very wholesome.

Bay Leaves: The leaves of the common laurel are used in cookery to give a kernel-like flavour to stocks, mirepoix sauces, custards, puddings, blancmanges, and to the milk which is used for mixing cakes. They are generally dried and used.

Carrots and turnips: Next to onions, these are considered to be the most important flavouring vegetables for soups and sauces. Besides being used for flavouring, carrots and turnips are largely used for garnishing certain dishes such, as ragouts, boiled meat, etc. They are also used as a vegetable and as a puree for soup. It plays an important part in sauces. The rind, juice and the essential oils contain valuable properties. The rind or peel is used for flavouring a variety of dishes. Generally the rind is grated, but the best way is to peel the rind with a very sharp knife as thinly as possible without touching the white part. Lemon rind is preserved in sugar. When sour limes are in season buy them in large quantities. Extract the juice and mix one cup of salt to every four cups of juice. Shake well and keep in an airtight bottle--under refrigeration it keeps for months. Use whenever fresh lime is required.

Savory: There are two varieties of this herb; one is

called the "summer variety". It is taken from a flowery herb. Both varieties are used extensively in Western cookery.

Marjoram: There are four kinds of marjoram. The sweet or knotted marjoram, original a native of Portugal, is the one which is commonly used. It is used for soups, sauces, stews etc., and used either fresh or dry.

Mint: This belongs to a family of plants called Labiatae. The spearmint or the 'Mentha viridis' commonly cultivated in gardens has a better flavour and is the one used popularly in cooking. It has the property of removing flatulence.

Onions: The name onion is given to all plants of the onion tribe, e.g., leeks, garlic and shallots. The onion is, next to salt, the most valuable of all flavouring substances used in cookery. When onions, shallots or garlic are used in cookery they should be well blended with other flavours. Whenever onion is used as a condiment or seasoning and the article properly treated, the strong smell is removed.

Basil: A favourite herb in French cookery. It has a flavour similar to that of cloves. It is used for making such things as mock turtle soup and clear soups made out of shellfish.It is also used for flavouring vinegar.

Garlic: This consists of groups of several bulbs called cloves, all enclosed in one membranous skin. When used carefully and sparingly, garlic is an excellent condiment. It is considered to be very wholesome and is a stimulant.

Shallots: This bulbous root resembles garlic. It is a native of Palestine and was introduced to England by the Crusaders.

Vanilla: This was first discovered by the Spaniards. It is the fruit of an orchid. The best variety is grown in Mexico. It has a delicious flavour and is largely used for flavouring puddings, custards, liquor chocolate, etc. For flavouring purposes it is better to use the vanilla pod or vanilla sugar rather than the essence of vanilla, since the odour of the essence escapes rapidly.

Thus, spices, if used in right quanityt as per demand of a particular dish, make the foods much palatable. They have medical value too.

5

The World of Delicacies

> The superior man thinks always of virtue; the common man thinks of comfort.
>
> —*Confucius*

Different regions of the world have different varieties of delicacies and cuisines. Here, we are giving brief introduction of these with special features of preparation Indian and oriental cuisines being given more emphasis.

French Cuisine

It is recognised by the world as one of the finest cuisines. The French are known for their artistic temperament and so is their cuisine.

History of French Cuisine: At the end of the Merovigian period, the convents which had preserved all the traditions of the gourmands increased in France; it was the beginning of culinary art.

Violet le Due, in the course of his studies, said that the kitchens were large and high spit roasting was common, dishes were cooked on the fire itself. Ovens were installed in the twelfth century for preparing roasts. From the fourteenth century, sauces were a much appreciated part of culinary art. Menu was varied which included game, fish, fowl, butcher's meat. Vegetables were featured less. At the end of the sixteenth century, Italian cooks and pastry cooks were employed. They taught and prepared a number of dishes, which since then, remained in the French repertoire, e.g. cannelloni, revioli, (Farinaceous dishes).

In the seventeenth and eighteenth century, Royalty and high ranking people took great interest in food and the cooks in gratitude named dishes after them. The cooks during feasts or banquets were honoured if the food was good and appreciated. If something went wrong, they were flogged in front of the guests. Confectionery, foreign dishes such as Caviare, Punch, etc. became popular.

Since the close of 19th century, French culinary art has reached the highest point of perfection. Chefs like Escoffier and Prosper Salles, etc. published books on cookery, which had far-reaching influence and are known throughout the world.

France's contribution to the international culinary repertoire is well known. She has bestowed her own names on the majority of dishes creating technical terminology of international usage.

Gastronomy (style or custom of cooking or eating) is an art with defined rules; the same is true of its presentation. For French Cuisine- cooking and law are quite similar. With both, there is the challenge of problem solving, logic and reasoning.

Style of Cooking: French cooking is less complicated while cooking the garnishes served are more complex. It has a delicate flavour, as spices are used sparingly and they create a suspicion in one's mind, if they are incorporated in the dish. Great emphasis is laid on sauces, and it is even called sauce *cookery*. Every ingredient speaks its own language, Wines used for cooking enhance the taste, give an unusual flavour, this being a unique feature of French cuisine. The most important rule is to use only the best ingredients and the proper blend of colour and taste of ingredients.

Garnishes and Accompaniments: Garnishes and accompaniments play a key role in French Cuisine and dishes are identified by them. Food items are cooked in sauces or they accompany a dish, e.g. roast beef is served with Yorkshire pudding and is accompanied with horseradish sauce.

Great emphasis is laid on the presentation of the dishes, and garnishes and accompaniments make the dish colourful.

Ingredients play an important role as it has climatic variations in the South of France, the Mediterranean heat adds flavour and richness to fruits, vegetables and herbs. In the northern region, finest fish is available. In certain regions, mushrooms and hard cheese are popular. The wines for cooking come from Bordeaux, Champagne and Brittany. The cooking medium used is butter, olive oil or salad oil, thus the dishes are not greasy, but give a lightness to the taste.

Spices and herbs give a subtle flavour, taste and originality to the dishes. Some of the spices and herbs are--parsley, celery, basil, tarragon, thyme, rosemary, chives, shallots, allspice, bayleaf, paprika, pepper, nutmeg etc. Popular continental vegetables are--asparagus, artichokes, carrots, turnips, aubergines, broccoli, swede, seakale, cardoon, Brussels sprouts, Topinambow, mushroom, etc.

Vegetables are served with main courses and serve as one of the accompaniments, they act as fillers to meat dishes. They add colour to the menu and make them colourful. Vegetables are arranged as a painter arranges colour. A meal is completed with potatoes as they give a satiety value. They also accompany the main dish.

The main dish consists of flesh foods such as lamb, beef, veal, pork, chicken, duck, turkey, fish, etc. The fleshy foods should be of the best quality. Cheese is extensively used and can be used as a base of dish, garnish to soups, blended with sauces, or grated and sprinkled on top of the dishes and gratinated. Cheese in a French menu forms a separate course during the meals and is called *"Fromage"* in French. Almost every region of France has its own cheese and a few popular cheeses are Camembert, Neufchatel, Roquefort, Brie, etc.

Red and white wines are used for cooking. Wine is much more than just a flavouring agent, if used with discretion. It gives an unmistakable fillip to the simplest dishes, regouts, and in marinades. It acts as tenderizers for the drier and tougher cuts of meat. Sauces have the quality of giving contrast or blond with the ingredients, enhance taste, flavour and give colour to the dishes.

Chinese Cuisine

Chinese culture is the oldest civilization in the world. In unrecorded history, they were the first discoverers of fire. Friendship and food were inseparably linked. A gathering without food was considered incomplete and improper.

One thousand years before the birth of Christ, they were already experimenting with fancy cooking, recording their recipes on silk and bamboo. They are considered the best in the eastern World.

Famines greatly influenced Chinese cooking. Adversity forced the Chinese always to seek new sources of food. They have been gastronomically courageous, setting no limits. They put everything edible to use, finding wonderful ways to utilize strange plants and roots, lily bulbs, chrysanthemum petals, bamboo shoots, jasmine flowers, etc.

The Chinese have a strong sense of artistry which finds impression in Chinese cooking. Every aspect of food is taken into consideration palatability, texture, fragrance and colour. Every dish is given proportion, balance and harmony.

A few factors are common in Chinese and French cuisine. The French and Chinese are skilful cooks. Both seek simplicity as their ultimate goal, the simplicity that comes with the art of diligence. They both recognise that second class ingredients can never produce first class dishes.

Chinese cooking calls for maximum preparations of raw ingredients and minimum cooking method. "Fan & Cai"--he dishes have balance, combination and blend of colour, flavour, texture, shape and size.

Techniques of Chinese Cooking: The Chinese saute, steam, deep fry and roast with a difference. Baking is rarely done. Stir frying is the most popular method of cooking. It is similar to sauteing but it is done on intense heat. It is because of the short cooking time that fresh foods have to be used as *they need less cooking time.* The heat seals the juices and preserves colour, texture. Ingredients are cut into beautiful shapes, yet flavour is never sacrificed to appearance as it brings joy to eating. The ingredients are combined and contrasted--cold, tiny ingredients against big ones, dry dishes against those with gravies, sweet taste is contrasted with sour taste. They set crunchiness against smoothness. Crisp tender vegetables surrounded with exquisitely smooth sauces, stimulate the senses with contrasting tastes.

Various Ingredients: Basic ingredients that give Chinese cooking its characteristic and subtle taste are soya sauce, peanut oil, sherry, garlic, ginger root, pepper, chilli sauce, vinegar, corn-flour, noodles and sodium glutamate, bamboo shoots, bean sprouts, dried shrimps, shark's fin, pork, ham, eggs, scallops, etc.

The ingredients are usually combined and seldom cooked well. The bite size pieces in the dish aids the use of chopsticks for eating.

Five regional cuisines predominate, i.e. the South-Eastern--Canton, Western-- Szechwan, sometimes called Chungking, North Eastern-- Peking or Shantung, Central--Honan, and East Coast--Fahien.

Cantonese (South-East): The various regional cuisines were influenced by many factors, such as in Cantonese, it was influenced by Western travellers. When they migrated, they established Chinese restaurants outside China.

Shantung Style: Shanghai was influenced by the active trade between Peking and Shantung. Peking, now called Beijing, was the site of Imperial Palace. Concentration of wealth attracted the country's best chefs, which brought cooking to its highest level. It had a reputation for mammoth feasts and banquets.

Szechwan Style: The province is hot, almost tropical. The food is highly spiced, peppery and somewhat oily. Deep frying is popular. Chicken Chilli Fry, Szechwan Duck is a favourite dish of this region.

Hunan Style: The yellow river runs through the Hunan province which is famous for its Yellow River Crop. It's known for its spiced concoctions, sweet and sour dishes and rich seasonings.

Fukien Style: Fukien province on China's east coast is famous for seafood and for clear light soups. They are known for their quality. Wine is sometimes used for its cooking.

Jiangsu in the last represents the four major original cooking styles of China.

The Chinese divide the temperature of heat into

'Military' (high or fierce, and medium) and 'Civil' (low or gentle, and weak) heat. Proper control of temperature and cooking time is the key to success or failure.

High or Fierce Heat: It is usually used for quick cooking of crisp and tender foods. Different kinds of frying, steaming, instant boiling, etc. all call for a high heat.

Medium or Moderate Heat: It can be used for quick-braising, stewing and boiling.

Low or Gentle Heat: It is used for slow cooking, allowing the flavours to penetrate through all the ingredients such as roasting and simmering.

Weak Heat: It is used for long-cooking, turning hard ingredients to soft ones. It is used for simmering, braising and stewing.

Here are some commonly used methods in Chinese Cooking.

One dish may require one, two or three methods; each will produce a different effect.

Chuan--Quick or Rapid Boiling: This simple cooking method is often used for making soups. Bring the water or slock to boil over high heat, add the ingredients and seasonings, serve as soon as the soup reboils. No thickening agent is added and the vegetable will be crisp and fresh.

Shuan--Instant Boiling or Rinsing: Thinly sliced ingredients are dipped into boiling water for a second or two, occasionally dunking it as if rinsing. Then serve with a dip sauce. This cooking method keeps the ingredients fresh and tender.

Ao--Stewing or Braising: Flavour a little hot oil with spring onions and ginger root, then stir-fry the ingredients for a short time.

Now add stock or water and seasonings. Simmer over a low heat. The food should be soft and tender.

Hui--Braising or Assembling: It is a method of cooking a dish that consists of several different ingredients. Stir-fry the ingredients first, add stock or water and seasonings, boil over high heat for a short while, then thicken the gravy before serving. Alternatively, prepare the gravy first, then add the partly cooked ingredients (deep fried or steamed), cook over low heat, thicken the gravy and serve.

Ban--Mixing Salads: This method does not actually involve cooking, but simply calls for cutting the raw or cooked ingredients, and dressing it with seasonings.

Giang--Hot Salads: Here the raw ingredients are parboiled or blanched first, then dressed with seasonings.

The difference between cold salad's and hot salad's dressing is as follows:

Cold Salad Dressing: Soya sauce, vinegar and sesame seed oil.

Hot Salad Dressing: Ginger shreds, sickwan peppercorn, salt, sugar and sesame seed oil.

Yan--Pickling: Pickle the food with salt and sugar, or with salt and wine. Dishes prepared this way have a subtle fragrance and crispness.

Jian--Shallow Frying: A flat-bottomed pan is used with little oil and medium or low heat. Seasonings are added when food is half done. The pan should be turned from time to time during cooking so that heat is evenly distributed.

The Chinese restaurants serve dishes which have mixed the styles of cooking. Cantonese is the most popular all over the world with Szechwan being the second popular style.

Indian Cuisine

No doubt, Indian cuisine can be said to have evolved along lines parallel to Indian history. India has ancient cultural heritage which is dependent on religion, geography and socio-economic conditions. Traditionally Indian cooking has been handed down through the generations by demonstrations and word of mouth. Strong impact was made on Indian cuisine during the reign of Mughals in the sixteenth century, who were fond of good living, cooking and eating. Muslim cooking was based on meat. Their influence was strongest in North and Central India. Since then, well-known Mughlai dishes were evolved which have soon developed into an important culinary art and is part of Indian cuisine. Extreme South, the Mughal influence was less, where cooking is mainly vegetarian. The regional dishes from different parts of India are influenced by religion, availability of ingredients and old traditions and customs, many of them being influenced by the different invasions. Thus, it is a combination of cookery of many nationalities. The preparations of various dishes have been handed down from one generation to another, from mother to daughter in homes, father to son working in Maharajah's kitchen, or those working as *Khansamas* and *Halwais* in catering establishments. Pictures depict the keen interest the kings took in the preparation of food as they would sit giving instructions and supervising the cooking. It is the knowledge of our ancestors that has been handed down from one generation to another. The cooking habits of India vary not within the religious communities but from area to area.

Regional cooking is influenced by the staple food of the area--in the North, wheat grows, the food is drier and the gravy is thicker. In the South, where rice is the staple diet, gravies are thinner. Climate too plays its role and because of the heavy rainfall, vegetables grow in abundance and make vegetarian cuisine varied and exciting.

Various Ingredients: The heart of Indian cooking is *masala,* the combination of spices and herbs which gives each dish its individuality. It is a fresh mixture of spices, mild and delicate or sharp and strong that may bring tears to the eyes. Masala may be in paste or powder form; spices are ground with vinegar, water or curd to form a paste. Masalas are dried in the sun or roasted on tawa and pounded into a powder form and kept in airtight containers. The combination of spices is endless and each cook follows his own taste and regional preference. Garam *masala* usually contains black pepper, cardamom, cinnamon, cloves, cumin seeds and javitri. It is ground into powder and is sprinkled over a dish just before serving. Red chillies and green chillies are essential to most Indian dishes. The common spices are ginger, garlic, onions, haldi (turmeric), dhaniya powder, jeera, methi, rai, hing. Fresh herbs are dhaniya leaves, curry patta, pudina and tulsi.

Acidic ingredients used are tamarind, curd (yoghurt), anardana (dried pomegranate seeds), lemon juice, vinegar and amchur (raw mango dried and powdered).

Hindus never eat beef, because the cow is sacred for them. Pork, mutton, chicken and vegetables are widely used. Indian Muslims do not eat pork but eat beef. Game birds are a delicacy; teetur and batair is a special favourite dish. The people staying in coastal areas eat fish because it is cheap, delicious and plentiful. Some of the popular fishes eaten are: pomfret, rohu, Mumbai duck, malli, carps, bhetki, surmai, Indian salmon, trout, shrimps, prawns, sole, tuna, crayfish, crab, etc.

Breads in India are prepared with different methods of cooking: poories, kachories, lucchies, bhaturas are deep fried, parathas are shallow fried and bhakar khani, nan and tandoori rotis are baked.

Pulse (*dal*) is important and necessary component of

every Indian meal and there are a variety of dals such as moong, channa, urad, arhar, masoor, lobia, rajma, gram, etc.

Vegetarian Cookery: As vegetables and fruits are found in profusion, there is an accent on vegetarian cookery in India. Many of the vegetables that are available in the West are found in India. The Indian vegetables are -- laisvai, karondas, plantain stem and flowers, kamal kakri, khol khol, snake gourd, amaranth leaves, sarson ka saag, ganth gobi, tindas, parval, kathal and amla etc. The cooking mediums used in various regions of India are--pure ghee-(clarified butter), vanaspati (hydrogenated oil), mustard oil, sesame oil, coconut oil, peanut oil etc.

Popular methods of cooking are frying and boiling. Traditional method used is spit roasting. A tandoor is a small Indian oven made of mud. Bread is flattened with wet hands and stuck to the inner sides of the heated tandoor and cooked. Chicken boti kabab, seekh kababs are skewered on an iron rod and it is placed in the hot tandoor and cooked.

Every Indian meal is a feast in itself. Typical way of serving Indian meals is in a thali (round metal plate) with small katoris (small metal bowls) placed all round in it. There are no different courses, all the dishes are served at one time including the sweet dish.

Commonly, a complete meal consists of dal (bland), mutton or vegetable curry (spicy, rich) sookhi bhaji (dry vegetable), raita (curd with mint to potato, etc), pickle/ chutney (sour and spicy), papad (crisp and crunchy), rice/ bread/(chapaties, parathas, etc.) which is the base of a meal. Sweet dishes--kheer, srikhand or halwa or sayvain or phirni, etc. The Indian dishes look exotic, colourful and rich.

Tandoor is a mud oven shaped like a drum, with the top side open which is narrow compared to the base. The inner sides are plastered with mud. Wood is the fuel used.

Some popular regional dishes come from different parts of India such as:

Bengal	Ponch, Sukhto, Phooraner, Charchari, Macherjhal, Rasgullasm and Sandesh.
Kashmir	Muthanjan, Gushtaba, Rishta, Kamargah, Methi and Chaman.
Gujarat	Amti, Srikhand, Khaman Dokla, Patrail, Irani
Maharashtra	Khandvi, Samosas, Dhansak and Baffat.
South India	Sambar, Dosa, Pulio darai, Murukku, Avial, Pachadi, Bondas, Bisi-bela--Huliyana, Appam and Mysore pak, etc.
Punjab	Makki ki Roti, Sarson ka saag, Mukandwadi, Bhature and Chhole etc.

Middle Eastern Cuisine

The Middle East countries are inextricably linked culinary-wise. Middle Eastern cooking, though sometimes elaborate, is easy. Some of the dishes, such as stuffed vine leaves may take some time to prepare. Lamb and mince are the favourite meat eaten. Cheap cuts of meat are used extensively. Alcohol is not used owing to the Muslim dietary law. Vegetables are used in abundance. Vine leaves, pine nuts, cabbage, baniva (okra) lentils, chick peas, bitter herbs, olives, figs, grapes, raisinc, dates, almonds are extensively used. Fish are eaten widely along the coast line.

A dish for the King consisted of hot and cold meats, rice jelly, stuffed vine leaves, marinated chicken and a sweet date puree. Some of the popular dishes are: meat grilled on the spit, meat fried in butter with a sauce, pudding made of eggs, honey, milk, butter, rice and sugar. A Dehkan dish, consisted of slices of salted mutton with pomegranate juice served with eggs. Veal and beef are cooked with spinach and vinegar. All kinds of game and poultry are also performed. Meats are usually marinated in yoghurt and flavoured with spices. Almond pastry is popular. Jams are made with quinces, dates are stuffed with almonds and walnuts. Pastries such as baklavas and Konafa are prepared.

Couscous and Burghul (cracked wheat) were adopted in most Middle Eastern countries.

The activities of cooking and eating reflect many subtly intricate facets of Middle Eastern character and ways of life. They are social activities.

The following is forbidden:

1. Use of animals dead before they are slaughtered, or those killed for reasons other than that of food.
2. Blood
3. Pig's flesh
4. Forbidden is the use of alcoholic or fermented liquids.
5. An animal that is being killed, the butcher will have to say "in the name of God, God is most great! and then cut its throat, "halaal" and let it bleed.

Cooking fats used were "alya" rendered tat from sheep or lamb. Nowadays oil, ghee, Samna i.e. butter, are used. Oils used are olive, sesame and corn oil,

A large variety of spices are used. Favourite combinations of spices or herbs are packed together and sold. Commonly used are; cumin, coriander, cinnamon, ginger, hot pepper (ayene) aniseed, sesame seed (taklia), ground coriander fried and crushed garlic.

Another mixture is cinnamon, nutmeg, cloves and ginger (four spices). The herbs used are coriander leaves, dill, mint, chervil, oregano and marjoram. Saffron is highly prized. Middle Eastern countries are -- Syria, Lebanon, Egypt, Iran, Turkey, Iraq, Saudi Arabia, Kuwait, Yemen, Sudan, UAE, Algeria, Tunisia and Morocco. All are inextricably linked culinary wise.

The early origins of Middle Eastern food can be found in Bedouin dishes. The ancient inhabitants of the Middle East were prosperous and highly civilised states have developed luxurious culinary traditions, undoubtedly influenced by Greek and Roman customs because of the invasions and conquests.

Australian Cuisine

It's a fine cuisine, took centuries to establish and it requires an indolent aristocracy to refine it. Australians have superb produce--marvellous beef and lamb, wonderful fish, first class vegetables and exotic tropical fruits. Nevertheless, these democratic people have never been much concerned with food.

There was no native cuisine to build on, the aborigines being nomadic and given to half roasting whole kangaroos and eating them dripping with blood. The settlers themselves were too busy settling to bother with anything but solid food to give them energy. Many of the interesting terms which describe uniquely Australian cuisine, are inherited from early pioneers and Bushmen who moved from place to place carrying their swag and billycan.

Since the war, there has been a wave of immigrants from Europe and things looked up.

Most Australian meals have as their main ingredients, meat, chicken or sea food. The quality of Australian produce is high so even a simple meal of grilled chops and vegetables is a culinary treat.

Famous Australian dish carpet bag steak, a giant piece of thick rump steak slit down the middle and stuffed with few oysters seasoned with salt, pepper and lemon juice and baked dishes made from Sydney rock oysters, snapper and Baramundi fish are popular. Plain steaks, roast lamb are eaten in abundance by Australians.

You will constantly encounter Peache Melba invented in England by Escoffier for Dame Nellie Melba, the great Australian soprano. You will also see the meringue and passion -- fruit cake made for Anna Pavlova. Good wines are produced in Australia.

New Zealand Cuisine

New Zealand settlers unlike their Australian counterparts, managed to graft onto the dreary "home" cooking which they brought from less well fed houses of Britain, a little livelier tradition they found in the land they took over.

Their produce is superb when fresh (rather than shipped, chilled or frozen halfway round the world) especially the dairy produce and the lamb. As in Australia, it is at its best when simply prepared.

The Maori influence however produces lots of interest, marinated raw fish is common. Paua (Abalone) pipis (which tastes like cockles) and toheroas (like clams) are excellent shellfish. The white bait in batter, paties are good. Maori vegetables are unusual puha and rauriki (sow thistle) are a little like spinach. Kumara is the sweet potato.

The Maori way of cooking meat, fish and root vegetable is in an earth oven or hangi. A hole dug in the ground. They are wrapped in flax leaves and placed on fiery stone on top mnuka or tea tree wood which gives a special flavour. Water is poured in to produce steam and then the oven is sealed with special mats and earth. Several hours later the food is supposedly cooked to perfection.

The climate guarantees an extensive range of fruits, the most exotic being the Kiwi fruit, tamrillos (tree tomatoes) and passion fruit.

Australian Food

Kangaroo Steak: Loin of Kangaroo filled are used and roasted.

Anzac Biscuits: They are made with rolled oats, coconut, flour, sugar, golden syrup, batter, bicarbonate of soda and water. They were made and sent in tins to Australian soldiers at the battlefields during World War I.

Meat Pie: Individual mince meat pies, small in size. They are traditionally sold at sporting and other community events, usually smothered with tomato sauce.

Balmain Bugs: Unusually shaped flat crustaceans found in Sydney harbour. They have a mild flavoured white flesh and are usually barbecued or boiled.

Billy Tea: Tea made in a metal can called a billy, over an open fire. The billy has a wire handle and a tight fitting lid. Water is brought to the boil, the lid removed and tea added. The billy is then removed from the fire and tea drunk from metal cups.

Cockys Joy: A tin of either golden syrup or treacle was one of the basics that swagness used to carry with them. It had many uses like sweetening billy tea, spreading on damper or pouring over puddings.

Cuppa: A cup of tea.

Damper: A basic bread originally, made simply with flour and water, kneaded, shaped into a round and cooked on the coals of a fire made on the ground. Raising agents are now used to make damper nowadays.

Some campers made the dough and moulded a small

amount around one end of a thick stick. The stick is then held over a fire. When the damper is cooked, golden syrup is poured in the hole left by the stick. It is also known as bush tucker. Tucker is a colloquial term for food.

Fish: Australia's coastline is a breeding ground for large fish like snapper, garfish, leather jacket, jewfish and flat head are some of the most common types available. John Dory and Barramundi, both flavoured fish are very popular and highly regarded.

Granny & Smith Apples: Greens Kinned variety with crisp juicy flesh. Extensively used in cooking and are also an excellent eating apples.

Jūmbuck: Young sheep.

Lamingtons: Pieces of light sponge cake dipped in chocolate icing and coconut.

Rock Oysters: Popular edible molluscs found on Australian seashores. Eaten straight from the shell, but some like them grilled or poached.

Pavlova: Basically a large meringue served with fruit and cream. Australian claim it was invented by a chef in Western Australia for the touring Russian dancer--Pavlova.

Tropical Fruits: When in season, mangoes, paw paws and pineapples are available. Kiwis and passion fruits are very popular.

Nouvelle Cuisine: In the early 70's chefs wanted to bring about a change in French Cuisine. It was done by H. Gault and C. Millan, as they were fed up to eat the same classical food everyday.

P. and J. Troisgros (brothers), M. Guerard, A. Chapel, R. Verce and Paul Bocuse spoke of changes and the revolution was started by emphasising on serving original salads, vegetable terrines, fish just cooked on the bone; and the prices were high. It took about 20 years for people to take Nouvelle Cuisine dishes. It was easier to get the recognition as many restaurants were not offering the French classical dishes.

The Nouvelle Cuisine was influenced greatly by the monthly publication by Gault and Millan. They increased from 10,000 copies to 20 lakh copies per month.

The change from the classical cuisine was brought about by the following points:

(1) A variety of dishes were served on the menu but smaller portions were served.
(2) Presentation of the food was given a lot of importance by serving it on a plate, so that the presentation was not spoilt by the service personal. Individual portions were placed on the plate and served.
(3) The sauces were served thinner, flour was not added for thickening.
(4) The cooking time was reduced, by stir-frying, frying, grilling, etc.
(5) Fresh foodstuffs had to be used and emphasis was laid on seasonal vegetables, fishes, etc. The items should be bought from the best suppliers.
(6) Unusual flavours, combinations were prepared. The dishes served by Paul Bocuse spit roasted, chicken and items like veal chops, steaks, fish are cooked in its own juices. The dishes were influenced by Chinese cuisine by preparing dishes with plenty of good quality crisp vegetables, tender meat items and cooking by stir-frying and steaming. To give a different taste, some Indian spices were used such as ginger, coriander, jeera and saffron. The latest equipment such as microwave ovens, high pressure steamers, vacuum cooking and inferred grillers are used. The Nouvelle cuisine has created interest but

it has not got the same popularity as French classical cuisine; in India, only few restaurants are serving Nouvelle cuisine. Abroad, some of the Indian restaurants are offering Nouvelle Indian cuisine, less spicy and greasy, etc.

6

Kitchen Equipments

The kitchen is used for cooking/preparing foods. Hence a number of utensils and equipments are required for preparing foods.

Kitchen equipment is expensive and to justify the expense it is essential that maximum use is made of it. This can be done only if the equipment works efficiently and this depends upon care and maintenance. The type of fuel to be used is an important factor. Though solid fuel and oil both have their place under certain circumstances, for professional cookery the choice lies between electricity and gas. In India, salt coke is used in small establishments sometimes. Firewood is used for tandoor. The routine use, care and cleaning of all items of equipment are important and this should be appreciated and understood.

When selecting equipment, capacity, trade name, good quality, simple design and ease to clean should be the criteria. The purpose and price is also considered.

Kitchen equipment may be divided into three categories:

1. Large equipment: Ranges, steamers, boiling pans, fish fryers, sinks and tables.
2. Mechanical equipment: Peelers, mincers, mixers, refrigerators, dishwashers.
3. Utensils and small equipment: Pots, pans, whisks, bowls, spoons, palate knives, graters.

Necessary Equipments

Stoves: A large variety of stoves is available fired by gas, electricity, solid fuel or oil.

Solid tops should be washed clean, or wiped clean with a cleaning pad. When cool, the stove can be more thoroughly cleaned by washing and using an abrasive such as emery-paper. After any kind of cleaning, a slid top should always be lightly greased.

On the open type of stove, all the bars and racks should be removed, immersed in hot water with a detergent, scrubbed clean, dried and put back in place on the stove. All gas jets should then be lit to check that none are blocked. All enamel parts of the stove should be cleaned while warm with hot detergent water, rinsed and dried.

The insides of ovens and oven racks should be cleaned while slightly warm, using detergent water and a mild abrasive. In cases of extreme dirt or grease being stuck on to the stove or oven, a caustic jelly may be used, but thorough rinsing must take place afterwards. Oven doors should not be slammed as this is liable to cause damage. The unnecessary lighting or the lighting of ovens too early can cause wastage of fuel, which is a waste of money.

Steamers: Steaming ovens that work from a main steam supply need little maintenance. The door controls should be greased occasionally. The steamer trays and runners should be washed in hot detergent water.

This type of equipment is usually fitted with a gauge which registers steam pressure ($^1/_2$lb. per square inch), also an overflow valve which gives a warning whistle, if the pressure reaches danger point. These should be periodically checked by a qualified engineer to ensure that they are working correctly. A constant supply of water should be maintained in the generating tank.

Steamer trays and the inside of the steamer should be cleaned with detergent water and rinsed.

Boiling Pans I Steam-jacket Kettle: Many types are available in different metals and various sizes (10, 15, 20 and 40 litres or more capacity). They may be heated by gas, electricity or steam from the main supply. As they are used for cooking large quantities of food, it is important that they do not allow the food to burn. It is for this reason that the steam-jacket type (double walled) boiler is most suitable. Many of these boilers are fitted with a tilting device to facilitate the emptying of the contents. After use, the pan and lid should be thoroughly washed with a mild detergent solution and then rinsed well. Any moving parts should be greased occasionally and checked to see that they are in good working order.

If gas fired, the gas jets and pilot should be inspected to ensure correct working. If a pressure gauge and safety valve are fitted, these should be checked to see that they are working correctly.

Deep Fat Fryers / Fritures: These are among the items of equipment that are commonly used in catering establishments. An unskilled or careless worker can cause money to be lost by food or fat being spoilt through misuse of the friture.

Modern fryers are heated by gas or electricity. Most incorporate a thermostatic control in order to save fuel and prevent overheating. A fairly recent development is the "cool zone". This is where the heating elements are at the sides of the fire but the lower part is kept at a reduced temperature. This stops particles that may fall off the food being fried from dropping to the bottom of the friture, burning and so spoiling other foods cooked. This form of heating also saves fat. Frying baskets can also be used.

Deep fat fryers should be cleaned daily after use by:

1. Turning off the heat and allowing the fat to cool.
2. Draining off and straining the fat.
3. Closing the stopcock, filling the fryer with hot water containing detergent and boiling for 10-15 minutes.
4. Draining off the detergent water, refilling with clean water plus vinegar and water, and reboiling for 10-15 minutes.
5. Draining off the water, drying the fryer, closing the stopcock and refill with clean fat.

Hot Cupboards and Bain-marie: Hot cupboards (commonly referred to in the trade as the hot plates) are used for heating plates and serving dishes and for keeping food hot. Care should be taken to see that the amount of heat fed into the hot cupboards and a thermostat is necessary in maintaining this. Hot cupboards may be heated by gas, electricity or steam. The doors should slide easily and essential greasing may be necessary. The tops of most cupboards are used as serving counters and should be heated to a higher temperature than the inside. These tops are usually made of stainless steel and should be cleaned thoroughly after each service.

Bain-marie in this case are open walls of water used for keeping foods hot and are available in many designs, some of which are incorporated into the hot cupboards, some in serving counters, and there is a type which is fitted at the end of the cooking range.

They may be heated by steam, gas or electricity, and sufficient heat to boil the water in the bain-marie should be available. Care should be taken to see that a bain-marie is never allowed to burn dry when the heat is turned on. After use, the heat must be turned off, the water drained away and the bain-marie cleaned thoroughly inside and outside with hot detergent water, rinsed and dried. And drain off tap should then be checked for any blockage and then closed.

Grills and Salamanders: The salamander, heated from above, probably causes more wastage of fuel than any other item of kitchen equipment, through being allowed to burn unnecessarily for long unused periods. Most salamanders have more than one set of heating elements or jets, and it is not always necessary to have them all turned on. Salamanders are heated by gas or electricity or a combination of the two. Bars and draining trays should be cleaned regularly with hot water containing grease solvent such as soda. After rinsing thoroughly, they should be replaced and the salamander lit for a few minutes to dry the bars.

For an under fried grill to work effectively, it must be capable of cooking food quickly and it should reach a high temperature (within 15-20 minutes) after lighting and the heat should be turned off immediately after use. When the bars are cool, they should be removed and washed in hot water containing a grease solvent, thoroughly rinsed and dried, and replaced upon the grill. Care should be taken with the fire-bricks if they are used for lining the grill as they are easily broken.

Fry Plates, Griddle Plates: These are solid metal plates heated from below. They are used for cooking individual portions of meat, eggs, bacons, etc. They can be heated to a high temperature and are suitable for rapid and continuous cooking. When cooking is commenced, a light film of oil should be applied to the food and the griddle plate. After use, the heat should be turned off and the plate scraped clean, allowed to cool and left lightly oiled.

Contact Grills: These are sometimes referred to as a double-sided or infra-grills, having two heated surfaces facing each other. These grills are electrically heated and are capable of cooking certain foods very quickly. The electricity should be turned off after use. When the grill is cool, the cooking surface should be cleaned with a stiff wire-brush. The surfaces are then wiped clean with a damp cloth and lightly oiled to prevent rusting.

Sinks: Different materials are used for sinks according to the purpose for which they are intended:

1. Teak or other hard wood for glass or china wash. (If hard wood sinks are left unused for long periods of time, they should be filled with cold water to prevent shrinkage of the timber.)
2. Heavy galvanised iron for heavy pot wash.
3. Stainless steel for general purposes.
4. Glazed earthenware for general light purposes.

Sinks, drainers, waste and overflow outlets should be cleaned with a suitable abrasive power cleaner, thoroughly rinsed with plenty of clean water and left to dry.

Tables: Wooden tables should be scrubbed clean with hot soda water, rinsed and wiped dry as soon as possible to prevent warping.

Formica or stainless steel topped tables should be washed with hot detergent water, rinsed with hot water and dried.

Marble slabs should be scrubbed with hot water and rinsed. All excess moisture should be removed with a dry cloth. No cutting or chopping should be allowed on table-tops; chopping boards must be used. Hot pans must not be placed upon tables, triangles must be used to protect the table-tops. The legs and racks or shelves of tables are cleaned with hot detergent water and then dried. Wooden table legs require scrubbing.

Butcher's Block: A scraper should be used to keep the block clean. After scraping, the block should be sprinkled with a few handfuls of common salt in order to absorb any moisture which may have penetrated during the day. Do not use water or liquids for cleaning unless absolutely necessary as water will be absorbed into the wood and may cause swelling.

Storage Racks: All types of racks should be emptied and scrubbed or washed periodically.

Handling of Equipments

When a new item of equipment is installed, it should be tested by a qualified fitter before being used by the catering staff. The manufacturer's instructions must be displayed in a prominent place near the machine. The manufacturer's advice regarding servicing should be followed and a record book kept showing when and what maintenance the machine is receiving. Before cleaning, the machine should be switched off and the plug removed from the socket.

Potato Peelers

1. Potatoes should be free of earth and stones before loading into the machine, otherwise damage to the machine will result.
2. Before any potatoes are loaded, the water spray should be turned on and the abrasive plates set in motion.
3. The interior should be cleaned daily and the abrasive plate removed to ensure that small particles are not lodged below.
4. The peel trap should be emptied as frequently as required.
5. The waste outlet should be kept free from obstructions.

Refrigerators: In order to maintain a refrigerator at peak efficiency, the following points should be observed:

1. Defrost weekly. The control should be turned to defrost, the racks should be emptied and racks and interior surfaces washed, rinsed and dried. If the refrigerator is not defrosted regularly, excess frost accumulates on the cooling system, acts as an insulator and causes the refrigerator motor to work longer than is necessary, thus shortening the life of the components.
2. The door or doors should be kept closed as much as possible. If too much warm air is allowed to enter the refrigerator plant, it overworks and excess frost can accumulate on the cooling system.
3. Food should be stored sensibly and in such a way that the cold air can circulate all around. Excessive packing of food into a refrigerator should be avoided.
4. A qualified engineer should be called in at the first sign of any defect in the machinery operating a refrigerator.

Food Mixer: This is an important labour-saving, electrically operated piece of equipment used for many purposes, for example, mixing pastry, cakes, mashing potatoes, beating egg whites, mayonnaise, cream, mincing or chopping meat and vegetables.

1. It should be lubricated frequently in accordance with manufacturer's instructions.
2. The motor should not be overloaded. Overloading can be caused by an obstruction to the rotary components. For example, if dried bread is being passed through the mincer attachment without sufficient care, the rotary cog can become so clogged with bread that it is unable to move. If the motor is allowed to run, damage can be caused to the machine.

3. All components as well as the main machine should be thoroughly washed and dried. Care should be taken to see that no rust occurs on any part. The mincer attachment knife and plates will rust if not given sufficient care.

Masher (Hand or Electric): The hand type should be washed immediately after use, then rinsed and dried. The electric masher should have the removable sections and the main machine washed and dried after use, extra care being taken over those parts which come into contact with food. Lubrication as for all electrical appliances.

Mechanical equipments are slicer, grinder, bowl cutter, food processor, etc.

Food Slicers and Choppers: Food slicers available are both manually and electrically operated. They are labour-saving devices which can be dangerous if not operated with care. Because of this, the working instructions should be placed in a prominent position near the machine.

1. Care should be taken that no material likely to damage the blades is included in the food to be sliced and chopped. If a piece of bone comes into contact with the cutting blade, severe damage will result.
2. Each section that comes into contact with food, should be cleaned carefully and dried after use.
3. The blade or blades should be sharpened regularly.
4. Moving parts should be lubricated, but oil must not be allowed to come into contact with any food.
5. Extra care must be taken when blades are exposed.

Chopper (Hand or Electric): The manual type should be washed and dried after- use. Care should be taken with the interior blades; they should be cleaned with a folded cloth. The electric chopper should be thoroughly cleaned and dried after use, particular attention being paid to those parts which come into contact with food. Care should be taken that no obstruction prevents the motor from operating at its normal speed. Moving parts should be lubricated regularly in accordance with the manufacturer's instructions.

Tea Making Appliances: There are two main types of boilers. Bulk boilers from which boiling water can only be drawn when all the contents are boiling and automatic boilers which provide a continuous flow of boiling water.

Bulk Boilers: Used mainly where large quantities of boiling water is required for a given time. They should be kept scrupulously clean, covered with the correct lid to prevent anything from falling in and when not in use they should be left filled with clean water.

Pressure Boilers: This is the type that operates many still sets, consisting of steam-heating milk boilers and pressure boilers providing boiling water. Care should be taken with the pilot light to see that it is working efficiently. As with all gas-fired equipment, it is essential that regular inspection and maintenance is carried out by gas company fitters.

Automatic Boilers: These boilers have automatic water supplies and can give freshly boiled water at intervals. It is important to see that the water supply is efficiently maintained, otherwise there is a danger of the boiler burning dry and being damaged.

Energy Saving

Energy can be saved in the kitchen by:

1. Turning gas flames once the food is cooked.
2. Using the lowest possible gas flame at all times, to correctly achieve the task.

3. Placing lids on pots when boiling water or cooking.
4. Turning off gas flames, ovens, and hot plates when work is finished.
5. Cooking food no longer than is absolutely necessary.
6. Preheating ovens only when needed, don't let them be on standby all day.
7. Keeping refrigerators and deep freeze compartment doors closed.
8. Keeping oven door closed to prevent loss of temperature.
9. Checking the effectiveness of oven's doors and the seals to prevent loss of oven heat.

Safety Precautions

(a) Excessive haste should be prevented.
(b) Distraction should be avoided.
(c) Failure to apply safety rules.

Excessive haste may cause people to take chances which inevitably lead to mishaps. Disconnect the power.

Accidents may be caused by not concentrating on the job in hand. It is the responsibility of everyone to observe the safety rules.

Ensure operational procedure for all machines and equipments which should be in good working order.

Prevention of Cuts and Scratches: Knives

1. Use the right knife for right job.
2. Use a sharp knife.
3. Handles should be free from grease.
4. When carrying these the points must be downwards.
5. Keep these flat on the board or table.
6. When cleaning, keep the sharp edge away from the hand.

Cutting Blades on Machines: Guard should always be in place when the machine is in use.

Never place hand under the blade. Before the guards are removed for cleaning, stop the revolving blades.

Cut from Meat or Fish Bones: Much care should be taken and cuts from bone should not be neglected. Always seek medical help.

Prevention of Burns and Scalds

1. Roll down the sleeves of jackets and overall. Use aprons of a suitable length so as to give adequate protection.
2. Trays containing hot liquid should be handled carefully. (Put one hand on the side and other on the end of the tray.)
3. A good thick dry cloth is very useful.
4. Put some white thing, e.g. flour on handle and lid to indicate that it is hot.
5. Handles of pans, etc. should not protrude over the edge of the stove.
6. Carry the large full pan correctly.
7. Take extra care with certain foods, e.g. when boiling sugar.
8. Frying, specially deep frying, needs special attention.

   The pan should not be more than 2/3 full. Drain the wet food first before putting in the fat. If the fat in pan bubbles over on to a gas stove, then turn off the gas taps.

   Fire blankets and fire extinguishers should be provided in the kitchen.
9. Keep the steamer in proper working condition. Clean the drain hole. Never open the door immediately the steam is turned off. It is better to wait for about half a minute before doing so.

10. When pouring boiling, liquid, keep your face away as far as possible.

Machinery

1. See that the machine is in correct running order before use.
2. The machine should be operated only by the person who is engaged for it.
3. Use a particular machine for a particular type of job.
4. When using mixing machine, never put your hand in the bowl until the balance hook or whisk have stopped revolving.
5. Remove the plug first before cleaning.
6. There should be proper earth connection of the electrical machines.
7. In case of any doubt, always inform the maintenance department.

Handling of Gas Cylinders: The risk of explosion from gas is considerable. To avoid this, it is necessary to ensure that gas is properly lit. Never allow the gas to collect in the oven, or on range. See that there is no leakage on the gas pipe or any connection with gas supply.

Floors: Accidents are caused by grease and water being spilled on floors and not being cleaned up. See that the floor is always clean. Never keep anything on the kitchen floor.

Never keep liquid items in containers on the shelves or racks beyond the eye-level specially when hot.

Keep the kitchen well lit, well ventilated and dry.

Safety in Restaurant: It is essential that people working in the restaurant are capable of using the tools and equipments in a manner which will neither harm themselves nor those with whom they are in contact. They should be aware of the causes of accidents and be able to deal with any which occurs.

Accident may come in various ways.

1. Excessive haste.
2. Distraction/carelessness.
3. Failure to apply safety rules or lack of knowledge.

Everybody must take greatest care to observe the rules of safety to avoid great pain and loss of time.

The waiter when engaged with carving, filleting, must use the correct sharp knife and must see that the handle is free from grease. When carrying a knife, he must keep the point downward and try to avoid movement with the knife. When not in use, keep the knife on its side on the table or sideboard preferably in the drawer. After every use, wipe the knife with the edge away from the handle.

During carving and filleting meat, fish, take care of bones which may be dangerous. Try to use a glove when dealing with such items.

Use a good dry thick folded cloth for carrying. Soup, roast gravy, etc. should be handled carefully.

When preparing flambe dishes, do not bring your face near to the pan when flaming the dish.

When dealing with gas stove, always check the gas first. Also check if there is any leakage in the pipe. Never allow the gas to collect on the stove by switching on the stove in advance. This will cause explosion.

Keep the floor as clean as possible. Never keep anything on the floor which may cause accident.

Safety From Fire

Fire Precautions: Fires in hotels and catering establishments are common and all too often can result in injury to the employee and in serious cases either injury or loss of life to employees and customers.

Fire Prevention: A basic knowledge regarding fire should assist in preventing fires and handling them if they do occur. Three components are necessary for a fire to start, if one of the three is not present, or is removed, then the fire does not happen or it is extinguished. The three parts are:

1. Fuel--something to burn.
2. Air--oxygen to sustain combustion (to keep the fire going).
3. Heat--gas, electricity, etc.

Fire Fighting Measures

To extinguish a fire, the three principal methods are:

1. Starving--removing the fuel.
2. Smothering--removing the air (oxygen).
3. Cooling--removing the heat.

Therefore one of the sides of the triangle is removed.

The Fire Triangle: The fuel is that which burns, heat is that which sets the fuel alight and oxygen is needed for fire to burn. Eliminate one of these and the fire is put out. Oxygen is present in the air, so if air is excluded from the fuel and the heat then the fire goes out. For example, should the clothes of someone working in the kitchen catch fire then the action to be taken is to quickly wrap a fire blanket round the person and roll them on the floor. In doing so, the flames have been cut off from the source of air. (The oxygen has been taken away from the triangle.) In the event of fire, windows and doors are to be closed so as to restrict the amount of air getting to the fire. Foam extinguishers work on the principle that the foam forms a 'blanket' thus excluding air from coming into contact with the fuel. Should fat or oil in a pan ignite, then the pan should be quickly covered with a lid or other item or fire blanket so as to exclude air. It is also essential to turn off the source of heat, gas or electricity, etc. so that the heat is taken away from the triangle. Water extinguishes fire by dousing the flames thus taking the heat out of the triangle provided the fuel is material such as wood, paper, etc.

If fat or oil is alight, water must not be used as it causes the ignited fat to spread thus increasing the heat. Water extinguishers must not be used on live electrical equipment because water is a conductor of heat. In the event of a small fire in a store, it may be possible to remove items in the store to prevent fire from spreading. Fire doors are installed for the purpose of restricting an area so that in the event of a fire, the fuel is limited.

Precaution in the Event of a Fire

1. Do not panic.
2. Warn other people in the vicinity.
3. - Do not jeopardise your own safety or that of others.
4. Follow the fire instructions of the establishment.
5. If it is a small fire, use appropriate fire extinguisher.
6. Do close doors and windows, turn off gas, electricity and fans.
7. Do not wait for the fire to get out of control before calling the fire brigade.

It is important that in all catering establishments, passageways are kept clear and that doors open outwards. Fire-escape doors and windows should be clearly marked and fire-fighting equipment must be readily available and in working order. Periodic fire-drills should occur and be taken seriously since lives may be endangered if there is a fire. Fire-alarm bells must be tested at least four times a year and the staff should be instructed in the use of fire-fighting equipment. All extinguishers should be refilled immediately after use.

All fire extinguishers should have been manufactured in accordance with ISI specifications; they should be red with an additional colour code to indicate the type and with operating instructions on them.

Red	- -	water
Cream	- -	foam
Black	- -	carbon dioxide
Blue	- -	dry powder
Green	- -	halons (vapourising liquid).

Fire Extinguishers

Foam (Cream): Foam puts out fires by forming a blanket of foam over the top of the fire. It is particularly good for putting out fat fires because the foam stays in position and so stops the fire-reigniting. Foam can also be used on fires of natural materials.

Carbon Dioxide (CO_2) (Black): Carbon dioxide gas is used on fires on inflammable liquids and has the advantage that it does not conduct electricity.

Disadvantage: CO_2 gas has limited cooling properties and therefore is not the most efficient way of putting out a fat lire.

Dry Powder (Blue): Dry powder is commonly used for fat fires. It does not conduct electricity, and some all-purpose powders can be used on fires in natural materials. Powders based on bicarbonate of soda are used in most extinguishers.

Disadvantage: Dry powders usually have limited cooling properties.

Fire-hoses: Fire-hoses are used for similar fires to those classified under water fire extinguishers. It is necessary to be familiar with the instructions displayed by the firehose before using it.

Water Sprinkler Systems: These consist of sprinklers from the main water supply fitted in the ceiling. The system is designed to automatically spray water over the whole area when the temperature rises above a pre-set level, e.g. 75° (167°F). Each extinguisher should be fixed on a suitable bracket, be properly maintained and should be always available for use. It should be immediately refilled after use. It is important that the staff must learn how to use them.

7

Preparing Some Popular Foods

> Complicated machines have a habit of frightening men. Inventors have been persecuted, progressive managements have been criticized, and the machines themselves have been blamed for all manner of evils. Laws have been proposed which would outlaw machines because they would throw men out of work. This is ridiculous, for statistics show that the higher the degree of mechanization the higher the total labour force.
>
> —*R. Bowling Barnes*

For the benefit of professionals in the catering department, we are presenting the procedure for preparing some popular food items. In fact, the information is gathered from different sources, to make it more useful and acceptable.

Stocks

It is a liquid in which meat or meat bones, fish or fish bones and various vegetables have been cooked to extract flavour. Fonds de Cuisine is a kitchen stock. Stocks are nutritious, strongly-flavoured liquids. They are important foundation liquids that are used in the preparation of various dishes such as soups, sauces, gravies, stews, curries, braisings, rice and cold dishes.

The preparation of stocks call for understanding, care and discerning taste. Long, slow simmering of food and cold water used for stock (except for fish stock) is required to draw out the flavour-- and nutrients into the liquids. After cooking is properly stored for a day it ripens and gives a fuller flavour. To improve taste of Indian curries, pulaos, etc. it is important that stocks should be used.

As stock is an important ingredient in various dishes, care should be taken in the preparation as follows:

(a) All fat should be removed from bones at the outset, as the stock becomes very greasy and becomes rancid soon.

(b) Marrow must be removed and put aside for use as a separate dish (marrow toast) or as a garnish (petite marmite, i.e. a soup).

(c) Stock should only simmer. If allowed to boil, the agitation and particles of fat cause an emulsification and it becomes milky or cloudy.

(d) Bouquet garni should be tied to a handle of the stock-pot. Cut large pieces of vegetables, should be added later on, as it flavours the stock. If allowed to remain in the pot too long, the vegetables will begin to disintegrate, discolouring the stock.

(e) The scum should be discarded.

(f) For storing, the stock should be strained and the liquid should be cooled. No fat should be allowed to remain on the surface, as heat is prevented from escaping and may cause the stock to turn, i.e. become sour.

(g) Stock could be stored in a refrigerator or cold room.

(h) Stocks turn cloudy, if boiled too rapidly and if a lid is used and not carefully strained and not skimmed properly.

Generally, stocks are of following varities:

White Stocks	Brown Stocks

White beef stock
White mutton stock
White veal stock
White chicken stock
Fish stock
Brown beef stock (stuffed)
Brown mutton stock
Brown veal stock
Brown game stock

Preparation of Stocks

For the stocks or bouillon, use chuckribs, neck, short ribs, skin and knuckle bones, and other body cartilagineous or gristly parts. These contain flavour, albumen and gelatine.

Basic Aromatics used are carrots, turnips, leeks, celery, onions, bay leaves, thyme and parsley.

Bones should be placed in cold water and then brought to boll. The layer of coagulated albumen that forms on the surface should be removed.

Recipes

Basic beef/veal/mutton stock (Fr. Fonds blanc/de boeuf /veau/ mutton)

Ingredients	*5 litres*	*1 litre*
Beef bones	216 kg	500 gins
Carrots	250 gms	50 gms
Onions	130 gms	25 gms

Bouquet Garni

Leeks	130 gms	25 gms
Celery	130 gms	25 gms
Parsley stalk and roots	30 gms	6 gms
Bay leaf	1	1/2
Thyme	1 sprig	1 sprig
Water	8 litres	2 litres

Method

(1) Cut or break the bones into 3" to 4" pieces and remove any marrow.

(2) Wash and place into stock-pot and add cold water.

(3) Bring to the boil and skim off the scum, add cold water and wipe the sides of the stock-pot clean with a clean damp cloth.

(4) Add vegetables whole and the bouquet garni.

(5) Allow the stock to simmer gently for 6 hours, during which time the fat that will rise to the surface must be constantly skimmed off. (The vegetables should be removed from stock after 3 hours.)

(6) Pass through a muslin, reboil and place aside to cool.

NB: 6 to 8 hours is the maximum time required to extract full flavour; if cooked too long, the flavour will suffer. Bones from which the flavour has been extracted may be reboiled for 6 hrs. to produce jelly.

Veal stock is made the same way as beef stock using veal bones instead of beef bones. Gelatin is released from veal bones more quickly than from beef. A good veal stock will get when cold.

Mutton stock is made the same way as beef stock. A boiling fowl is added for better taste and flavour.

White Chicken Stock *[Fonds blanc de Volatile (Fr.)]*

Ingredients	*5 litres*	*1 litres*
Chicken bones, trimming	3 Kg	600 gms
giblets/Boiling fowl Carrots	350 gms	70 gms
Onions	180 gms	35 gms
Leeks	120 gms	25 gms
Celery	60 gms	12 gms
Parsley stalk and roots	30 gms	6 gms
Bay leaf	1	$^1/_2$
Thyme	1 sprig	$^1/_2$ sprig
Water	6 litres	1 $^1/_2$ litres

Method is the same as beef stock, water is less and cooking time is 2 hours.

White chicken or meat stocks are used for the preparations of white soups, sauces, stews, braises, court bouillon (cooking liquor).

White Fish Stock [Fonds de poisson blank (Fr.)]

Ingredients	*5 litres*	*1 litre*
Butter	75 gms	15 gms
Finely sliced onions	250 gms	50 gms
Bay leaf	1	$^1/_2$
Peppercorns	8	2
Parsley stalk	20 gms	4 gms
Fish bones and trimming of Beckti, Surmai or Rahu	2kg	400 gms
White mushroom trimmings	15 gms	3 gms
Juice of lemon	1 lime	$^1/_4$ lime
Cold water	5 $^1/_4$ litres	$1^1/_2$ litre

Method

(1) Place the aromatics in the bottom of a buttered saucepan on top of the blanched shredded onions.
(2) Add the cleaned and cut fish bones and trimmings.
(3) Add the lemon juice and sweat the bones, etc. Place a cartouche (grease-proof paper).
(4) Moisten with water, bring to the boil, skim, allow to simmer for 20 minutes (maximum).
(5) Strain through a muslin, reboil and cool or use as required.

NB: 20 minutes will extract all the flavours from the bones, excess cooking will make the stock bitter and cause It to deteriorate. Care must be taken over the simmering as a fish stock will "cloud" much more quickly than a meat stock.

Brown Stocks

Brown beef/veal/mutton Stock (*Fr. Stuffed or Fonds brun*)

	Ingredients	*5 litres 1 litre*
Beef, veal, or mutton		
bones	1,800 gms	500 gms
Ham bone	200 gms	40 gms
Carrots	360 gms	75 gms
Onions	120 gms	25 gms

Bouquet Garni

Celery	60 gms	12 gms
Parsley stalk	30 gms	6 gms
Bay leaf	1	
Thyme	1 sprig	$^1/_2$ sprig
Beef fat or any other	a little to brown the bones	
Water	7 litres	1 $^1/_2$ litres

Method

(1) Cut or break the bones into 3" to 4" pieces and place with fat in a roasting tray.

(2) Roast the bones or trimmings until rich brown in a hot oven. Remove bones from oven, place in a stock-pot.

(3) Cover with water, bring to boil and skim.

(4) Add the fried carrot and onion, the bouquet garni and the ham bone.

(5) The stock should simmer for 6 hrs., skimming form time to time.

(6) Strain, reboil and use as required.

NB: Brown stock is used for soups, braises, gravies, curries, stews and sauces.

Glazes (Fr. Glaces)

Glazes in classical cookery are used for enhancing the flavour of sauces, enriching sauteed meats and for decorating finished hot or cold dishes. It gives a brilliant and unctuous coating to dishes and improves their appearance. The common glazes are: meat, chicken and fish glazes.

Meat Glaze: Brown stock is put in a large stew-pan on an open fire and reduced, skimming the scum that comes up. As the volume reduces, smaller stew-pan should be used and heat lowered. It should be strained through a muslin cloth. For testing, a wooden spoon should be dipped into the reduced stock and if it has an even coat, then the glaze is ready. Strain in a bowl and place in a cold place.

Chicken Glaze: Chicken stock is used and prepared the same way as meat glaze.

Fish Glaze: Fish fumet is prepared the same way as fish glaze, it is less concentrated and its flavour is more delicate than that of meat glaze.

Chinois: Is a conical strainer which is used for straining stocks, consommes, etc. *Storage:* The correct storage temperature for stocks is 1°C-4°C. The holding temperature for warm emulsion sauce is 30°C-37°C.

Tasty Sauces

Sauces are liquids or semi-liquid mixtures. A keen sense of smell, delicate sense of taste, a light, strong hand for the blending--all contribute to the perfect sauce.

Long ago, Grimande de la Royere, philosopher and gastronomer wrote: "The sauce is to culinary art, what grammar is to language."

A perfect sauce has a colourful appearance, is glowing in its rich smoothness, its texture is that of velvet, and it has a definite taste. It has a natural flavour and complements the food it accompanies, rather than mask its taste.

It provides moisture, colour and shine to food.

Importance of Sauces in Food Preparation

(1) Enhances flavours.

(2) Some sauces help in digestion, e.g. mint sauce, apple sauce with roast pork.

(3) It gives moistness to the food, e.g. white sauce adds creaminess to firm and dry food.

(4) Adds colour to the food. Hollandaise sauce served on a vegetable adds colour. Tomato sauce goes with *Fish a I' orly*.

(5) Served as an accompaniment, sometimes gives a contrast taste to another food, e.g. cranberry sauce with roast turkey.

(6) Sometimes gives the name to the dish, e.g. Madeira wine when added to the brown sauce, it is called sauce Madeira.

(7) Enhances nutritional value of the dish.

(8) Dresses and complements food that need some additional quality and makes the food more palatable, e.g. Chaudfroid sauce is used to coat various food items, and gives a good appearance.

(9) Gives tartness and contrasts or balances a bland food, e.g. Devil sauce served with eggs give appealing tartness. Thickening agents or liaisons that are used to thicken sauces are:

   (i) Roux,

   (ii) Starch,

   (iii) Beurre manie,

   (iv) Yolks of eggs,

   (v) Blood,

(10) A liaison (thickening agent) thickens at 80°C-88°C.

Roux is fat and flour mixture, which are cooked together. It is cooked to various degrees, namely white, blond or brown. Equal quantities of flour and butter and margarine are taken to prepare the different coloured roux. The colour acquired depends upon the degree of cooking of the flour, and the colour of the sauce depends upon the liquid and roux used.

While preparing the sauce, boiling liquid should never be added to a hot roux, as it may become lumpy, a cold liquid to a hot roux, or a hot liquid to an old roux may be added to get smooth texture.

Starch: Arrowroot, cornflour, fecule (potato-starch), tapioca are used to thicken the sauce. A paste should be made of cold liquid and starch, and then stirred into boiling liquid and allowed to boil, till the starch is cooked. It gelatinises at 93°C (200°F). Starch contains no gluten and gives a clear sauce and thickens more as it cools.

Manie Butter (Beurre Maine Fr.}: Chiefly used for fish sauces. Equal quantities of flour and butter are kneaded, and very little quantity is added at a time to the boiling liquid and stirred well to form a smooth consistency.

Yolks of Eggs and Cream: It is a liaison, added as a finishing agent at the end of cooking. The product is never boiled, when the liaison is added, or it would curdle. The liaison is added to thicken delicate cream or volute sauces or cream soups. Yolks of eggs are used to prepare mayonnaise by emulsifying it with oil.

Blood: It is usually used for game cooking. It thickens the sauce and gives a particular flavour, e.g. preparation of Jugged Hare. Sauces could be grouped as follows:

(1) Basic sauces
(2) Cold basic sauces

(3) A class of their own (miscellaneous)

(4) Butter sauces

Yield: 4 litres of sauce yields 80 portions. The service temperature of hot sauce is 85°C.

Basic Sauces

(1) *Bechamel or White Sauce:* Bechamel sauce is named after Louis de Bechamel.

It is prepared with white roux and mildly flavoured with onion.

Recipe of Bechamel Sauce

Ingredients	*5 litres*	*1 litre*
Flour	450 gms	90 gms
Butter	450 gms	90 gms
Milk	5 litres	1 litre
Onion studded with clove and bay leaf	125 gms	1 litre

Method

(1) Bring milk to boil with studded onion and set aside.

(2) Melt butter in a thick-bottomed pan.

(3) Add flour, stir and cook the roux over a gentle fire without colouring till it gets a sandy texture. Pour the milk into the roux stirring with a wooden spoon to avoid lumps. Simmer gently for half-an-hour. Remove the studded onion and pass through a fine strainer, cover with butter to prevent the formation of a skin.

Volute

It is a basic blond sauce. It is prepared from blond (light brown) roux and stock. Volute gets its name from the type of stock used, e.g. fish stock and blond roux--Fish volute.

Chicken stock and blond roux--Chicken volute.

Allemande, a derivative of volute sauce, strictly speaking, is not a basic sauce, but is very often used in the preparation of other sauces.

Recipe of Volute

Ingredients	*5 litres*	*1 litre*
Butter	400 gms	90 gms
Flour	400 gms	90 gms
Stock (chicken or veal or fish)	5 litres	1 litre
Mushroom trimmings	125 gms	25 gms

Method

(1) In a thick bottomed pan, prepare blond roux.

(2) Add cold stock into the roux, stir vigorously to avoid lumps.

(3) Add mushroom trimmings.

(4) Simmer gently for one hour, stirring frequently with a wooden spoon.

(5) Pass through a fine strainer and cover with butter, to prevent the formation of skin.

NB: Fish volute should be cooked for 20 minutes only and wine should be added at a later stage.

Brown or Espagnole Sauce

Brown sauce is made from brown roux and brown stock, or glaze of brown stock. It is one of the most widely used basic or mother sauces. Demi-glaze is a derivative of brown stock and is widely used for the preparation of other brown sauce derivatives.

Recipe of Brown Sauce or Espagnole

Ingredients	*5 litres*	*1 litre*
Fat	300 gms	60gms
Flour	350 gms	70gms
Tomato puree	150 gms	30gms
Blown stock	8 litres	$1^1/_4$ litres
Fat	75 gms	15gms
Carrots Roughly	350 gms	70gms
Onions chopped	350 gms	70gms
Mirepoix for Bacon trimmings	175 gms	30 gms
Flavouring Finely chopped		
Fresh pork rind finely chopped		
Parsley, celery and bay leaf	10 gms	3 gms

Method

(1) Prepare brown roux in a heavy-bottomed pan and cool.

(2) Add tomato puree, stirring to prevent lumps.

(3) Gradually mix in hot stock, stirring vigorously to blend well and cook on a genti fire.

(4) Saute the mirepoix in fat and add the sauteed vegetables to the sauce.

(5) Simmer gently for 4 to 6 hrs.

(6) Remove the scum when it comes to the top.

(7) Strain and cover with a thin layer of butter.

NB: Overbrowning should be avoided, as this tends to make the sauce taste bitte.

Recipe of Demi-glaze (Basic Derivative of Brown Sauce)

Ingredients	*5 litres*	*1 litre*
Brown sauce	5 litres	1 litre
First class brown stock or stuffed	5 litres	1 litre

Method

(1) Mix the above ingredients in a pan and place on the stove.

(2) Reduce it fifty per cent and add a little sherry (optional) and mix.

(3) Slightly butter the top to avoid the formation of a skin.

Tomato Sauce

It is a red kitchen sauce and has some piquancy. It is served with ravioli or spaghetti, eggs, fish and meat, it adds colour to the dish.

Recipe of Tomato Sauce

Ingredients	*5 litres 1 litre*	
Flouf	400 gms	80 gms
Butter	350 gms	70 gms
Dices of bacon trimmings	200 gms	40 gms
Onions	400 gms	80 gms
Carrots Roughly	400 gms	80 gms
Celery Chopped	200 gms	40 gms
Bay leaf	1	$^1/_2$
Garlic crushed	5 cloves	1 clove
Tomato puree	450 gms	100 gms
Tomatoes chopped	250 gms	50 gms
Brown stock	$4^1/_2$ litres	450ml
Sugar	50 gms	10 gms
Salt	15 gms	3 gms

Method

(1) Melt butter in a pan.

(2) Add roughly chopped vegetables, crushed garlic and saute, till slightly brown

(3) Mix in flour and fry till it gets a sandy texture and gets a slightly brown colour

(4) Add tomato puree and chopped tomatoes, and stir.

(5) Add cold stock, stirring to prevent lumps and bring to boil.

(6) Add seasoning and cook for 1V£ hrs.

(7) Skim frequently.

(8) Strain and cover with butter.

NB: If the tomato sauce is being served separately in a sauce boat, it should have a fairly thick consistency. Many of the sauces finished with butter oil is known as Monter au beurre.

Hollandaise Sauce

It is a warm yellow and rich sauce. It contains a high percentage of fat and egg yolks. It is an emulsion of butter, lemon juice and egg yolks. Hollandaise is served over grilled or baked fish, vegetables and egg. It is an accompaniment to cauliflower, asparagus, broccoli, salmon, trout.

Recipe of Hollandaise Sauce

Ingredients	500 *gms*	200 gms
Butter	500 gms	200 gms
Egg yolks	5	2
Crushed peppercorns	8	5
Vinegar	30 ml	15 ml
Lemon juice	2	$^1/_2$

Method

(1) Melt butter in a pan and keep aside.

(2) Place crushed peppercorns and vinegar in a pan and reduce completely.

(3) Add one tablespoon of water and cool.
(4) Add egg yolks and whisk.
(5) Place the pan in a double boiler and whisk the egg yolks till a sabayon is formed (thickens). Then gradually add the melted butter until it is blended and forms a smooth sauce. Add lemon juice.
(6) Strain through a fine strainer, correct seasoning.
(7) Store at 30°-37°, if necessary.

NB: If Hollandaise turns or curdles or is too thick, beat in a little hot water, a little at a time. If too thin, add a teaspoon of lemon juice to a tablespoon of the sauce in a warm bowl and whisk until it is thick, then add the remaining mixture, a little at a time, whisking all the time. If this method does not rectify the same, then in a clean bowl add egg yolk, a few drops of hot vinegar and whisk while adding the curdled Hollandaise.

Cold Sauces

Mayonnaise is a basic cold sauce. It is used as a salad dressing and as accompaniment. It has a wide variety of uses, particularly in hors d'oeuvres and sate It is a rich sauce, as it is thickened with egg yolk and has a high percentage of fat. Sometimes it is thickened with gelatine and is used as a shiny flavourful coating decorate cold dishes or buffets.

Basic Recipe of Mayonnaise

Ingredients	*5 litres*	*1 litre*
Salad or olive oil	5 litres	1. litre
Egg yolks	35	8
French mustard	1 tspn.	$^1/_2$ tspn.
Vinegar	100 ml	25 ml
Lemon	5	1
Seasoning	as required	to taste

Method

(1) Place of yolks of eggs, vinegar, seasoning in a clean bowl and whisk well.

(2) Add oil slowly, a little at a time, whisking continuously, until all the oil is incorporated.

(3) Finish the sauce by adding the juice of lemon and warm water.

This is done to ensure coherence of the sauce and to prevent its turning or curdling. Mayonnaise is suitable for serving with cold fish, meat and hors d'oeuvres.

The following must be kept in mind:

(1) Do not expose mayonnaise to too low a temperature after making it.

(2) Initially, the oil should not be added rapidly.

(3) Do not use congealed or too cold an oil.

(4) The oil should be in proportion to the egg yolks.

(5) Use hot water when necessary as it acts as a stabiliser.

(6) Cover the sauce with a lid, and store in a cool place.

Rectification of a Turned or Curdled Mayonnaise

(1) Take a clean bowl, add boiling water or vinegar and gradually whisk in the curdled sauce.

(2) Place an egg yolk and gradually whisk in the curdled sauce.

(3) If a small quantity of mayonnaise is to be rectified, then put mustard powder in a clean bowl and add in drop by drop, whisking the curdled mayonnaise.

Sauces, a Class of their Own

These sauces have an individuality of their own in colour and flavour. They blend with the food items they accompany or give a contrasting sharpness. The sauces are bread, apple, mint, cranberry and horseradish sauces.

Butter Sauces

They are served melted, in a liquid form or as hard butter sauces. Butter is mixed with different ingredients, set and cut in fancy shapes and served with food items. They are placed on the hot food items, just before serving and allowed to melt. It can be served separately, along with the dish in a sauce-boat and crushed ice. The other name for butter sauces is compound butter, e.g. anchovy, colbert, brown butter, etc.

Sauces play a very important part in Western cuisine. Various dishes are named after the sauce that is used. Sometimes very slight variations change the name of sauce and some derivative sauces are used to make other sauces, e.g. demi-glaze, Allemande Normande, Bearnaise, tartare etc.

Basic Sauces White Sauce	*Empagnole*	*Volute*	*Hollandaise*	*Tomato sauce*		*Mayonnaise*
Colour White	*Brown* *Fish*	*Blond* *Chicken*	*Meat*	*Yellow*	*Red*	*Cold Yellow*
Derivatives						
	Bordelaise					
Mornay Cambridge	Demi-glaze	Normande	Allemande	Supreme	Bearnaise	Barbecue
Cheese Gloucester	Madere	Joinville	Aurore	Hongroise	Noisette	Italienne
Cream Remoulade	Piquante	Vin			Mustard	Milanaise
Scotch Egg Tartare	Diable	Diplomat	Poulette	Chivry	Mousseline	Bretonne
Mustard Vincent	Robert	Shrimp	Fine herbs	Ivory	Maltaise tomated	Chaudfroid
Parsley	Chasseur	Caper	Riche	Foyot	Provencale	Verte
Soubise	Charcutiere	Bercy	Chaudfroid	Choron	Portugaise	Andalouse
Anchovy	Chaudfroid (brown)	Curry	Ravigote	Rachel		Cocktail Tyroliene
Onion Sauce	Lyonnise	Grimod				Thousand Island

There are numerous cold and hot sauces, but only certain sauces are commonly used.

Derivatives of Basic Sauces Brown or Espagnole Sauce

Name of Sauce	*Ingrediente*	*Foods with which cooked or served*
Demi-Glaze (Fr. Demi-glace)	50% of brown stock + 50% of brown sauce reduced to half.	Used for preparation other sauces.
Bercy	emi-glaze + meat glaze + minced shallots. + white wine + sliced bone marrow.	Grilled meat, fish.
Chasseur	Minced mushrooms, sauteed chopped shallots + white wine reduced + demi-glaze + butter + chopped parsley.	Poultry, eggs, grilled or sauteed meat.
Charcutiere	Robert sauce, garnished with juliennes of gherkins.	Grilled pork chops.
Bordelaise	Chopped shallots + Mig nonette pepper + thyme + bay leaves + red wine.	Steaks, grilled and sauteed cuts of beef, chicken.
Chaudfroid	Demi-glaze + aspic jelly + essence of truffles + Madeira.	Poultry, meat, cold dishes.
Devil (Diable) tongue,	Chopped shallots + white wine + vinegar + peppercorns, salt, reduced + demi-glaze strained + chopped parsley (prominent flavour of pepper).	Vegetables, boiled veal, beef, grilled fish, meat and poultry.
Madeira beef, (Madere Fr.)	Demi-glaze + Madeira wine.	Small items of veal, poultry, game, ham. Eggs.

Piquant chops,	Chopped shallots + vinegar + white wine + demi-glaze and strain, garnish with gherkins, chervil, chopped tarragon and pepper the of	Grilled pork rice, pastas.
	Chopped onions sauteed + white wine + vinegar + pepper reduced + demi-glaze + mustard to finish.	Grilled pork, chops, fish.

Glace de Viande is a meat glaze. The stock is concentrated and used as a glaze for cold dishes and roasts.

Bechamel Sauce

Name of Sauce	*Ingredients*	*Foods with which cooked or served*
Scotch egg sauce (Escossaise)	Thin Bechamel sauce, mixed with hard-boiled yolk, sieved, garnished with white of eggs cut into strips.	Poached fish or boiled fish, eggs, lamb.
Mornay	Bechamel + Parmesan and Gruyere + cream + egg yolks.	Fish, eggs and vegetables.
Cream	Bechamel + fresh cream + butter.	Poached fish, boiled vegetables.
Soubise	Bechamel + sauteed, minced onions + pepper + nutmeg and strained.	Eggs, boiled fish.
Cardinal	Bechamel + fish stock + truffle essence + lobster butter + cayenne pepper.	Fish.
Parsley	Bechamel + fresh cream + butter + chopped and blanched parsley.	Vegetables, calfs' head and boiled fish.
Mustard	Bechamel + fresh cream + butter + mustard (also prepared with Hollandaise).	Grilled herrings.
Anchovy	Bechamel + anchovy essence + anchovy fillets + cream + butter + lemon juice (also prepared with fish volute).	Poached, fried or boiled fish.

Onion sauce	Bechamel + minced onions cooked in milk + seasoning + nutmeg.	Roast mutton and eggs.
Chicken Volute		
Allemande	Chicken volute + egg yolks + mushroom trimmings + cream + juice of lemon.	Poached chicken.
Supreme	Chicken volute + white wine + parsley + shallots + mushroom trimmings and strain. Add fresh cream + yolk of eggs + juice of lemon.	Fish, chicken.
Mushroom	Sauce supreme + sliced button mushrooms, poached chicken and sweet	Bitoks, escalopes of veal, supremes of chicken, breads.
Hongroise	Chicken volute + paprika + white wine + cream.	Poached chicken escalopes of veal.
Ivory	Sauce supreme + meat glaze.	Poached chicken, boiled chicken.
Aurore	Chicken volute + tomato sauce + butter.	Poached chicken, boiled chicken, poached eggs.
White chaud-froid sauce	Chicken volute + chicken glaze + cream.	Cold dishes, boiled chicken, boiled leg of mutton.
Chivry	Chicken volute + tarragon + parsley + chives + strain + green butter.	Boiled or poached poultry.
Curry sauce	Dices of onions + apples sauteed in butter + curry powder + coconut milk + add volute + strain.	Eggs, fish, chicken.
Fish/Meat Volute		
Shrimp	Fish volute + fish fumet + cream + shelled shrimp tails + shrimp butter.	Fish, shrimps.
Normande	Fish volute + mushrooms + oyster liquor + fish'fumet + finish with egg yolks, cream + shelled shrimp tails + shrimp butter.	Fish, shellfish,
Joinville	Normande sauce + crayfish + cooking liquor of shrimps, juliennes of truffles.	Shellfish, fish,

Vin blanc	Thin fish volute + yolk of eggs and finished with butter (pour the butter in mixture in a double boiler).	Fish,
Nantua	Fish volute + fried mirepoix fish in crayfish butter.	Fish, shellfish,
Diplomate	Normande sauce + lobster butter, garnished with dices of lobster and truffles.	Shellfish, fish,
Caper	Mutton volute + capers.	Boiled leg of mutton.
Bercy	Allemande sauce + 'chopped shallots + white wine + meat glaze + butter, garnished with dices of marrow and chopped parsley.	Grilled meats.
Ravigote	Veal volute + white wine + vinegar + shallot butter, garnished with chervil chives and tarragon.	Boiled meat, fish and shellfish.
Poulette	Allemande sauce + mushroom essence + lemon juice + chopped parsley.	Boiled meat, eggs.
Tomato Sauce		
Bretonne	Tomato sauce + sauteed chopped onions + white wine reduced, strained + butter + chopped parsley.	Haricots.
Tomated Chaudfroid	Tomato sauce + aspic jelly.	Cold chicken, eggs.
Provencale	Thin tomato sauce + sauteed sliced mushrooms + chopped parsley + garlic + tomato concasse + sugar.	Eggs, fish and shellfish cold sauce is served with cold meats hors d'oeuvres.
Portugaise	Tomato sauce + white wine + tomato concasse + garlic.	Eggs, fish, shellfish.
Italienne	Tomato sauce + demi-glaze + chopped shallots + mush rooms + lean ham + fine herbs.	Small entrees, brains, lamb, cutlets and liver.
Barbecue	Tomato sauce + ketchup + vinegar + sugar.	Barbecued meats. It is an American sauce. There are different recipes.

Hollandaise		
Mousseline	Hollandaise sauce mixed with stiffly whipped cream.	Fish, eggs, vegetables and meat.
Maltaise	Hollandaise sauce + zest + juice of blood oranges.	Served with hot asparagus.
Noisette	Hollandaise + nut brown cooked butter.	Poached salmon and trout.
Bearnaise	Hollandaise sauce + chopped tarragon + chervil.	Grilled fish, meats, i.e. steaks.
Choron	Bearnaise sauce + tomato puree.	Grilled or sauteed meat.
Foyot	Bearnaise sauce + meat glaze.	Grilled and sauteed meat.
Mustard	Hollandaise sauce + mustard.	Meat, steaks.
Mayonnaise		
Chantilly	Mayonnaise + lemon juice ins- tead of vinegar, mixed with whipped cream.	Vegetables, cold dishes.
Gribiche	Mayonnaise + chopped hard- boiled eggs + mustard, garni- shed with chopped gherkins, capers, chervil, tarragon.	Calf's head and cold fish. Prepared, like mayonnaise, cold meat.
Cambridge	Pounded hard-boiled eggs + anchovy fillets + capers + chervil + tarragon + chives + vinegar + Cayenne pepper, add oil gradually as for may - onnaise, strain + chopped parsley.	
Gloucester	Mayonnaise + sour cream + lemon juice + chopped fennel + Worcestershire sauce.	Cold meat.
Remoulade	Mayonnaise + mustard garnished with capers, parsley, gherkins, chervil, tarragon and finished with anchovy essence.	Fried fish, spiny, lobster, cold meet and poultry.
Andalouse	Mayonnaise + tomato puree garnished with sweet capsicums.	Served with cold meet
Tartare	Mayonnaise + hard yolk of eggs, garnished with finely chopped onion and chives.	Fried fish and shellfish.
Green Sauce	Mayonnaise sauce mixed with	Cold trout, salmon

	puree of blanched herbs, spinach, water parsley, chervil, tarragon. Pass through very fine sieve.	trout and shelfish.
Vincent	Half tartare sauce + half green sauce mixed together.	Cold fish, shellfish
Thousand Island Dressing	Mayonnaise + hard-boiled eggs + tomato ketchup + chopped gherkins + onions -+ pimentos, olives + paprika powder.	Cold meat.
Cocktail	Mayonnaise + tomato ketchup + Worcester sauce + tabasco + cream + lemon juice.	Shellfish.
A Class of their Own		
Roast gravy	It is not a sauce, but is an accompaniment to roasts. Essence of roast meat + brown stock.	All roast items of meat, game and poultry.
Horseradish	Finely grated horseradish + vinegar + seasoning + cream. Vinegar + sugar + seasoning + chopped mint.	Roast or braised joints of beef, especially fillets. Mint Roast lamb or cold lamb dishes.
Apple	Apple puree + cinnamon powder + butter + sugar + water.	Roast joints, joints of port, duck, roast hare.
Bread	Flavoured milk with onions + bread crumbs + butter + cream + seasoning.	Roast poultry and roast feathered game.
Curry	Blond roux + garlic + chopped apple, onions + coconut powder + curry powder + tomato puree + stock + sultanas.	Rice, prawns, vegetables, and eggs.
Cranberry	Cranberries + sugar + water.	Roast turkey.
Oxford	Red currant jelly + chopped shallots + port wine + orange juice + chopped blanched orange and lemon zest.	Cold ham, cold version.
Butter Sauces		
Parsley butter Beurre Maitre' d'hotel (Fr.)	Butter + lemon juice parsley + seasoning.	Grilled meats, fish and fried fish.
Anchovy	Butter + seasoning + anchovy essence.	Grilled and fried fish.
Colbert	Parsley butter + dissolved pale meat glaze + chopped tarragon.	Fish colbert.

Shrimp butter	Half of finely pounded shrimp and half butter sieved.	Shellfish,
Beurre Manie	Prepare a paste of equal quantities of butter and flour and break into small pieces of boiling liquid for thickening and stir constantly, till a smooth texture is acquired.	Vegetables, fish,
Brown Butter	Brown the butter on gentle heat and get an even brown colour, pour over the food immediately.	Fish meuniere.
Garlic Butter	Soften butter, add garlic paste and lemon juice. Compound butter is a flavoured butter.	Grilled steaks,

Appetisers and Salads

Appetisers are small portions of food items, served as the first course to stimulate the appetite. They may be served in a liquid or solid form.

It is important that an appetiser should be colourful, dainty, decorated and well presented. Appetisers are classified into the following categories:

(1) Cocktails

(2) Canapes

(3) Hors d'oeuvres

(4) Petite Salads

Cocktails

They are generally served chilled and could be in a liquid form or solid. Juices of fruit or vegetables or seafood, cut into bite size, mixed with Worcestershire sauce and lemon juice, jal jeera (Indian).

They must be fresh in appearance and arranged attractively to have an eye appeal. The various cocktails are:

(1) Juices of orange, pineapple, grapefruit or tomato served with cold salad dressings are served as cocktails.

(2) Mixed fruit cocktail is dices of pineapple, orange, grapefruit, and grapes served with lemon juice squeezed on top. A cherry placed in the middle, served in cocktail glasses.

(3) Melon cocktail has small balls of melon served in a cocktail glass, melon juice poured on top and a cherry placed in the centre.

(4) Grapefruit--Cut into half the segments loosened with grape- fruit knife, placed in a grapefruit cup, cherry placed in the centre and castor sugar served separately. (Marashchino cherry)

(5) Avacado and Melon Cocktail--Dices or balls of avocado and melon, topped with cherry and lemon.

(6) Shellfish Cocktail (prawns, shrimps, crabs, etc.)--Dices of cooked shellfish, placed on shredded lettuce in a cocktail glass, cocktail sauce poured on top, garnished with wedges of tomatoes, slices of boiled egg, lemon slices and parsley.

(7) Orange Cocktail--Orange segments.

(8) Florida Cocktail--Orange and grapefruit segments, orange and grapefruit juice poured on top. A cherry placed on top.

Special Points for the Serving and Preparation of Cocktails

(1) Cocktails should be served well chilled, they could be single or assorted.

(2) The fruits should be cut in an attractive manner into segments, balls, or dices.

(3) The ingredients should be arranged in an attractive manner to create an eye appeal, a cherry placed on top adds colour.

(4) If greens are used, they should be crisp.

(5) Cocktails should be served in cocktail glasses.

Canapes

Canapes are savoury tit bits of food. They could be served hot or cold. The items should be dainty, petite, fresh, having an eye appeal and colour contrasts. There are not set recipes for the making of canapes. Individual or a combination of several different coloured items are used on the small fancifully cut pieces of bread, toasted or fried, and biscuits, etc. For the preparation of canapes, one should have an artistic sense, imagination, skill and flair for presentation.

Different butter spreads could be used, decorated and garnished with capers, hard-boiled eggs, gherkins, cucumber peel, olives, pimentos, radish, piped butter or mayonnaise, truffles, mushrooms, parsley, chervil. Base bread cut outs, toast, crackers, melba toast and pastry bases, etc.

Hot canapes are made similar to the cold variety, but they are not garnished as highly. Canapes could be served as a hors d'oeuvre course, for tea, cocktails, supper or during an evenings's entertainment. Canapes are eaten by hand.

Special Points to be Observed for the Preparation of Canapes

(1) The canape spreads should be colourful, butter or mayonnaise mixed with colour ingredients.

(2) The bread should be cut into thin slices.

(3) Toast fancifully, cut pieces of bread on both sides or it will become soggy.

(4) Use different breads, brown, white, rye, coloured breads to give a variety.

Zakuski

It originated in Russia in 1890s. They are like canapes and are made with classical filling, e.g. toast covered with smoked fish and aspic. It has original presentation and fillings. Chef Zakuski invented them. Zakuskis are larger than canapes and look attractive.

Hors D'oeuvres

The origin of hors d'oeuvres has been traced back to the Romans who enjoyed eating spicy foods before a big dinner.

Hors d'oeuvres are meant to stimulate appetite, so the presentation and taste is very important. Simplicity should be the watchword. They could be made with leftovers and fresh items so that they look appealing to the customers, tasty and well presented. Discretion, common sense, imagination and good taste should determine the selection. Although most hors d'oeuvres are served cold, there are also hot hors d'oeuvres.

Single Hors d'oeuvres

Caviar: Fresh caviar is certainly the finest and the most luxurious hors d'oeuvre, provided that it is fresh and of the best quality. It is the salted roe of the sturgeon fish and its allied species. The container is placed in a deep dish surrounded by crushed ice. It is served with quarters of lemon, sieved white and yolk of hard-boiled egg, finely chopped onion, and Blinis.

Smoked Salmon: It is classified among the more delicate hors d'oeuvres. Thin slices of salmon are served with lemon slices, brown bread and butter.

Plovers' Eggs: They are nutritious and are regarded as a delicacy.

Oysters (Huitres): Oysters should be bought with their

shells tightly closed. They are opened with a special oyster knife at the hinged end levering it open. The oysters are released from the shell by cutting the muscle that is attached to it. Place the shell with the oyster on a dish of crushed ice. Serve it with brown bread, butter and lemon.

Foie Gras: It is a ready-made delicacy made from goose liver and is served in its original dish or pastry case.

Potted Shrimp: They are peeled shrimps cooked and served in butter, dressed on lettuce leaves, accompanied with brown bread and butter.

Grapefruit: These are halved, segments are loosened with a grape fruit knife and chilled. They are served with a cherry in the centre and castor sugar is served separately.

Pate de Foie (Liver Paste): It is prepared with liver, pork fat, chopped onions, herbs, butter, seasoning, cooked and passed through a mincer and put in a mould which has been lined with slices of fat bacon. It is first poached and then it is sliced and served on a silver flat. It is accompanied with toast.

Cold Globe Artichokes: Cook the globe artichokes, refresh, drain and dress on a folded serviette. It is garnished with parsley served with French dressing.

Avocado Pears with French Dressing: Cut avocado pears lengthwise, destone and place on lettuce leaves with French Salad Dressing.

Cold Asparagus: Cook asparagus, refresh, drain and dress on a folded serviette, and serve with mayonnaise.

Assorted Hors d'oeuvres: The recipes are practically inexhaustible. Standard hors d'oeuvres are prepared with vegetables, fruits, eggs, shellfish, fish, chicken and meat.

Egg Mayonnaise (Oeufs durs mayonnaise Fr.): Arrange lengthwise halved hard-boiled eggs or lettuce leaves and coat with mayonnaise. Garnish with slices of olives and fanciful cuts of tomatoes. Garnish with quarters of tomatoes and slices of cucumbers.

Fish Mayonnaise: Poach fish and shred it, place on lettuce leaves and coat with mayonnaise. Decorate with strips of anchovy fillets, capers, and stoned olives.

NB: Flaked fish could be mixed with mayonnaise and then placed on lettuce leaves and decorated the same way as above.

Stuffed Eggs (Oeufs Farcis Fr.): Cut the hard-boiled eggs lengthwise or breadth wise. Cut in a *zigzag* manner all around the egg, remove the egg yolk and sieve it, mix butter or mayonnaise to get the correct piping consistency. Put it in a piping bag with a star nozzle and pipe in the hollow of the egg.

Goujons a la Russe: Poach fish mix aspic to mayonnaise and coat, sprinkle chopped parsley and serve cold.

Escqffier Onions (Oignons Escoffier Fr.): Small button onions are sauteed in refined or salad oil in a pan, then excess fat is drained off. Vinegar is added and reduced, then tomato puree and a little sugar seasoning is added. Bay leaf, peppercorns and a little stock is also added. When the onions are half cooked, then sultanas are added. After the onions are cooked, it is chilled, then served cold.

Cauliflower Portugaise (Choufleur Portugaise Fr.): The cauliflower flowerets are cooked in boiling water to which vinegar has been added. Portugaise sauce is prepared by sauteing chopped onions in a pan, and crushed garlic is added, then vinegar is added and reduced. The tomato puree, sugar, a little salt, bay leaf, and peppercorns are added.

To this sauce blanched cauliflower flowerettes are added and allowed to simmer and then chilled and served cold.

Tomato Antibois: Tomatoes stuffed with a mixture of tuna fish, chopped boiled eggs, capers, chopped onions, anchovy fillets and mayonnaise.

Tuna *Marinette:* Thick slices of tuna fish placed alternately, with slices of tomato with onion rings and parsley, dressed with vinaigrette dressing, border of potatoes placed all around.

Hot Hors d'oeuvres: At certain times they can be served as small entrees. They may be served as cocktail savouries, or as a first course. A number of them are usually made with paste and different kinds of filling. The other popular preparations are cheese puffs, cheese balls, bouchees, croquettes, fritters, mini shasliks, small shami kababs, boti, kababs, etc.

Small Salads

They are dainty, artistically arranged and consist of a base, body and garnish, as an appetiser. Salads are served in small quantities.

The preparation of salads for hors d'oeuvres can be left to one's imagination, the variety is endless and almost everything in the kitchen can be used for them. Some of the salads used as an hors d'oeuvre course are:

Peas and Rice Salad

Equal parts of rice and very green peas mixed with vinaigrette dressing (vinegar, oil and seasoning mixed) to which chopped parsley is added.

Salad Nicoise: (Salade de Nicoise Fr.)

Tuna fish, tomato, anchovy fillets, cut into cubes, mixed with vinaigrette dressing with chopped chervil and chives.

Potato Salad: (Salade do pommes de terre Fr.)

Cubes of boiled potatoes or slices and chopped onions mixed together, and vinaigrette dressing.

Apple and Potato Salad: (Salad de deux pommes Fr.)

Cubes of potatoes and apples mixed with mayonnaise. Garnished and decorated with chopped parsley.

Meat Salad: (Salade de Viande Fr.)

Boiled meat, chopped onions, boiled eggs and blanched tomatoes, cut into dices and chopped parsley. Mix all the ingredients and add vinaigrette dressing. Garnish with tomato rosettes and sprigs of parsley.

Indian Rice Salad (Salade Orientale Fr.)

Recipe I

Curried boiled rice, chopped onions, mixed with mayonnaise. Garnished with slices of tomatoes.

Recipe II

Rice, asparagus tips, strips of pimentos, dices of apples and curry cream.

Midinette Salad

Juliennes (strips) of apples, cooked chicken, celery, mixed with mayonnaise and grated cheese added to it.

Tasty Salads

A salad is a food served with a dressing. The food can be a cold dish, or green vegetables or mixture of fruits, or hot mixture of piquant food, or frozen mixture of bland fruits, or chopped food in aspic, coleslaw, potato, or meat.

The difference between hors d'oeuvres and salads is, that the hors d'oeuvre is an important course and it is always the first course. It is served in small quantities, and is a light, appetising, colourful and stimulating dish.

Hors d'oeuvre, is not served as any other course. Salad can be served as the first course, in small quantities; it can also be served as a salad course or as an accompaniment with the entree or roast course. Salads maybe served in substantial quantity. Freshness and stimulating flavours are characteristics desired in salads. To qualify as a salad, food must possess piquancy or relish value. In some food, flavour has to be developed with marinades, spices and herbs.

Salads should be cold, crisp, piquant, colourful, well seasoned and attractive. They supply nutrients to the dish, especially when they are made of fresh fruits and vegetables. The preparation involves working with food that possess highly perishable qualities in ways that may readily result in contamination. In order to ensure safety and good quality, cleanliness, continuous refrigeration is essential. A large share of preparation calls for cutting and arranging food by hand.

Materials selected for salads and the size of the portions, need to be governed by the salad's role on the menu. Their arrangement should be simple with a natural rather than a set appearance. Arrangements that are exact, uniform or perfect, tend to lead to overhandling of materials.

The other ways of serving salads are:

1. As *a Main Dish*--It is substantial enough as a main dish. One of the body-building food, such as meat, fish, eggs or cheese, forms the base. The volume and richness of these salads are adequate to satisfy the normal appetite.
2. *Salad Course*--Salads are served as a separate course following the main course, in the more formal types of service. The salad that follows a heavy course is light and refreshing. It provides a change from the main course and refreshes the appetite. Well-dressed

salad greens and savoury vegetables are popular choices.

3. *Salads as Accompaniments--The* salads are served with the main course and provide relish with the main course food.

Salads are of two types: Plain or Simple salads, and Compound or Composite salads. *Simple Salads*

These can be sub-divided into green salad or salad in season, which is served raw or cooked, consisting usually of a single kind of vegetable as a base. One or two ingredients, in small quantities are used for decoration or as a garnish. Examples of some of the simple salads are:

Name of salad	*Ingredients*	*Dressings*
Chicory	Wild chicory	Mustard cream
Celery	Chopped celery	Vinaigrette
Endive	Curly of other endive	Vinaigrette, garlic flavoured
Cabbage	Juliennes of cabbage	Vinaigrette or Mustard cream
Cucumber	Roundels of cucumber	Vinaigrette
Lettuce	Salad leaves	Vinaigrette
Artichoke	Cooked artichoke bottoms	Vinaigrette
Potatoes	Dices or roundels of cooked potatoes, with onion rings or chopped onions.	Vinaigrette or mayonnaise
Beetroots	Roundels or dices of cooked beetroots with parsley	Mustard cream
Tomatoes	Slices of tomatoes and parsley	Vinaigrette

Compound Salads

They are more elaborate salads and consist of more than one ingredients. They are divided into four groups:

(1) Fish based

(2) Vegetables based
(3) Poultry, game or meat based
(4) Fruit based

The Salad has four basic parts: Underliner or base, body, dressing and garnish. While composing a salad, each part plays an important role, and if one part is omitted or done poorly, the finished salad will not be up to the standard.

Base

The underliner is usually a leafy vegetable such as lettuce of different kinds as romaine or cos, watercress, cabbage, etc. There are not many varieties cultivated and only one variety is used. The tossed salads do not have an underline; they are piled in bowls. The main purpose is to keep the plate or bowl from looking bare and to provide contrast colour to the other parts of the salad.

Body

This is the most important part of the salad. The salad gets its name from the ingredients that are used for the body. This part gets the most attention and its appearance is enhanced by decorations. The ingredients used have a balance of flavours and taste. The body consists of broken salad greens, fruit in moulded aspic, sliced cooked potatoes, raw cabbage, tomato stuffed with tuna fish, chicken or meat dices or strips, etc.

Garnish

The main purpose of the garnish is to add an eye appeal to the finished product but in some cases it improves the taste and form (border). It may be a part of the body or it can be an additional item that will blend and complement. If the garnish is simple it will attract and not distract.

Dressings

A dressing is usually served with all types of salads. It

adds flavour, provides food value, helps digestion, improves palatability and appearance. Dressing is in a liquid or semi-liqued form, a mixture of oil-vinegar, seasonings or eggs or cream, etc.

The basic dressings are:

Mayonnaise, vinaigrette or French dressing, lemon dressing, mustard cream and acidulated cream.

Mayonnaise is also known as a basic cold sauce and has numerous derivatives. It is used for cold dishes, the coating of fish, meat, eggs, etc. (Please refer to the chapter on Sauces)

Vinaigrette can be made, in the French, English or American style. The ratio of ingredient vary.

French--3 parts oil and one part vinegar and French mustard and seasonings.

*English--*1 part oil and 2 parts vinegar, mustard and seasonings.

*American--*Equal quantities of vinegar and oil, seasonings and sugar.

*Lemon Dressing--*Same as vinaigrette using lemon juice instead of vinegar.

Acidulated Cream

3 parts thin cream and 1 part vinegar or lemon juice, salt and pepper.

Compound or Composite Salads: Some of the examples of the salads with many ingredients are:

Vegetable Based

Name of salad	*Ingredients*	*Dressings*
Tossed Salads	Prepared of salad 'greens and are tossed in large bowls, in the	Vinaigrette or Mayonnaise

	kitchen or before the customers. They consist of celery, lettuce, cabbage, herbs, onions, shallots, chives, etc.	
Coleslaw	Sliced cabbage, capsicum, carrots	Vinaigrette or Mayonnaise
Orientale	Rice, tomato, dices, chopped garlic and green beans, pimentos, fillets of anchovies	Vinaigrette
Aida	Curly chicory (endive) tomatoes and sliced artichoke, artichoke bottoms, julienne of sweet pimentos and whites of hard-boiled eggs, covered with hard boiled yolks, passed through a sieve	Vinaigrette mustard
Andalouse	Quarters of tomatoes, julienne of sweet pimentos, plain boiled rice, crushed garlic, onions and chopped parsley French beans, juliennes of Duchesse	Vinaigrette
Meat Based		
Carmen	Rice, red pimentos, cold chicken, green peas	Mayonnaise potatoes and celery
Hongroise	Bacon juliennes, cabbage, potatoes, grated radish, crisp lettuce, paprika	Mayonnaise
Laperouse	Tomatoes + Dices of ham + French beans + artichoke bottoms + onions	Mayonnaise
Bagration	Julienne of celery and chicken + artichoke bottoms + macaroni + tomatoes, decorated with truffles, eggs and chopped parsley	
Chatelaine	Hard-boiled eggs, truffles, artichoke bottoms, potatoes, chopped tarragoan	Vinaigrette
Fish Based		
Parisienne	Fish aspic, vegetable salads macedoine, lobster flesh, truffles, lobster coral, herbs, lettuce	Mayonnaise with
Fish	Fish mayonnaise, tomato, parsley mayonnaise	Mayonnaise for decoration
Belles de Nuit	Slices of truffles and crayfish	Vinaigrette
Favourite	Crayfish tails, slices of white truffles, asparagus tips, celery and chopped parsley and seasonings	Lemon Dressing
Hollandaise	Smoked salmon in dices, potatoes, caviar and onions	Lemon Dressing

Fruit Based		
Creole	Small melons, take out the flesh, cut into dices, salt, ginger and cooked rice	Acidulated cream dressing
Japonnaise	Tomatoes, pineapple, orange dices and lettuce	Lemon Dressing or cream dressing
Dalila	Bananas, apples, juliennes of celery	Mayonnaise
Eve	Prepare apples, scoop and fill with balls of apples, bananas and pineapple	Accidulated cream
Waldorf	Pieces of celery, apples, halved and shelled walnuts	Thin Mayonnaise

Accompaniments and Garnishes

Many dishes have separate accompaniments whose flavour, taste and colour blend or give contrast to the principal dish. Food items such as sauces, vegetables, salads and certain meat items, cheese or bread are accompaniments that make a dish complete. They add to the bulk of the dish and give greater satisfaction, improve the satiety value and enhance the taste, e.g. bland poached fish accompanied by Hollandaise sauce. They also help to digest food, sometimes provide moistness, and give piquancy to the dish, e.g. roast lamb accompanied by mint sauce, fried fish with tartare sauce, etc.

Foods and Their Usual Accompaniments

food items	*Accompaniments*
Grapefruit	Castor sugar.
Oysters	Tabasco sauce (commercial chilli, vinegar, cayenne pepper, brown bread and butter, pepper-mill, lemon.
Melon	Castor sugar and ginger powder.
Caviare	Hot buttered breakfast toast.
Smoked salmon	Red pepper, pepper-mill, brown bread and butter.
Foie gras	Hot butter breakfast toast.
Tomato juice	Worcestershire sauce (commercial sauce).
Tasty Soups	
Puree soups	Croutons (fried).

Bortsch a la Russe	Sour cream, beetroot juice, duck forcemeat, bouchees.
French onion soup	Slices of dry French bread, Parmesan cheese.
Potage Bonne Femme	Flutes.
Minestone	Parmesan cheese.
Pitite Marmite	Sippets, Parmesan cheese.
Fish	
Fried fish (egg and bread crumbed and deep fried)	Tatare sauce, lemon slices.
Fish Orly (Orly batter and deep fried)	Tomato sauce.
Grilled fish	Tartare or Hollandaise sauce.
Poached fish	Hollandaise sauce or egg sauce and melted butter.
Poached fresh	Cucumber salad, Hollandaise sauce, salmon or cold salmon.
Fish Meuniere	Tomato sauce, Noisette butter.
Cold lobster or any other fish	Mayonnaise.
Meat	
Roast beef	Yorkshire pudding, Horseradish sauce and roast gravy.
Roast lamb	Mint sauce, roast gravy.
Roast mutton	Onion sauce or Red current jelly, roast gravy.
Roast pork	Sage and onion stuffing, apple sauce, roast gravy.
Roast veal	Savoury herb stuffing, grilled bacon, roast gravy.
Roast Venison:	
Hot	Red currant jelly, roast gravy.
Cold	Cumberland sauce.
Boiled mutton	Caper sauce, mashed turnips, mustard.
Boiled fresh beef	Spinach, madeira or peach sauce.
Grilled ham	Sauce will appear on the menu.
Cold meats	Mustards, pickles, chutney, relishes and proprietary sauces.
Poultry and Game	
Roast chicken	Bread sauce, roast gravy, roast potatoes.sauce, roast gravy.

Roast duck	Sage and onion stuffing, apple sauce,
Roast turkey	Herb stuffing, chestnut stuffing, chipolatas, cranberry sauce, roast, gravy.
Vegetables	
Vegetables served hot	Hollandaise sauce, melted butter
Vegetables served cold	Mayonnaise or vinaigrette sauce.

The Garnishes

Garnishes can be defined as "food items placed around or on top of a principal dish for adornment or relish." Classical dishes are garnished by their creator for the naming of public personalities, whether political, professional or merely a name of the establishment. The popularity of an establishment has often been made by the Chef (Head cook, specialising on his garnishing alone). His aim is to present perfect dishes.

The constituents of garnishes are supplied by farinaceous products, quenelles of all kinds, cock's combs, kidneys, truffles, mushrooms, plain or stuffed olives, shellfish, bone marrow, etc. Vegetables for garnishing are treated in accordance with the use and shape, implied by the name of the dish, e.g. for consomme juliennes, the vegetables will be cut into juliennes.

A careful selection of garnishes that have flavour, colour and eye appeal is appreciated and it is accepted as a finished dish. The purpose of garnishing food is to supply some appropriate and suitable adjunct to the dish. e.g. maitre d'hotel and straw potatoes with mixed grill. It makes the dish attractive in appearance and enhances flavour, e.g. lemon wedges and parsley with fried fish. It helps to improve the colour of the principal dishes and it is seen that the colourful ingredients blend well with the dish. The subtle touch of colour well used will increase the attractiveness of a dish whereas if uncontrolled, the result can be disastrous. Omission of any constituent is to be avoided, as the garnish would thereby be out of keeping with its specified character. The neatness is of prime importance and from the service point of view, arranging of garnish must be planned to facilitate the servicing. Many a dressed and garnished dish has its appearance spoilt after only one portion having been served, simply because the garnish has not been carefully considered with the service in mind. There is no specific design to work to, although the classical dishes are always garnished as their originator intended.

There are two types of garnishes, simple and composite. Simple garnishes consist of a single element, most commonly a vegetable, braised, sauteed or fried, ice croutons, flutes, e.g. tomato soup with croutons. Composite garnishes are made from a number of ingredients varying according to the basic dish, e.g. Chicken Maryland with corn galettes (thick corn pancakes), bacon rasher, banana fritters, potato croquette, and grilled tomatoes.

The garnishes for cold buffet for decorating cold dishes must be glazed with aspic jelly before they are arranged on the dish. After the garnish has been arranged on the dish, a final coating of aspic jelly will ensure that they become set on the dish and do not move when being carried for service. A few specific garnishes for cold buffets are eggs, stuffed tomatoes, barquettes with various fillings, fanciful shapes, cuts of vegetables, used wherever appropriate. The important role is that the garnishes are neat, tastefully decorated and in keeping with the item of food which they accompany. The number of pieces should be in keeping with the number of portions of the dish.

While compiling menus, it should be borne in mind that the garnish used must be in keeping with the nature of dish. The garnish should not be repeated between courses nor should it form an accompaniment to any course. There are hundreds of garnishes, but only some of the common garnishes are given below.

Suggested Garnishes

Tomato juice	Lemon wedges.
Shellfish cocktail	Parsley, lemon, boiled egg.
Fruit cocktail	Cherry.
For soups	Juliennes of vegetables, brunoise of vegetables, egg royal, cooked tongue, ham, spaghetti, vermicelli, croutons, rice, etc.
For fish	Parsley, lemon, truffles, prawns, shrimps, tomatoes, grapes and bababas, etc.
For meats:	
Grills	Maitre d'hotel butter and straw potatoes.
Stews	Dices or turned vegetables, grilled tomatoes, mushrooms, peas, French beans.
Roast	A salad, orange, greens, etc.
Sandwiches	Lettuce or watercress.
Tandoori murgh	Sliced onions, green chillies, lemon slices.
Seekh kababs	Sliced onions, lemon wedges and chutney.
Pulaos	Silver foil, fried, cashewnuts and fried onions.
Curries	Silver foil, chopped coriander leaves,
Masala fish	Lemon wedges and coriander leaves.
Dals	Whole red chillies or fried onions, coriander leaves.

Terms which Feature Dishes: When the featured dishes are served, they must match the build up provided by the menu description. Mention has been made of standard terms. Here is a selection which is understood the world over:

Terms	*Indicators*
Africaine	Egg plant, tomatoes, and mushrooms.
Americaine	Tomatoes, bacon, watercress.
Argenteuil	Asparagus.
Bohemierme	Onions, tomatoes, rice.
Bouquetiere	Carrots, turnips, peas, beans and cauliflower. Bouquet of vegetables.
Bourgeoise	Carrots, small onions, lardons.

Clamart	Green peas.
Conti	Lentils.
Crecy	Carrots.
Danoise	Cucumber.
Doria	Cucumber, cooked in butter.
Dieppoise	Shrimps, mussels, mushrooms.
Dubarry	Cauliflower.
Fiananciere	Cock's combs, kidneys, mushrooms, olives, quenelles.
Fleuriste	Carrots, turnips, peas, beans.
Florentine	Spinach
Forestiere	Mushrooms.
Hongroise	Paprika.
Indienne	Curry sauce, rice.
Jardiniere	Carrots, turnips, peas, beans (garden vegetables)
Judic	Stuffed tomatoes, braised lettuce, chateau potatoes.
Lyonnaise	Onions.
Marechale	Asparagus, noisettes, potatoes, truffles.
Maryland	Sweet corn, banana, bacon, potatoes, croquettes.
Milanaise	Spaghetti, ham, tongue, mushrooms.
Montmorency	Cherries.
Niscoise	Tomatoes, beans, chateau potatoes.
Parmentiere	Potatoes.
Perigueaux	Foie gras, truffles.
Portugaise	Tomatoes, chateau potatoes.
Princesse	Asparagus, artichokes, noisette potatoes.
Reforme	Ham, tongue, gherkin, mushrooms.
Rossini	Foie gras, truffles.
Soubise	Onions.
St. Germaine	Green peas.
Toulousaine	Cock's comb, kidneys, sweetbread, mushrooms, quenelles.
Tourtne	Quenelles, mushrooms, gherkin, brain, fried eggs, crouton.

Tyrolienne	Tomatoes, onions.
Vichy	Carrots.
Viennoise	Lemon, hard-boiled egg, olives and anchovy.
Walewska (Fish)	Slices of lobster tails and truffles.
Washington	Sweet corn.
Zingara	Ham, tongue, mushrooms, truffles.

Soups

It is probable that soup in its earliest form was a complete meal because it was found hearty, nourishing, economical and wholesome.

Soup is a liquid food consisting of meat, seafood, vegetables, cereals or poultry. They play an important role on the menu and are regarded as appetisers as they stimulate the appetite for the heavier food to follow. On the menu, they are served as the first course, if hors d'oeuvres are not being served. If hors d'oeuvre is served them soup is served as the second course.

Special Points for the Service and Preparation of the Soups

(1) First-class, clean, strong and flavourful stock should be used, as it would help in producing good quality soup.

(2) If there is a heavy entree, the soup should be thin or light.

(3) If a heavy soup is served, the portion should be small.

(4) The soups should not in any way be filling or consist of food particles that require much chewing.

(5) Garnish should be small and dainty, so that they can be picked up easily by a soupspoon.

(6) Soup should be always moderately seasoned.

(7) Serve hot soups piping hot, and cold soups very cold.

(8) A little sugar should be added to tone the acidity of the soup, before mixing cream as it prevents curdling.

(9) Consomme should be amber in colour. (Onions halved and browned on hot plate are added to the soup for colour.)

(10) Accompaniments of the soups should be of a crisp character, e.g. Melba toast, various crackers, bread-sticks, cheese croutons, bread rolls, etc.

(11) Entree portions of one litre of soup yields five portions.

Commonly Used Garnishes for Soups

Croutons	Dices or other shapes made from bread, toast, pastry.
Profitroles	Prepared from chou paste. They are miniature cream puffs which may be filled or used plain.
Cereals	Rice or barley.
Cheese	Cheese balls, or grated Parmesan served with croutons on one side.
Cream	Unsweetened whipped cream or sour cream.
Meats	Usually small dices or juliennes.
Poultry	Same as meat.
Seafood	Diced or flaked, Large enough pieces distinguishable.
Pastas	Noodles, spaghetti, other pasta products such as star letters, cornets, etc.
Vegetables	Cut in various sizes, shapes--juliennes, round slices, dices of sprig, printaniere vegetables.

There is no set standard for the classification of soups, as there are virtually thousands of soup preparations. In order to learn about them easily, soups may be classified in the following manner:

Thin Soups

Most of the thin soups are clear, flavoured nutritious liquids and are prepared without the use of starch. The soup is a thin liquid with garnish or with small, daintily cut food items floating in it. Some of the consommes are slightly thickened with tapioca.

Consomme--Comes from the word 'consummate', which means to bring to completion or perfect. It is a strongly-flavoured, clarified soup, its flavour is heightened by the adding of meat, vegetables, poultry and seasonings. The foundation liquid used is rich, of cold beef, mutton or chicken stock, to which raw lean minced meat, finely diced or chopped carrots, turnips, onions, celery seasonings and egg whites are added and mixed well. This mixture is placed on heat and allowed to come to boil and then simmered. The protein in the eggs and meat coagulates and binds in most of the clouding materials.

This coagulated mass, rises slowly to the top and forms a raft. When the consomme is clear and cooked, the soup is strained, through several thicknesses of cloth. Consommes are varied and the soup gets its name from the additional ingredients that are added to the consomme. Sometimes it is named after historical figures, people or events in the form of accompanying garnish.

Consumers should be sparkling, clear and well flavoured and they are varied. They can be served hot or cold.

Recipe of Consomme (1 Litre)

Minced meat	225 gms
Onions	70 gms
Carrots	50 gms
Turnips	30 gms
Stock	$1^1/_2$ litres
Egg whites	2

Celery	40 gms
Thyme	1/4 tspn.
Bay leaf	1/2
Peppercorns	3

Method

Mix minced meat and chopped onions, carrots, turnips, celery and mix well with egg whites. Add cold stock, thyme, bay leaf and peppercorns. Place on fire, go on stirring so that the ingredients do not stick to the bottom of the pan and articles are suspended. When the mixture starts boiling, lower the temperature and let it simmer until the coagulated mass (raft) comes to the top. Simmer for one and a half hours.

When consomme is clear and tasty, strain through a double muslin cloth. Add seasoning.

NB: Beef stock is good for consomme as it is full of flavour and has body.

Consommes

Alexandra Chicken consomme thickened with tapioca garnished with juliennes of chicken, quenelles and shredded lettuce.

Andalouse Consomme blended with tomato puree garnished with dices of Royale and dices of tomato, juliennes of ham, boiled rice + vermicelli and threaded eggs.

Bretonne Consomme garnished with juliennes of leeks, celery, onions, mushrooms and chervil shreds.

Carmen Consomme garnished with tomato puree and capsicum garnished with juliennes of tomatoes and capsicum, rice and chervil shreds.

Colbert Consomme garnished with printaniere of vegetables and small poached eggs.

Consomme Variations

Garnishes	*Ingredients*
Breton	Juliennes of celery, onion and leeks.
Brunnoise	Small diced vegetables.
Dubarry	Flowerettes of cauliflower.
Florentine	Juliennes (strips) of blanched spinach.
Julienne	Juliennes of cut vegetables (3 cm strips).
Madrilene	Tomato dices and green peas.
Paysanne	Uniform size cut fresh vegetables.
Printaniere	Mixed fresh spring vegetables, cut in small dices.
St. Germain	Fresh green peas.
Celestine	Juliennes of thin pancakes.
Cereals	Rice and barley.
Diablotin	Diamonds of cheese biscuits.
Egg drops	Pour into the boiling consomme, beaten eggs.
Royal	Dices of savoury egg custard (egg, stock and seasoning poached)
Tapioca	Pearls of tapioca.
Vermicelli	Fine noodles.

Consommes could be named by the garnishes used.

Bouillon and Broths are terms that are interchangeable and practically mean the same. They are unpassed soups.

Bouillon comes from the world "boil"'. It has a more pronounced strong meaty flavour and is clear soup with pieces of vegetables, meat, seafood, etc. floating in the soup.

Broths are similar to bouillons but the liquid is a little cloudy and contains all types of vegetables, meat, chicken, etc. These should be cut into regular shapes, floating in the soup.

The broths usually have the cheaper cuts of meat, such as the scrag end of mutton, boiling fowls. Some of the popular broths are: Scotch broth, mutton broth, chicken broth, petite marmite, soup bonne femme, soup paysanne and potage fermiere.

Thick Soups

They are passed thick soups and in this category are purees, cream, veloutes, bisques and chowders.

Purees

Starchy vegetables such as leguminous plants, potatoes or cereals when pureed in soups, usually act as self-thickeners and need no further thickening ingredients. Many vegetables like carrots, pumpkins, turnips, peas, celery, leafy greens need an additional thickening agent as their own purees do not cohere and so the above thickening agents are added. The cooked soup is strained through a sieve and the consistency of the soup is thick. Water or stock in which the pureed product was cooked is usually used as the liquid in the soup. The soup is served with fried golden brown croutons (fried small dices of bread). Common puree soups are--Puree parmentiere, pea soup, lentils puree, tomato soup.

Puree Soups

Compiegne	Puree of white rajma (haricot beans) garnished with sorrel and chervil shreds and butter added at the last minute.
Conde	Puree of red kidney beans with red wine and butter added before serving.
Conti	Puree of lentils (malka masoor) garnished with bacon chervil and butter added at the last minute.
Grecque	Puree of green peas and garnished with shreds of carrots, leeks, cabbage and butter added before serving.
Lamballe	Half of fresh peas puree and half of tapioca puree, and butter added just before serving.

Cream Soups

They are composed of a puree of vegetables, fish, poultry, or meat, thickened with bechamel sauce or given a cream finish. Milk is used to dilute and achieve correct consistency. Various cream soups are: cream of Germaine (peas), cream of tomato, cream of argenteuil (asparagus), cream of mushrooms soup, cream of chicken soup, cream of lentil soup.

Ambassadeur	Prepare puree of fresh peas and garnish with rice, shredded sorrel, chervil, lettuce, add butter and cream just before serving.
Bretonne	Puree of white rajma (haricot beans) with onions and spring onions. Add tomato puree, add butter and cream before serving.
Chantilly	Puree of lentils, add cream, garnish with quenelles of chicken.
Crecy	Puree of carrots and rice and add butter and cream just before serving.
Washington	Puree of maize, add cream and just before serving, add whisky and port and garnish with maize grains.

Veloutes

Volute sauces have already been discussed. Veloutes as soups are similar to other veloutes, but differ from purees, as they require a thickening element and a roux. Volute is made by preparing roux and adding stock and the pureed vegetable or meat and hot milk is blended in, to produce a smooth soup. Generally proportions for a volute soup are half basic volute, ½ puree (main ingredients characterising the soup), ¼ stock or white consomme used to dilute the mixture of puree and volute to the correct consistency. Finishing of veloutes is done by a liaison, i.e. cream and egg yolks, as it enhances the taste and texture. Examples of veloutes are: chicken volute, celery volute, almond volute, etc.

Volute	Chicken volute with barley flour, garnish
Marie Louisa	with dices of spring vegetables, cooked macaroni and cream and egg liaison.
Volute Celeris	Volute supreme and celery puree and add cream.
Volute Princesse	Equal quantities of chicken volute and asparagus puree, garnish with dices of chicken and asparagus heads and pluches of chervil and cream.
Volute Montoruetl	Chicken volute, garnished printaniere of vegetables, shreds of sorrel and chervil.
Volute Indienne	Volute supreme with coconut milk, flavoured with curry powder, garnished with rice.

Bisques--These are shellfish puree soups, thickened with rice or cream. It is a slightly thick rice cream type of soup with small particles of cooked shellfish floating in It, to add flavour and colour. A small amount of wine is added to enhance the flavour. Examples of bisques are: Crayfish bisque, Lobster bisque.

Chowders--Originated from America. They are thick heavy soups, owing their consistency to potatoes. Chowders consist of potatoes, onions, pieces of bacon, various seasonings, and seafood. They can be milk or tomato based. Crackers are generally added just before serving. Examples are: Clam chowder, seafood chowder, oyster chowder, etc.

Cold Soups

Chilled soups include those that are jellied by the natural gelatin in the meat stock or by addition of gelatin powder or those that are thickened with a starch or puree. Cold consomme Madrilene is popular. Vichyssoise is a rich cream of potato soup, which is served cold, and garnished with chopped chives. Borscht can be served cold or hot. Scandinavians love cold fruit soup which contains a blend of assorted fruit and juices, usually garnished with mint leaves.

Andalouse gazpacho is a refreshing tomato and cucumber soup with a garnish of thin strips of pimentos, cumin seeds for flavour accompanied with croutons.

Cold soups have become popular and a summer menu is incomplete without it.

Volute de Prepare chicken volute and serve cold.

Volatile Froid

Gelee de Strong tomate chicken consomme iellied.

Velaille aux

tomate

Gelee de Strong chicken/consomme with dices of tomatoes and pimentos. Served very cold.

Volatile Strong consomme and celery flavoured with tomatoes and pimentos.

Napolitaine Served very cold.

Consomme Leeks and potatoes, milk, stock

Madriliene and butter.

Vichyssoise Cook all the ingredients, strain, add cream and add chopped chives, and cool. Serve very cold.

Convenience Soups

These are marketed in dried, liquid or frozen form. They are available in many varieties. The soups are sold in cans or bottles, some in ready to use forms, others in concentrated forms. These liquid soups can be classed as deluxe, e.g. turtle, kangaroo's tail, oxtail, etc. They are a consistent product.

International Soups

There are many varieties, cold or hot, thin or thick soups. They have been placed in a special category, as they have different origins. There are soups that originated in a certain locality and are associated with that particular place. In some cases, these soups have a great tradition, as the New England clam chowder, helped the early colonists survive many winters. Crecy soup originated when nothing was available at the site of the Battle of Crecy. The carrots that were grown in the land were taken and cooked. Most of the national soups are unpassed soups.

Popular International Soups

Name of Soups	*Origin*
Minestrone	Italy
Green turtle soup	England
French onion soup	France
Petite marmite	France
Scotch broth and Cock-a-leekie	Scotland
Creole	New Orleans
Mulligatawny	India
Bortsch Polonais	Polland
Olla-podrida and Gazpacho	Spain
Manhattan Clam Chowder	America
Hotch Pot Flamanda	Belgium
Camaro	Brazil
Laberkroedel	Germany
Paprika	Hungary
Bouillabaise	French (salt-water and shellfish stew)

Acknowledgement

The elaborate foregoing discussion will definitely be useful to readers and practitioners in the field. To conclude, we owe a deep sense of gratitude to the original sources of information contained in this chapter

8

The Beverages

> All of us must be drank once, youth is drunkenness without wine.
>
> —*Johann Wolfgang Von Goethe*

Generally, by beverage, we mean drinks—alcoholic or non-alcoholic. Here in this chapter, we are giving information about non alcoholic drinks, that too most popular-like tea and cofee.

Functions of Beverages

To Prevent Water Depletion: Water being one of the essential constituents of beverages it is very useful in making good the loss of water content in the blood stream, specially after heavy physical exertion. Adequate supply of water is essential for the healthy functioning of all the tissues in the body. For an adult doing no manual work and when the weather is pleasant enough not to cause any excessive perspiration, three litres of water daily are necessary for good health. Two litres are obtained from food so one litre must be taken in the form of water and other beverages.

Refreshing and Restorative: Cold drinks in summer and hot drinks in winter have a greatly refreshing and restorative effect on the body particularly when fatigued.

Supplies vitamins: Certain beverages like lime juice, Ovaltine, etc., are a source of vitamin supply.

Stimulating: Alcoholic beverages are stimulating and have a definite value in case of illness, but if taken regularly even in moderate quantities, lessen the power of resistance to disease, and if taken in excess are very harmful.

Beverages such as tea, coffee and cocoa besides being refreshing are also stimulating but they do not have any aftereffects.

Rechauffe Cooking: Although freshly cooked food is better than reheated food, in the interests of economy and food management, reheating of food forms an important part of cooking. A clever cook should take pride in seeing that the second appearance is appetizing and that the maximum amount of nourishment is retained. Great care must be taken in reheating food, particularly meat. Since it is already cooked, further cooking will toughen the fibres and harden the proteins, thus making the food indigestible. Therefore, the first rule is never recook, only reheat.

Food may be warmed in a moderate oven if carefully covered. If the vessel containing food can be placed in a tin containing water, over-drying is prevented. Steaming is one of the best methods of reheating as the heat is gentle and does not dry the food. A covering is necessary to prevent the condensed steam from falling on the food. Frequently it may be necessary to do more than just reheat and, therefore, an ingenious cook must find ways and means of using up cooked food to make new dishes, e.g., cutlets, minced coilops, shepherd's pie, hash, and curry can be made without having to recook.

Tea

The most popular non-alcoholic beverage, tea consists of the dried leaves of the tea plant grown in India, Ceylon, China and Japan. Chinese tea contains less tannin than the other varieties. Tea leaves have a characteristic oval shape and serrated edge. The younger the leaves the better the quality of the tea. The treatment of the leaves after they are picked varies according to the tea required.

For black tea the leaves are withered, then rolled till they become soft and mushy. This is done to break up the fibre and cells of the leaf to liberate the constituents so that extraction is easy. The leaves are then fermented. During the process of fermentation some of the tannic acid in the leaves oxidizes and is converted into less soluble forms while more essential oils develop. After fermentation is complete, the leaves are fired in a drying machine. For green tea the leaves are withered in hot pans at a temperature of 71°C (about 160°F) or steamed, then rolled to break them up and liberate their juices, and then fired. The main difference between black tea and green tea is that the former, is fermented while the latter is not. Since the purpose of fermentation is to make the tannin less soluble, an infusion of green tea has more tannin in it.

The best tea generally produces a pale-coloured infusion and the depth of colour is not necessarily a sign of strength. Freshly infused tea is harmless to normal digestion; continued infusion extracts the tannin, a bitter substance with a decidedly harmful effect upon the digestive organs.

Storage of Dry Tea: Tea very quickly absorbs odours and moisture. So it should be kept in airtight containers, whether in the store or on the counter.

If the tea is in chests, they should be kept off the ground and at least 16 cm. or 6 inches away from the walls. This allows a current of air to circulate round the tea chest and averts dampness. Once a chest is opened it is advisable to put a close- fitting lid over it. When issuing tea from it, be sure that it is sent out in a tin fitted with a lid that can be firmly replaced after use, so that the natural aroma of the tea is retained.

Next in importance to the tea leaf is water, which is used for the preparation of tea. Water varies in different parts of the country. In some places water is hard and at other places it is soft. Tea which gives good results in soft water may not necessarily do so in hard water. For this reason samples of water drawn from different areas of the country are used for blending teas.

Water should not be too hard or too soft for making good tea. Artificially softened water is unsuitable for making tea and should be avoided.

Water should be freshly drawn before it is put on to boil.

Water which has been lying in the kettle for several hours or which has been boiled previously makes tea flat and insipid, as also, water which is allowed to continue boiling for some time before it is used. When the water used is off the boil, approximately half the leaves float and remain floating throughout the infusion. The rest remain at the bottom from the time the water is added. The movement of the leaves is very slight and tends to be from the bottom upwards. The flavour of the tea is poor.

With freshly boiled water approximately two-thirds of the leaves float from the start. There is a marked circulation of the leaves from the bottom to the top and from the top to the bottom. The liquor has good body and good flavour.When water is over-boiled all the leaves remain clotted at the bottom from the start of the infusion to the end. The liquor is thin and lacks flavour and character.

Preparation of Tea

(i) *Use Good Tea and Remember the Recipe:* one teaspoonful per person and one for the pot. The ideal is 60 gm of good tea to 4 litres of boiling water. There should be no guesswork; weigh or measure tea for each brew.

(ii) *Use Freshly Drawn, Freshly Boiling Water:* Take water from a cold water tap, use it when it bubbles fiercely. An automatic boiler provides this, but if bulk boilers are used, two small ones are better and more economical than one large. Measlired water may be boiled in metal pots (degchis) and transferred to another pot (already heated and containing tea leaves), or tea leaves can be put directly into · the pot in which water has reached boiling temperature. Remove the pot from the fire and allow the tea to infuse for 5 minutes.

(iii) *Heat the Pot:* Tea pots or urns in which tea is to be prepared should be heated before making tea. Unless this is done the water will go off the boil rapidly, thus preventing correct infusion of the tea leaves.

(iv) *Take the Teapot to the Boiling Water:* The water must be at boiling point to enable the leaves to infuse properly, so the teapot should be brought near the boiling water outlet to ensure the shortest length of pour possible. To a measured quantity of water add a measured quantity of tea leaves and remove the pot immediately from the fire. Allow it to infuse for 5 minutes and strain. If electric or other boilers are used for boiling water, their outlet taps should be such that the maximum water can flow through them in the minimum of time.

(v) *Brew for 5 Minutes:* Never more, never less. Tea should be made of good average strength to allow being watered down if necessary, as nothing can be done about strengthening tea which is too weak to start with. Removable infusers enable the leaves to be with draw easily and prevent stewing. Stir well before pouring.

Approximately 190 to 200 cups of tea can be obtained from 500 gm of tea leaves.

Adding of milk first or last does not make any significant difference in the taste of tea--but let people have their choice--some like to add milk first and some afterwards. Sugar must be added last. Tea is also taken hot with sugar and slices of lemon. This is known as Russian Tea.

Iced Tea: Prepare strong tea. Pour over crushed ice on which is placed a sprig of mint. Top with lemon slices.

Tea contains the stimulating principle caffeine, tannin and some volatile oils.

Coffee

Coffee is the berry of a plant grown in Kenya, Ceylon, Brazil, West Indies, India and other places.

Coffee has become one of the important beverages in India. There has been a steady increase in the consumption of coffee in recent years. It is also one of the major plantation crops of India, particularly South India. The two main varieties of coffee grown in India are, Coffee Arabica and Coffee Robusta. Coffee Arabica originated in Yemen in Arabia and was brought to India in the seventeenth century by a Muslim called Bababudan Sahib on his return from his visit to the Mecca, Coffee Robusta was brought to India from Java in 1910.

After the fully ripe berries are harvested, they are processed in two ways, by the 'wet' method or by the 'dry' method.

The 'wet' process is very elaborate. Ripe berries called cherries are first passed through pulpers where their outer skin is removed. The pulped beans are then allowed to ferment for about 12 to 36 hours. They are then washed in running water. This leaves the beans encased in a soft parchment covering. They are then dried in the drying yard. Great care is taken at this stage to see that only a little moisture remains and the parchment covering becomes brittle. This produces what is known as Plantation or Parchment Coffee.

The 'dry' method is a simpler process. Immediately after harvesting, the coffee berries are dried in the sun until the three layers--the outer skin, the sticky layer and the inner parchment covering--dry into a husk, leaving the beans loose inside. The beans are separated from the husk by being pounded in a mortar or passed through a huller. This is then graded and is called Native Coffee or Cherry Coffee.

In the days of sailing ships when a voyage to Europe took about six months or so, Native (Cherry) Coffee stowed away in damp holds lost its colour and became white. Later, when steamships went speedily through the Suez Canal, coffee drinkers in Europe complained that the coffee had lost its flavour. To overcome this, a new process known as 'monsooning coffee' was evolved. This is done in Mangalore and Tellicherry on the west coast of India.

When the monsoons break in early May or June, Native (Cherry) Coffee is evenly spread in layers from four to six inches thick, in airy godowns which are open on all sides. Every four or five days the beans are raked. They are then packed in gunny bags and stacked in piles so that the monsoon breeze can blow continuously on each bag. Once a week the beans are repacked or poured from one bag to another, so that they do not develop moulds and also to ensure uniform monsooning. After six weeks of this treatment the coffee becomes silvery white in colour and is considered fully matured and ready for export.

After the beans have been treated to make either 'parchment' or 'cherry types, they are sent to the curing houses for the final process required to prepare the coffee for the market. It is here that the parchment is peeled off Parchment Coffee.

The stimulating principle in coffee is caffeine. It also contains tannin and some volatile and aromatic oils. As long as coffee is in good condition the distinctive aroma remains. It should always be stored in airtight containers. Refrigerated storage is best for keeping coffee.

Roasting and grinding: The aroma and flavour associated with coffee is brought about by roasting. Roasting must be done evenly without any scorching. It should be done on a slow fire and the beans should be uniformly roasted. When the beans stop swelling and obtain a golden-brown colour, the roasting is complete. If roasting goes beyond this point the essential oils exude and the beans turn shiny. When it reaches this stage the coffee has no value. Roasting can be done in a charcoal roaster or in an electric roaster. A medium roast and grind is considered to give the best results.

Roasted beans keep fresh much longer than powder and so grinding must be done just before use. Too finely ground powder clogs up the filter if used, and deteriorates rapidly when stored. The coarser the powder, the less the extraction. As a standard for brewing coffee, 450 gms. (16 oz.) gives 53 cups [187.5 ml (6 fl.oz.) coffee, 62.5 ml (2 fl.oz.) milk per cup].

Coffee can be prepared by many methods. The pot method, the filter method, the urn brewing method and the vacuum brewing method are commonly used.

Just one cup of coffee does some amazing things to the body. The temperature of the stomach jumps up by 10-15%. Salivary glands double their flow; the heart beats 15% faster; the lungs work 13% harder; blood vessels dilate in the brain and near the heart; the metabolism rate goes up 25%; and the work-load of the kidney doubles.

Rules for Making Coffee

(i) Fresh coffee is the best; so buy quantities to last

not more than a week,

(ii) Use the quantity required for making coffee,

(iii) Use freshly drawn water,

(iv) The coffee-maker must be rinsed with hot water before use and thoroughly washed and dried before being put away. Never brew less than three-fourths of the coffee-maker's capacity; use a smaller one instead.

Pot Method

(i) Warm an earthenware pot or jug. Put in 3 level teaspoons of fresh coffee powder (coarse grind) for each 250 ml (8 oz.) cup.

(ii) Pour water which has started to boil over the powder and stir. Cover the pot and let it stand near the fire for 5 to 7 minutes.

(iii) Pour the coffee through a fine meshed sieve or cloth. Add milk and sugar to taste.

Filter Method: Several types of filters are available. Stainless steel or brass filters are the best but the latter should be properly tinned, or else the coffee will be spoilt. Glass or china containers are good but are fragile. Copper should not be used.

(i) Put in 3 level teaspoons of coffee powder (fine or medium grind) to each 250 ml or 8 oz. cup. Press the plunger down lightly over the powder.

(ii) Pour water which has just come to boil over the plunger in a circular motion. Let it stand for 5 to 7 minutes.

(iii) Coffee can be poured out straight from the lower vessel and milk and sugar added as required.

Percolator Method

(i) Place the ground beans in the centre section of a clean warm percolator on a fine strainer fitted inside and resting on a paper filter (a pinch of salt is mixed with the coffee).

(ii) Pour fresh boiling water slowly through the top section,

(iii) The water passes through the coffee, is strained and collects in the bottom section of the apparatus.

Cona coffee machine (a patent percolator) consists of two flameproof glass bowls joined by a glass drainer tube which also acts as a filter. A measured amount of ground coffee is placed in the top receptacle and water in the lower one. Heat is applied, causing the water to rise, meet and mix with the coffee. The whole operation is automatic, and the beverage returns to the lower bowl and is served immediately or placed on a warming unit to be held at 85°-88°C (about 185°-190°F) (never allow coffee to boil).

Coffee is made in large quantities in the urns using the filter or percolator method. It is then held at 85°-88°C (about 185°-190°F) temperature and should be served within the hour.

All equipment used for the preparation of coffee should be kept scrupulously clean. When using a Cona or other mechanical percolator be sure to:

(i) Scrub upper tube regularly with a stiff brush.

(ii) Remove rubber collars and wash all parts thoroughly,

(iii) Replace rubber collars when they become heat softened.

If a coffee urn is used

(i) Clean inside of urn after each batch,

(ii) Clean faucets at close of each day.

(iii) Leave plenty of water in urn when not in use.

(iv) Clean gauge glasses twice a week,

(v) Give urn a thorough cleaning twice a week.

Turkish Coffee: Turkish coffee is rich and syrupy and has a peculiar aroma of its own, caused by the preliminary method of drying coffee: the 'wet' method. The ground coffee is first mixed with sugar in a small china or copper pot fitted with a long handle. Water is added, heat applied and the coffee is flavoured with rose water. It is served piping hot.

Cocoa: Cocoa, besides being a stimulant, is also a food. It is prepared from the seeds of a tree grown in South and Central America, the West and East Indies and along the Gold Coast and adjacent areas in Africa.

The pods are gathered in heaps and cut open with sharp rounded knives. The cocoa beans which are covered with a moist glistening white pulp are scooped out. Oxidation begiris almost at once causing the beans to become brown. Therefore, as soon as possible, they must be placed on fermenting heaps or spread in the sun to remove the moisture so that they are not spoilt. However, fermentation is necessary to get the finest possible flavour. This is accompanied by a rise in temperature and the transformation of natural sugars to acetic and other acids. After several days, this operation is complete and the beans are allowed to dry. They are then ready to be packed and shipped.

In the manufacture of cocoa and chocolate the first step is thorough cleaning to remove any foreign substance which may be present. The beans are then roasted in revolving cylinders by currents of air heated to a temperature above 204.4°C (about 400°F). At exactly the right moment they pass from the roaster and are quickly cooled to prevent further change.

The beans are then conveyed into chambers where they are broken into fragments called nibs. At the same time the shells are lifted away from the nibs by air currents and removed from the chambers. The nibs are quite dry. They are then milled to reduce their size. In this process they pass between three sets of steel-encased grinding stones. Here the cocoa butter, the natural fat of the cocoa bean averaging about 55 per, cent, is released from the cells in the form of a free-flowing liquor of rich, dark colour and heavy, distinctive aroma. This product is the basic ingredient of all forms of chocolate and milk chocolate.

Cocoa is the second derivative of chocolate liquor. After undergoing heat treatment for flavour development, the liquor is pumped into powerful hydraulic presses which expel the free-flowing cocoa butter until the original 55 per cent is reduced to less than half that quantity. The solid cakes of cocoa remaining in the presses are then ejected and reduced to a fine dry powder in crushers and pulverizers. The powder is then cooled and wind-sifted to get the pleasing brown colour and extreme fitness essential for high quality. Cocoa contains the bromine and caffeine as well as starch, fats, nitrogenous bodies and salts, so it is both a stimulating drink, and a food.

Cocoa can be prepared in milk only, or in milk and water, mixed to suit the taste of the individual. The powder is mixed with sugar to avoid lumping. A little cold milk is added and a thick, even paste made. Either hot milk or hot milk and water are poured over. The preparation is then allowed to boil for a few minutes which improves the flavour. A pinch of salt added at the beginning enhances the flavour.

9

Food Preservation Practices

> Waste is worse than loss. The time is coming when every person who lays claim to ability will keep the question of waste before him constantly. The scope of thrift is limitless.
>
> —*Thomas A. Edison*

Although preservation in one form or another has been practised throughout the world, it developed scientifically into a technology only after the First World War when it was found convenient to use preserved food for the armed forces. The technology has continued to progress, and preserved food is used by rich and poor in everyday life in the West. Easy transportation, variety in food and convenience in use have all added on to the popularity of preserved foods. The development of this technology has now made it possible to have preserved food of practically the same nutritive value and palatability standards as fresh foods. Careful preservation of food eliminates waste which may happen otherwise during a time of glut. It also helps to prevent undue fluctuation of prices.

The object of food preservation is to destroy or inactivate spoilage by micro-organisms, toxins produced by them and the chemicals present which are responsible for the deterioration of food. This has to be done without affecting the palatability of the food to be preserved, its colour, flavour and nutritive value.

Various Types

Preservation can be divided into short or long period preservation.

Short Period Preservation: All moist foods are inclined to decompose rapidly and it is often necessary to use some temporary method of preservation to prevent food from deteriorating before use. In this type of preservation the spoiling agents are not killed but their growth is retarded or inactivated for a short period. This is done in the following ways:

Asepsis: The number of microorganisms is reduced by

(i) *Washing:* Along with the dirt some of the microorganism are removed,

(ii) *Careful Handling:* Crushing and bruising of fruits and vegetables is avoided and damaged ones are discarded.

(iii) *Packing in Sanitary Packages:* This reduces the number of microorganisms to a great extent. Nature preserves nuts, etc., by this method.

Low Temperature (chilling or cold storage): This is keeping food at refrigerated temperature. This is not a drastic method. The food is not altered but the bacteria is held dormant. This method keeps food whole only for short periods.

Some fruits such as bananas however, spoil under refrigeration so they must be kept at 12°C (about 54°F).

Apples and hard fruits will keep for a long time in cold storage as long as they are wrapped in greaseproof paper.

Cold storage has been practised for thousands of years. In old temples and caves (e.g. Kanheri Caves, Bombay) one can see niches surrounded by running water to keep them cool. In Pompeii in Roman times each house had a food storage compartment cut out of rock with running water playing on it.

By Heating: Cooking of food and boiling of milk helps to preserve these longer than if left fresh.

By *Mild Antiseptics:* Sugar and salt can be sprinkled over fruits and vegetables respectively that are to be used for the next day.

By Removal of Air: If butter is spread over potted meat or egg is dipped in a wax emulsion it can be kept for a longer period than if untreated as the air that is necessary for growth of microorganisms is not available.

Waxing fruits by means of sugarcane wax is another old method which is now being revived in India and is being developed on *a* commercial scale in Nagpur. The purpose is to exclude air by covering fruits and vegetables with wax emulsion. The results have been very encouraging.

Long Period Preservation: The storage life of foods is increased for a longer period by these methods:

Sun Drying: This is perhaps the oldest method of food preservation and has been used by hunters and travellers for generations. The method of preservation is the removal of moisture to render germs inactive. It has been extensively used in India and fish, meat, vegetables and fruits have been preserved by this method; e.g., dried fish, such as Bombay Duck, dried game meat, lentils, peas, chillies, etc., and dried fruits and nuts such as apricots, dates, raisins, cashewnuts, etc.

Dehydration: Whilst sun-drying is a method of dehydration, by using mechanical devices this process has been speeded up considerably. Dehydration is the removal of moisture to the extent that mould growth does not flourish under carefully controlled conditions of air flow, temperature, and humidity, in a special piece of apparatus known as a dehydrator. By using dehydrators a more standard product is also obtained. Milk and eggs, for example, are roller-dried or spray-dried. The products can be successfully reconstituted. Dehydrated vegetables such as potatoes, peas, carrots, cabbage, etc., are extensively used. All vegetables must be blanched before being dehydrated (except onion, garlic, etc.). Dehydrated food can be easily transported and does not need refrigerated storage. The storage space required is also reduced.

Salting: This very often accompanies dehydration. When foods are just salted, this must be done at as low a temperature as possible. In tropical countries it must be done under refrigeration. Use salt that is as pure as possible, or else the impurities cause a bitterness in the fish or meat being salted.

Two methods are used:

(i) Rubbing the salt on the flesh of fish or meat.

(ii) Soaking in a brine tub. This method is used particularly for tongue, beef, pig's trotters and pig's head. Sometimes the brine solution is injected into the meat. Microbes cannot grow in a strong salt medium.

Smoking: This is also a very old method of preservation. Fish or meat is exposed to the smoke of a slowly burning wood fire thus imparting a smoked flavour and assisting in the preservation of the food stuff.

Bacterial growth is stopped by the drying of the food surface and by the antiseptic action of certain constituents of the smoke, such as creosote, formaldehyde and acetic acid.

The wood must not contain any substance that will impart a foreign flavour to the food, nor must the temperature be too high, or else the food will become too dry, and the smoke will not be able to penetrate the food thoroughly.

Deep Freeze: This does not kill germs, but prevents them from being active. This method is being used more and more in recent years, with the advancement in refrigeration machinery.

Freezing is a relatively simple method of preserving food and is generally accepted as one of the most satisfactory ways of storing perishable foods. Research done in this field has shown that freezing food is the simplest and safest method of preservation provided one follows the five cardinal points: careful selection, proper packaging, freezing at -18°C (0°F) or lower, storage at -18°C (0°F) or lower with the minimum of fluctuation, and avoiding long storage.

Meat, poultry, products, game, fruits and vegetables and prepared and cooked foods can be preserved by this method.

(i) *Careful Selection.* Careful selection is the first step in successful preservation as freezing does not improve the natural product, except in the case of beef. If quality products are to be taken from the freezer, only quality products should be frozen. Slime or bruises must be trimmed carefully from meat before it is frozen.

(ii) *Proper Packaging.* Experience has demonstrated that special packaging materials are necessary. Inferior or low grade materials should be avoided. A good packaging material should be:

(a) Clean and sanitary.

(b) Odourless, flavourless, and impervious to odours.

(c) Mechanically practical.

(d) Attractive and easily labelled.

(e) Protective against desiccation (freezer burn).

(f) Resistant to oxidation.

(g) Tough and not brittle at low temperature, (h) Greaseproof and stain-proof.

Several papers, foils, plastic films, and waxes meet most of these requirements. Only materials that adequately protect the product should be used. There is quite a range in the prices of these materials. More expensive materials increase packaging costs, but the increased protection usually justifies the extra cost. Even the best available wrapping material must be applied properly. The following suggestions are offered for best results in packaging meat:

(a) Cut meat to suit needs. Avoid packages weighing more than 4.5 kgs. 2.5 kg. roasts are convenient.

(b) Interleave all pieces of meat with tissue paper.

(c) Be sure all sharp edges of bones are removed.

(d) Avoid rolling or folding steaks. Keep all packages as flat and square as possible.

(e) Maintain as complete contact between the meat and the paper as possible.

(f) Mark each package clearly with name, locker number, cut of meat, weight, and the date frozen.

(g) Eliminate air from the packages, wrap tightly and seal.

(iii) *Freezing at -18°C (about 0°F) or Lower:* Foods should be frozen at -18°C (about 0°F) or lower, and packages should be loosely arranged while freezing, but when completely frozen they may be tightly stacked in the home unit or locker. "Sharp freezing" often refers to freezing at temperatures between --18°C (about 0°F) and -28°C (about 20°F), while "quick freezing" applies to still lower temperatures.

(iv) *Storage at -18°C (about 0°F):* The palatability and nutritive value of food are best preserved at -18°C (about 0°F) or lower. The storage temperature should not fluctuate above this, but experiments indicate that fluctuation below that temperature is not serious. Fluctuation of the storage temperature above --18°C fosters dehydration even with the best of wrapping material. Ice or snow on the inside of the package usually indicates fluctuation above this temperature.

(v) *Avoid Long Storage:* Many people think that because freezing retards bacterial and enzymatic activity a frozen product will keep indefinitely. This is true only to a degree, as there is progressive deterioration in a frozen state. The rate is slow, but nevertheless specific; therefore time in storage should be limited. It is best to plan on a normal seasonal turnover. When meat is carefully handled, properly wrapped, sharp frozen, and stored at -18°C (about 0°F), it can be stored for a reasonable period of time, but deviation from the ideal in any one of the above factors may cause rapid deterioration.

It is recommended that beef be consumed within twelve months, fresh pork within six months and ground meat, especially pork sausages, within four to six months. Pork and pork products tend to develop rancidity early and cured pork products even earlier; therefore, it is a good practice to stock only a six months supply of pork at one time.

These are the five cardinal points for successful storage. They are not over-exacting and not beyond reach. It is believed that home freezer owners will be far wiser to have all their bulk processing done at the nearest commercial freezer plant and use the home unit only as a home reservoir. This will leave all processing to the professional at the plant, where adequate facilities and equipment are available ad thus relieve the householder. Where small quantities of food a to be handled, as a day's supply of peas beans or strawberries from the garden, the may be handled safely and without materially influencing the storage temperature; but large quantities should be done in units intended for volume. The home unit is essentially a storage unit and not a processing unit.

Hermetically Sealed Containers: The absence of air from any container is a principle of food storage. This method is used for biscuits, cereals and preserved food in bottles.

Canning and Bottling: In this method preservation of food is done in hermetically sealed containers sterilized by heat.

The word 'canning' is of American origin but is now used internationally in connection with preserving foods in tin containers. In its broader sense it also includes preservation by application of heat in glass containers as well. Tins are standardized. Al T A 2Vi and a_{10}, are the commonly used sizes in India. A_{10} has a capacity of about 3 litres and is used for the trade as it is an economical size.

The canning of vegetables, fruits, meat, fish, dairy products and most edible products cooked and uncooked, has reached a very high degree of efficiency. Each food item uses a special technique. Colouring agents if added in canned and bottled products are strictly controlled by the Food and Drugs Act. In India colouring agents are specially used for canning cherries and green vegetables.

By sugar: Food products containing 60% sugar do not ordinarily spoil. Jam, jelly, marmalade, preserves, candy fruits, fruit, syrups and confectionery are preserved by this method.

Gas Storage: Oxygen (air) is replaced by inert gases e.g. aerated water.

Acid: Acids preserve foods by virtue of their hydrogen ion concentration, which produces a toxic effect on microbial protoplasm, e.g., pickles in vinegar.

By Spices: Essential oils of spices produce a toxic effect on micro organisms, e.g., as in pickles.

By Vacuum Packing: Coffee powder, milk powder, etc. By fermentation Alcoholic beverages, etc.

By Chemical Preservatives: Sodium benzoate and potassium metabisulphite are the two preservatives permitted by the Food and Drugs Act.

Irradiation: Preservation by irradiation is a new technique which is being explored at present. This is done by radiation of various frequencies ranging from the low frequency electric current to the high frequency gamma rays. In 1957 it was reported that 100 food items have been cleared for human testing. The obvious advantage of food preserved by this method is that food can be stored without refrigeration. Bacon, beans, and peaches have been kept for one year at 22°C (about 72°F) storage temperature without spoilage after irradiation treatment.

Ionized radiation produces some destruction of nutritive value, but not sufficient to be nutritionally significant. Experiments on irradiated powdered milk showed no loss of vitamins. This may be due to a lack of moisture.

Colour changes were noticed in strawberry and milk powder amongst the foods studied. There was some flavour change in the foods, the most noticeable being in ground beef. It is believed, however, that acceptability of the strangeness in odour will be only a matter of time.

Work done hitherto does prove, however, that irradiation as a form of food preservation although still in its infancy, has great possibilities.

Preservation by Antibiotics: This is another method of preservation now under study. Much work has been done on Penicillin, Streptomycin, Aureomycin, Tyrrannizing, Chloromycetin, Subtlin, Tetracyclin, Oxytetracydin, Chlortetracyclin, etc.

Eviscerated chicken dipped in Aureomycin and stored at 4.4°C (about 40°F) was found fresh 7 to 14 days longer than untreated chicken.

Chlortetracyclin (aureomycin) is recognized as one of the most effective of the broad range of antibiotics.

This method is still in the experimental stage. Although food bacteriologists realize the advantage of the preservation of raw foods by means of a non-toxic antibiotic or the use of one in combination with reduced amounts of heat in the processing of canned foods, they are aware of certain problems that could arise with the use of antibiotics as preservatives.

(i) The effect of an antibiotic on a micro-organism is known to vary with the species or even with the strains of the organism. Hence the antibiotic may be effective against some spoilage organisms but not others, or against part of the population in a culture but not all.

(ii) Organisms are known to be able to adapt themselves to increasing concentrations of antibiotics, so that new resistant strains may develop. There is also the possibility that other organisms not yet significant in food spoilage but resistant to the antibiotic might assume new importance in food spoilage.

(iii) Effects of the antibiotic on the consumer, sensitization to it, changes in his intestinal flora and the development of strains of pathogen in the body resistant to that antibiotic, are all possibilities. It is, therefore, recommended that the antibiotics used for food preservation be other than those used for therapeutic reasons.

Glossary

A. WESTERN CULINARY TERMS

Abats: Butcher's supplies such as heads, hearts, liver, kidney, etc.

Aiguillettes: Thin slices of breast of poultry cut lengthwise.

A la: Meaning merely, "in the style of.

A la broche: Roasted in front of a fire on a spit or in a Dutch oven.

A la carte: Opposite of table d'hote, meaning that each dish is ordered and priced individually. A

La liable: The French way of saying "devilled", in other words, any very hot or highly seasoned dish.

A la frangais: Dishes that are prepared in the French way.

A peritif: A cocktail or other drink served before a meal to stimulate the appetite.

Appetizer: A tidbit served before a meal or as the first course. A drink such as sherry, cocktail, etc.

Aspic: A transparent savoury jelly, generally made of seasoned meat stock. It is used to garnish meat or fish, or to make moulds of meat, fish or game.

Au bleu: Applied to fish cooked in fish stock with wine added. Au four Baked in the oven.

Au gras Rich. Applied to dishes with meat in a rich gravy.

Au gratin: Any dish covered with sauce, breadwinners or cheese and afterwards baked or grilled. The food is served from the dish in which it is cooked.

Au maigre: Opposite of au gras. Applied to meatless or Lenten dishes.

Au naturel: Simply-cooked food, or food served raw, such as oysters. *Baba:* A light yeast cake, usually soaked in rum or spirit.

Bain-Marie: A large shallow pan to hold water in which several small sauce-pans can be heated without their contents boiling, an alternative to the double saucepan, but often used to keep cooked food warm.

Bake: To cook by dry heat, usually in an oven.

Barbecue: Meat basted with a highly- seasoned sauce, e.g., lamb basted with hot red-currant sauce.

Barquette: A boat-shaped pastry tartlet, filled with chicken, vegetables, oyster, fish mayonnaise, etc.

Baste: To spoon melted fat or liquid over food during cooking to keep it moist.

Batter: A mixture of flour and liquid such as milk, egg, etc., of such consistency that it can be beaten or stirred. Used to coat foods for frying, or as pancakes, etc. May be sweet or savoury.

Bearnaise: A rich sauce, resembling a Hollandaise sauce, made from butter, egg yolk and vinegar, and flavoured with peppercorns, shallots, chervil and tarragon

Beat: To mix air with food by vigorous motion; also used to make a mixture smooth and free from lumps. A wooden spoon is best for beating thick mixtures; an egg-whisk for thin ones.

Bechamel: a rich white sauce.

Beignets: Pancake batter fried in deep fat or fritters of different kinds.

Beurre: noir Browned butter.

Beurre manie: Equal quantities of flour and butter used

for thickening sauces. *Bisque: A* rich, thick, cream soup, usually made from shellfish, e.g. lobster.

Blanch: Literally to whiten, but used here to mean dipping food into boiling water for a few moments, and then into cold, to remove skin. To blanch almonds, boiling water is poured on them to whiten them and to remove the skins.

Blend: To combine two or more ingredients.

Bombe: glacee A mould lined with one kind of ice cream and then filled with ice cream of a different flavouring.

Bonbon: Sugar confectionery -- sweets.

Bouchees: Small patties of light pastry sufficient for one mouthful.

Bouillon: Unqualified broth or stock made from fresh meat.

Bradsot: Russian soup containing beetroot.

Bouquet garni: A small bunch of mixed herbs used for flovouring soups, stews, etc. Ideally, this should consist of a sprig each of parsley, thyme, basil, marjoram, with a bay leaf and a strip of lemon peel, tied together with cotton. It must always be removed before the dish is served. When fresh herbs are unobtainable, dried herbs tied in a piece of muslin may be used instead.

Brioche: Very light French rolls.

Broil to cook: By exposing food directly to heat; used synonymously with "grill".

Browning: A substitute added to stews and gravies to darken them.

Brunoise fashion: Cut into small dice.

Brush: A thin, even coating of beaten egg or milk applied to pies, buns, etc., immediately before they are put in the oven. It gives the pastry or bun a glossy appearance and helps it to brown more quickly and deeply. Pastry brushes are sold for this purpose. Dried egg is especially useful for brushing, as a very small quantity can be mixed instead of beating a whole egg.

Cafe au wait coffee with milk; white coffee.

Canapes: Small pieces of toast, fried bread or pastry on which light savouries are served.

Carte do jour: Menu for the day.

Canneloni: Small pasta rolls filled with mince (Italian). *Capon:* A castrated male chicken. It grows large and has tender meat.

Caramel: A substance made by heating sugar until it turns dark brown. Used for coating moulds, flavouring dishes, etc.

Caramelize: To heat sugar until it turns brown.

Casserole: a baking dish with a well-fitting lid used for cooking stews, etc. in the oven. Usually made of fireproof earthenware or glass, or of heavy enamel. The food is usually served from the casserole.

Cassolette: A kind of hot hors d'oeuvre moulded to the shape of a small drum.

Caviar: Salted roe of sturgeon or similar fish.

Cepes: A kind of mushroom.

Cereals: Grains such as wheat, including semolina, oats, barley, rye, rice etc.

Charlotte: A sweet made of alternate layers of fruit and either bread crumbs or slices of bread and butter.

Charlotte russe: Generally a mould lined with sponge cake or sponge fingers and filled with a mixture of cream and fruit, and jelly.

Chartreuse: Mould of fruit, jelly or savoury mixture.

Chateaubriand: Head of the fillet of beef. *Chaud-froid:* A cold sauce used for coating meat, game or fish.

Cheese fondue: Grated cheese melted in white wine, seasoned with pepper and flavoured at the last minute with a little kirsch.

Chiffonier: Mince of sorrel, lettuce, etc. Wash the leaves, remove veins, roll and cut into fine strips with a sharp knife.

Chinos: A conical strainer.

Chilopoda: A kind of small sausage.

Choux: A kind of pastry used for such things as cream buns and eclairs.

Chowder: An American soup made with pickled pork, shellfish, fish, potatoes, and other vegetables.

Cisel: Finely chopped vegetables.

Coat: To cover with a thin layer.

Cochineal: A red colouring matter Compote Fruit stewed in syrup.

Concass: To chop roughly, e.g., concassed tomatoes. *Condiments:* Spices and seasonings.

Confiture: Jam or fruit preserves.

Congalaise: Garnish of poached oysters and shrimps cohered with Normande sauce.

Consistency: The thickness or texture of mixture, such as a cake or batter mixture.

Consomme: A light-coloured clear soup.

Cotelettes: Cutlets.

Coupe: A cream or water ice served with fruit.

Court-bouillion: A well-flavoured cooking liquor for fish.

Crackling: The rind of roast pork.

Cream fat: To beat fat with a wooden spoon until it is light and fluffy.

Crazy (a la): Dishes containing carrots.

Creme: Anything of a creamy consistency can be described thus.

Crepe: Pancakes.

Croissants: French rolls, crisp and light.

Croquettes: Leftover meat, fish, poultry or game, finely minced and rolled into small sausage shapes. These are coated with egg and bread crumbs and fried a golden brown.

Croutes: Ovals or rounds of fried bread.

Croutons: Bread cut in small dice or fancy shapes and fried or toasted. Used as a garnish for serving with soup.

Cuisse: Leg, e.g., cuisses de volailles, cuisses de granules.

Custard: A cooked or baked mixture made of milk and eggs; it may be sweetened for dessert, or it may be flavoured with cheese, fish, etc., as an entree.

Cut and fold: To mix flour very gently into a mixture.

Cutlet: A small piece of meat cut usually from rib of veal or pork, mutton or lamb, usually grilled or fried.

Dariole: A small cup-shaped mould.

Darne: The middle slice of a fish.

Devilled: The same as 'a la doable', that is, any highly seasoned dish. Often this seasoning is done with some form of curry powder.

Dice: To cut into small even cubes. Cut food first into slices $^1/_2$ in thick, then into strips the same width and finally hold strips together and cut into cubes. Use a chopping board and a sharp knife.

Dieppoise: A garnish for fish consisting of shrimp's tails, mussels and mushrooms. *Dissolve:* To melt a solid food in a liquid.

Dot: To put small bits of butter, cheese, cream, etc., over the surface of a dish. Dough A mixture of a liquid, flour, etc., kneaded together into a stiff paste or roll.

Dredge: To cover with a thin sprinkling.

Dust: To sprinkle lightly with fine sugar, dried milk or flour.

Duxelle: A mixture of parsley, mushrooms and shallots used for flavouring sauces and purees or as a forcemeat.

Ecarlate: Salted meat is said to be a 1'ecarlate when it is covered with a coat of red jelly.

Eclair: Choux pastry filled with custard or cream. Can be coated with chocolate.

Emince: Finely sliced or shredded.

Entree: A dish served in the first part of a dinner, usually a made-up dish with sauce. Or it can be the main dish of a less formal meal.

Entremets: Hot or cold sweets.

*Escalopes :*Thin slices of meat dipped in egg and bread crumbs and then fried.

Estouffade: Brown stock.

Espagnole: A rich brown sauce.

Farci: Any kind of stuffing.

Fennel: A fragrant herb used for flavouring sauces (saunf).

Fillets: Fish with bone removed. Undercuts of veal or beef. Slices from the breast of a bird.

Fillet: To bone fish, etc., and cut into fillets.

Flan: A pastry case made in a flat tin and afterwards filled with a sweet or savoury mixture.

Flute: A long crisp roll of bread (French) used to garnish soups or to serve with soup. Foie gras Liver of a fat goose.

Fondant: Sugar boiled to 112°C (234°F) and then beaten to a "fudge-like" smoothness. It can be used as an icing on any kind of sweet.

Fool: A summer sweet made with sieved fruit and whipped into a frothy mixture and served with cream or custard. Forcemeat Savoury stuffing.

Frangipane: Confectioner's custard. Frappe Sweetened fruit juice, half frozen.

Fricadelles: Braised game or meat in very small pieces.

Fricassee: A stew generally made with chicken, veal, rabbit or lamb thickened with white sauce to which milk has been added.

Fritters: Fruit, meat, vegetables or fish coated with batter and fried, usually in deep fat. *Frosting:* A cooked or uncooked sugar icing used to cover and decorate cakes, etc.

Fry: To cook food in very hot fat in an open frying-pan. Furnet A kind of essence extracted from fish, game, etc.

Galantine: Cooked meat that has been boned, pressed into a mould with jelly and served cold.

Galette: A large quoit made from puff pastry or short pastry.

Garnish: To decorate *Garniture:* Decoration

Gateau: This can be a cake, an ice cream, or anything made in the shape of a cake and lavishly decorated.

Gelatine: A product made from refined cows' hoofs. Used

for jellies. Sold either granulated or in sheets. The strength varies with each brand. Allow 1/2 oz. to 1/3 oz. to each pint of liquid.

Genoese: A rich butter sponge used as a base for gateaux, and as a base for savoury fingers, etc.

Giblets: The heart, liver and gizzard of poultry used to make gravies, soups and pies.

Gild, gilding: (i) To cover an object with beaten eggs by means of a brush, (ii) To give a golden sheen to objects by means of heat.

Glace: Ice, ice-cream, icing, to make smooth or glossy with icing or jelly. Also crystallized or frozen foods.

Glaze: Meat glaze is made by reducing (by boiling) stock or gravy to the consistency of jelly. It is used for improving the appearance of cold meats, etc. Sugar and water glaze is brushed over fruit pies, buns, etc., when they are taken from the oven, to improve their surface appearance. Egg-and-water glaze is brushed on to savoury pies, buns, etc., before they are put in the oven.

Goulash: Hungarian meat stew, flavoured with paprika.

Haggis: A kind of bag pudding, made in Scotland, from liver, sheep's head, etc., finely minced and mixed with oatmeal, herbs, etc.

Haricot: A type of stew. Literally, "beans".

Hash: A made-up dish of meat that has been diced or minced. Usually a way of using leftovers.

Hollandaise: A rich sauce of Dutch origin made with butter or cream, egg yolks and lemon or vinegar served hot or cold with many kinds of vegetables or fish. Hors d'oeuvre Small savoury tidbits, usually cold, served as an appetizer at the beginning of a meal.

Indienne: A dish served in the Indian manner.

Infusion: The liquid extraction derived from steeping a substance such as coffee, tea, herbs, etc., in boiling water.

Jardiniere: Garnish of vegetables.

Julienne: Food cut into long strips. A clear soup of this name contains finely-shredded vegetables.

Junket: Milk coagulated by the addition of rennet. This makes *a* very light and digestible sweet. It can be served with fruit, and is a valuable nursery food.

Jus Gravy

Kebab: Small pieces of meat fixed on a skewer, braised or curried.

Kedgeree: Indian dish of cooked fish, often salted or smoked, with rice, eggs etc. Sometimes curried.

Kirsch: A favourite Continental drink is cafe kirsch; this is made with half a cup of black coffee and half a cup of cherry brandy, also a cherry cordial.

Knead: To work a dough lightly by bringing the outside of the dough into the centre, using the knuckles of the hand.

Kromeskils: Croquettes dipped in a yeast batter and fried.

Langoustine: A small variety of spiny lobster.

Liaison: Mixture of eggs and cream used for thickening white sauces and soups.

Larding: To place strips of fatty substance such as fat bacon on top of lean meat or on the breast of a dry bird. To run strips of fat bacon through lean meat with a larding needle.

Macaroni: An Italian pasta made of flour forced through a tube.

Macaroons: Small cakes made from almond paste, coconut, etc.

Macedoine: A mixture, usually consisting of vegetables or fruit.

Maltre d'hotel butter: A piquant sauce or butter flavoured with parsley and lemon.

Marinate: To soak meat or fish in a marinade.

Majoram: A lemon-scented herb.

Marzipan: A sweet or icing made of almonds ground to a paste with egg.

Mask: To coat a dish with sauce or line a mould with jelly.

Matignon: A mixture of finely minced carrot, celery, onion, ham, thyme and crushed bay leaf used to cover joints or poultry before being roasted or cooked to impart a good flavour.

Mayonnaise: A thick sauce made of egg yolks, oil and vinegar, mustard, etc. Used as a dressing for salads of all kinds.

Menu: List of fare.

Meringue: A mixture of stiffly beaten egg white and sugar, often used as a garnish when browned in the oven. It can be made into small sugar cakes and afterwards filled with cream.

Mignonette pepper: White peppercorns, coarsely ground.

Minestrone: Italian soup with many vegetables and macaroni added.

Mirepoix: Roughly cut onions, carrots, celery and a sprig of thyme and bay leaf.

Mise-en-place: A general name given to the elementary preparation area which is constantly resorted to during the various stages of most culinary operations.

Mocha: A flavouring usually made with a coffee infusion.

Mousse: A light spongy dish, made with sweetened and flavoured cream, then whipped .and frozen. Can also be made with a mixture of meat, vegetables, etc., mixed with gelatine.

Mousseline: Same as above but moulded in small quantities. Enough for one person at a time.

Muffin: A drop batter baked in small individual moulds and eaten hot with butter.

Navarin: Mutton or lamb stewed with turnips.

Noodles: A flour pasta served in small fancy shapes or in thin string-like tubes. Often fried in Chinese fashion.

Nougat: A sweet of a fairly rich kind made with almonds, sugar, nuts, cherries and honey.

Failles: Potato straws.

Panada: A thick paste of flour and liquid or flour and butter with a little liquid used to bind together ingredients which would fall apart by themselves. Paneer to coat in egg and breadcrumbs.

Papillate: Paper frills placed on chops for decorations. It also means food cooked in paper casings.

Parboil: To boil food until only partly cooked.

Pare: To peel. Parfait Ice-cream served in a tall glass and decorated with a variety of nuts and fruits.

Parmesan: A very hard cheese made in Italy from cow's milk. Used mainly for cooking.

Pate: Pie, pastry or raised pie, or a paste.

Paysanne: To cut into even, thin pieces, triangular or round or square.

Pimento: Red or green pepper pods used in salads or often as a colourful garnish.

Piquante: Sharply flavoured. Usually the word is applied to mustard or a sharp sauce.

Pistachio: Green-coloured nut kernels. Used as a garnish.

Plat do jour: Special dish of the day.

Pluck: To remove feathers from poultry and birds.

Poach: To cook just below boiling point in hot liquid in an open pan.

Poele: Roast done entirely or almost entirely in butter. It is a simplified process of old cookery. The joint or poultry is first fried and coated with a thick layer of matignon, wrapped in slices of pork fat covered with butter paper or aluminium foil and cooked in the oven. It is basted with melted butter during cooking.

Potage: A nourishing broth or soup.

Pot-au-feu: A beef soup made with vegetables, and poured over French bread or toast.

Potpourri: A stew of various meats and spices. Praline Burnt almond flavouring.

Pulses: Vegetables that grow in pods, e.g., peas, beans, lentils, etc.

Puree: A smooth mixture obtained by rubbing cooked fruit, vegetables, etc., through a sieve.

Quenelles: Forcemeat or meat, fish, game or poultry, pounded, rubbed through a sieve and formed into balls, then poached or fried.

Ragout: Well-flavoured meat stew. Thick, well-seasoned and rich.

Raising agents: Substances which produce a gas when acted on by heat or other substances, and make flour mixtures rise, e.g. baking powder, baking soda, yeast.

Ramekins: Individual small baking dishes.

Raspings: Very fine breadcrumbs obtained by grating stale or over,-dried bread on a fine grater.

Ratafia: A flavouring. Tiny biscuits for trifles, etc., flavoured with almonds.

Ravioli: A savoury meat mixture enclosed in dough and cooked in boiling water.

Rechauffe: A reheated dish.

Relish: A highly-seasoned food used as an accompaniment.

Rissole: A fried cake or meat or fish in a pastry case.

Roe: Eggs offish.

Rex: A thickening for soups or sauces made with flour and fat.

Royal: The name of a kind of icing.

Royale: A savoury egg custard cut into cubes and used as garnish for a soup.

Sabayon: Yolks of eggs and a little water cooked until creamy.

Saffron: The dried stigma of the crocus flower, used for adding colour and flavour.

Salmi: Partly roasted game made into a rich stew.

Sauce: A pouring mixture, sweet or savoury, to serve with, and enhance the flavour of another dish.

Saute: Toss and lightly brown in shallow fat.

Scald: To immerse food in boiling liquid for a short time. To heat a liquid (e.g. milk) to just under boiling point or to pour boiling water on (e.g. scald a jug).

Scallop: Food baked in layers with sauce and breadcrumbs.

Score: To make light cuts in a surface such as the outside of a fat piece of pork before roasting.

Sear: To form a hard coating on the surface of meat by exposing it to a fierce heat.

Seasoned flour: Flour flavoured with salt and pepper.

Sherbet: Frozen mixture of fruit juice, egg whites, sugar, milk or water.

Shortening: Fat suitable for baking is sometimes called this.

Shredded: Cut in fine strips e.g., lettuce, cabbage, etc.

Sift: To put dry ingredients through a fine sieve.

Simmer: To cook a liquid, or food in a liquid, at a temperature just below boiling point.

Singe: To brown or colour.

Skewer: A long pin of wood or metal used to secure meat or poultry while cooking.

Sorbet: A half-frozen water ice, served in the middle of a long dinner.

Souffle: Very light baked or steamed pudding, savoury or sweet, usually puffed up with egg whites.

Souse: Fish such as herrings, pickled in vinegar and spices.

Spaghetti: An Italian pasta, finer than macaroni, coarser than vermicule.

Steam: To cook in steam.

Steep: To soak in a hot or cold liquid.

Stew: To cook by simmering in a little liquid.

Stock: Well-flavoured liquid made from meat, vegetables, fish or poultry, etc., and used as a foundation for soups, sauces, stews, etc.

Supreme:.A name given to the fillet of fish or breast of fowl or game. *Table d'hote:* A set meal at a fixed price.

Tartare: A cold, sharp, savoury sauce with a base of mayonnaise served with fried fish or a meat dish.

Temperature: The degree of heat, usually measured in degrees Celsius (Centigrade) or Fahrenheit as °C or °F. Thus

Temperature of boiling water = 100°C or 212°F.

Temperature of simmering water = 85°C or 185°F.

Temperature of tepid water = 26.6°C or 80°F.

Tepid: The temperature of a mixture of 2 parts of cold water to 1 part of boiling water, i.e. about 26.6° or 80°F

Terrine: A baked, savoury meat or game mould which is cooked in the oven, usually in an earthenware dish.

Timbale: A cup-shaped mould, usually made from meat, fish or vegetables, added to a custard mixture, and finely decorated.

Tournedos: Small fillet steak cut from the middle of tenderloin (nearly 65 mm. (1/4") thick and about 6-7 cm. (2½ to $2^1/_3$") in diameter.

Tranche: A slice.

Trangon: A slice of flat fish on the bone.

Truss: To tie up or skewer a bird ready for the oven after plucking and drawing.

Tutti-frutti: Mixed fruit.

Vanilla: A flavouring generally used for cakes, ices or puddings.

Veloutes: A rich, creamy smooth sauce.

Vermicelli: A very fine Italian Pasta.

Vol-au-vent: Creamed game, meat or fish served in a pastry case.

Walewska: Garnish for fish or collops of lobster, slices of truffles.

Whisk: To beat cream or eggs until a stiff froth is obtained.

Zest: Thin outer skin of oranges and lemons. *Indian Culinary Terms*

B. INDIAN CULINARY TERMS

Akhni or Yakhni: Soup or stock.

Alu: Potato.

Amriti: A sweetmeat.

Atta: Wholemeal flour.

Baffad: A curry with meat and radish from Goa.

Baghar: Tempering done after the dish has been prepared. Onions and a few spices or herbs are fried in a spoonful of fat and added to the cooked dish to improve flavour.

Baked hilsa: An oily fish considered a delicacy. Smoked slightly--all bones removed and baked with anchovy essence, tomato sauce, salad oil, mustard, etc.

Balushai: A round ball made of dough, slightly flattened at the centre, fried and dipped in sugar syrup.

Barfi : A fudge-like sweet.

Basundi: Milk sweet.

Bhajjia: Slices of vegetables dipped in gram flour batter and fried crisp.

Bhaji: Another term for vegetable preparations.

Bhaturas: Slightly leavened bread baked on a grid and then fried. Generally served with 'Chhole', a dish prepared out of whole chickpeas.

Bhel puri: Crisp fried thin rounds of dough mixed with puffed rice, fried lentil, chopped onion, herbs and chutney.

Bhindi: Okra/gumbo, an Indian vegetable known as ladies fingers.

Bhujjia: A North Indian vegetable preparation.

Bhurta: Vegetable boiled or roasted in charcoal, peeled,

mashed and sauteed with a little chopped onion and chillies.

Biryani: A rich preparation of rice. Parboiled rice is put in layers with a rich meat or vegetable curry and the whole is baked till cooked.

Black Papper: The berry of the pepper vine dried with the skin on.

Bombay Duck: A small, phosphorescent, gelatinous fish, abundant at the surface of the salt waters of Bengal and Bombay. It is prepared fresh or dried. When dried, it is toasted crisp and served.

Bonda: Mashed potatoes, seasoned and formed into balls, dipped in batter and deep fried -- a South Indian snack.

Brinjal: Eggplant or aubergine. Also called baingan.

Cardamom: A spice--the fruit of the cardamom tree. The seeds are found in a pod which is dried. It has a pleasing taste and flavour.

Cashewnut: The nut of the cashew fruit. It is found outside the fruit, enclosed in a kidney-shaped shell.

Chapatti or Phulka: Wheat bread made of unfermented dough, round in shape and paper thin. Resembles a tortilla.

Charoli: An Indian nut.

Cheera: Amaranth leaves.

Chikkoo: A brown Indian fruit--a cross between a fig and a russet apple. Also known as sapota.

Chiwda: A mixture of nuts, fried pressed rice, fried lentils, gram preparations and spices.

Cocum: A sour fruit dried and used chiefly with fish. Acid in taste.

Coriander: A spice, the seed of a small herb. *Cumin:* A spice resembling caraway seeds.

Curry powder: A mixture of various spices such as coriander, chillies, turmeric, cumin etc., roasted and powdered together.

Custard apple: Resembles a leaf artichoke. A luscious custard-like fruit with hard black seeds inside.

Dahi: Yoghurt or curd.

Dahi Bhalla: Ground lentil, made into fried balls and then steeped in seasoned beaten yoghurt. Served with pulao or as a snack.

Dal Lentil: There is a large variety of lentils in India.

Dhansak: Literally meaning "rice & vegetables", a Parsi speciality. It is plain fried rice served with a curry rightly called "wide mouthed" as it contains an innumerable variety of ingredients--meat, lentils, vegetables, leafy vegetables, nuts and a variety of spices.

Doodh path: Sweetmeat made of rice and milk.

Do pays: Literally "twice onion". Ground and fried onion added to meat along with other spices. Hence Do (twice) and Pays (onion). It is not very hot and could form a tasty accompaniment to parathas and chapatties.

Dosa: A type of savoury pancake made with fermented batter of ground lentil and rice. Cooked on a griddle. A speciality of South India.

*Dura:*A process of cooking with heat from above as well as below.

Dum phukta: A dry rich meat dish prepared by cooking meat in pressurised steam.

Drumstick: A long type of bean with hard fibrous covering, resembling a drumstick.

Garam masala: A mixture of cloves, cinnamon, cardamom, pepper and cumin.

Gaujas: A fancy sweetmeat made of dough fried and dipped in sugar syrup.

Ghee: Clarified butter or vegetable shortening processed to resemble clarified butter.

Groundnut: Peanut or monkey-nut.

Guava: A popular fruit used to make guava cheese, jelly and stewed fruit.

Gulab: gamin Khoa or Mawa (milk evaporated to remove all moisture) is kneaded and flavoured and made into balls which are fried till golden brown and dropped immediately into hot sugar syrup.

Gustaba: Large meat balls (Kofta) in a gravy of curd, mixed with ground poppy seeds, nuts and onion, and lightly spiced.

Hing: Asafoetida, a strong flavouring agent. It also acts as a carminative.

Hopper: A counterpart of the American hot cake. For making it, the batter is fermented by the addition of toddy, an alcoholic beverage. Cooked in seasoned earthenware pots. Its subtle and pleasing flavour would appeal to all palates. Eaten with stew.

Halzva: A sweet dish made of lentils, semolina or wheat, or of vegetables such as beetroot, carrot and pumpkin, with butter, milk and sugar.

Idli: A fermented batter of ground lentil and rice steamed in moulds. A speciality of South India.

Jaggery: Refined and solidified molasses.

Jalebi: A golden-coloured, crisp sweet filled with sugar syrup, formed in rings.

Kababs: A savoury barbecue done on iron rods.

Kalia: A Bengali vegetable or fish dish with spices and yoghurt.

Kesari: A South Indian sweet dish made of vermicelli or semolina.

Kheema: Minced meat.

Kheer: A pudding-like preparation of milk with other ingredients such as rice or carrot.

Khoa Milk is boiled down till all moisture is removed, used as a base for a large number of Indian sweets.

Khorma: Rich, thickened brown curry of chicken, mutton or vegetables. Poppy seeds and desiccated coconut are added along with other condiments for thickening. The meat itself is made tender by marinading in curd (yoghurt) before cooking.

Khichdi: Mixture of rice and lentils.

Kofta: Minced meat ball.

Laddoo: A sweet ball made of gram or lentil flour, rice or semolina.

Lassi: A beverage made of beaten yoghurt diluted with water; sugar or salt may be added.

Litchi: A luscious Indian fruit. It looks like a bigger version of the strawberry and grows in Bengal, Dehra Dun and Delhi regions.

Lime: A smaller variety of lemon.

Much sharper: Loochi Bengali version of puri.

Macherjhal: A special Bengali fish curry where the fish is first fried and then curried. Mustard oil is the cooking medium used. Mackerels make excellent jhal.

Machhi: Fish.

Maida: Refined flour.

Maize: Indian corn.

Mango: A very luscious Indian fruit, which has several varieties-- Dasehri, Chausa, Langara, Alfonso, etc.

Marinate: To steep in a mixture of yoghurt or vinegar to soften.

Masala: Indian condiments and spices.

Moilee: Fish or prawn cooked in plenty of coconut milk-- lightly spiced.

Murgh Musallam: A spicy chicken preparation.

Mattar: Peas.

Mutanjan: Spiced rice with mutton sweetened with sugar. It is a speciality of Kashmir.

Mulligatawny Curry: Chicken or mutton curry with a flavour popularised in the West as Mulligatawny soup.

Nan: Indian bread made of slightly leavened dough, baked on the wall of a mud oven.

Nargisi Kofta Curry: Minced meat, mixed with spices and egg, covers a hardboiled egg (like scotch eggs) and it is fried and dropped in a spiced curry.

Neera: A non-fermented drink obtained from the coconut palm.

Pachadi: Seasoned yoghurt with vegetables--served in South India.

Palak Mutton or Palak Chicken: Meat or chicken cooked with spinach, lightly spiced and thick, without much gravy. The spinach is mashed and cooked with the meat.

Pani puri: A puff of dough fried and eaten with tamarind water and sprouted gram.

Panir: Cottage cheese made by curdling milk with lemon juice, curd etc., and the whey removed by straining and hanging in a muslin bag.

Papaya: A luscious Indian fruit; papaw or pawpaw.

Paratha: Fried bread made of unleavened wheat flour.

Plasma: A South Indian milk pudding made from cereal (such as rice or vermicelli) or pulse, and sugar.

Phirnee: A creamy milk pudding made of rice flour. Pinafore a type of white fish very popular in Bombay.

Prawn malai curry: Prawns cooked in spiced cream and coconut cream and baked in a coconut.

Pulao: A rice dish. Rice is fried in fat and cooked in stock and water.

Pulao rice: A special type of rice used in pulao -- thin and long and not as starchy as ordinary rice.

Pumpkin: A big, round vegetable of the squash variety.

Puri Deep-fried round wheat bread: About 5 cm. or 2 inches in diameter and puffed,

Quebracho: A type of meat kabab.

Rabri: Sweet, thickened milk.

Raita: Vegetable, raw or parboiled, mixed with beaten and seasoned yoghurt.

Rasam: A spicy soup made of lentils and tomatoes. Hot and sharp; served sometimes as an appetiser. A speciality of South India.

Rasgullas: Milk is curdled by the addition of curd and lime, the casein separated from whey which is then kneaded smooth and made into balls. A piece of sugar candy is usually kept in the centre. These balls are put into clarified simmering sugar syrup and cooked.

Rava: Semolina.

Reshmi chapatties: Unleavened bread resembling tortillas, but as thin as silk, and about 20 to 25 cm. or 8 to 10

inches in diameter. Baked over an upturned domelike iron vessel over live coal.

Rista: A minced meat ball curry, a speciality of Kashmir.

Rogan josh: A red curry with a thin gravy made from the leg of mutton cut with bones into fairly large pieces. The distinct flavour is that of saffron and nutmeg. Saffron is added just before removing from the fire. The red colour is obtained by the addition of saltpetre and rattanjog, a red coloured bark.

Sambar: A preparation of lentils with one or more types of vegetables-- served as a necessary accompaniment to rice in South Indian vegetarian food.

Samosa: A thin pastry cone filled with boiled or spiced vegetable or minced meat and deep fried.

Sandesh: Sweetened milk, condensed to solid form by slow cooking and flavoured.

Seekh kabab: Minced meat and spices ground together bound with egg and fixed on to a skewer and grilled.

See: A fried savoury resembling vermicelli. It is made of gram flour dough passed through a mould and deep fried till crisp.

Shami kabab: Cutlets made with minced meat and lentil.

Shrikhand: A sweet yoghurt based dish with liquid removed by straining, and flavoured with saffron and nuts.

Snake gourd: Vegetable with a long snakelike shape.

Tamarind: A sour fruit used for curries, chutneys, etc.

Tandoori Chicken or Fish: Spiced meat or fish barbecued in a specially designed tender oven.

Toddy: An alcoholic drink obtained from a variety of palm.

Turmeric: A yellow spice used for imparting a characteristic flavour and colour. The root of a plant belonging to the ginger family.

Uppuma: A savoury South Indian dish made out of semolina and lentils.

Vindaloo: A sharp and hot curry made of pork, prawn, chicken or mutton. Originated in Goa.

Wada or Pakora: A rissole of lentil or vegetable served as a snack.

Wark: Thin foil of silver or gold which is edible.

Yellow rice: Rice flavoured and coloured with saffron or turmeric.

Zarda: A sweet pulao served at the end of a meal.

Bibliography

Antil, F.H. (1984), "Career planning in the hospitality industry", *The Cornell Hotel and Restaurant Administrative Quarterly*, Vol. 25 No.1, pp. 46-52.

Arnaldo, M.J (1981), "Hotel general managers: a profile", *The Cornell Hotel and Restaurant Administrative Quarterly*, Vol. 22 No.3, pp. 53-6.

Arnold, J, Robertson, I.T, Cooper, G.L (1991), "Career choice and development", *Work Psychology: Understanding Human Behaviour in the Workplace*, Pitman, London, pp. 265-82.

Arthur, M.B, Hall, D.T, Lawrence, B.S (1989), *Handbook of Career Theory*, Cambridge University Press, Cambridge.

Bentivenger, A, Sluder, L (1989), "Hotel GMs bring diverse background to the job", *Lodging*, Vol. 14 No.10, pp. 61-2.

Brownell, J. (1992), "Personality and career development", *The Cornell Hotel and Restaurant Administrative Quarterly*, Vol. 35 No.2, pp. 36-43.

Carper, J (1993), "The painful truth: operations is no longer King", *Hotels*, Vol. 50.

Chartrand, J.M, Camp, C.C (1991), "Advancements in the measurement of career development constructs: a 20-year construct", *Journal of Vocational Behaviour*, Vol. 39 No.2, pp. 1-39.

Clark, M (1993), "Communications and social skills: perceptions of hospitality managers", *Employee Relations*, Vol. 15 No.2, pp. 51-60.

Cooper, C., Westlake, J. (1998), "Stakeholders and tourism education", *Industry and Higher Education.*

Cracknell, H.L., Kaufmann R.J., Nobis, G. (1983), *Practical Professional Catering* , Macmillan, Basingstoke, pp. 22.

Dex, S (1991), *Life and Work History Analyses: Qualitative and Quantitative Developments*, Routledge, London.

Doswell, R., Gamble, P.R. (1979), *Marketing and Planning Hotels and Tourism Projects*, Hutchinson, London, pp. 19-20.

Gamble, P.R, Lockwood, A, Messenger, S (1994), "European management skills in the hospitality industry", University of Surrey.

Guerrier, Y, Lockwood, A (1989), "Developing hotel managers - a reappraisal", *International Journal of Hospitality Management*, Vol. 8 No.2, pp. 82-9.

Guerrier, Y, Lockwood, A (1990), "Managers in hospitality: a review of current research", *Progress in Tourism, Recreation and Hospitality Research*, Vol. 2 pp. 151-67.

Guerrier, Y. (1987), "Hotel managers' careers and their impact on hotels in Britain", *International Journal of Hospitality Management*, Vol. 6 No.3, pp. 121-30.

Harris, N. (1989), *Service Operations Management*, Cassell, London, pp. 3.

Hay, J (1990), "Managerial competencies or managerial characteristics", *Journal of Management Education and Development*, Vol. 21 No.5, pp. 305-15.

Haywood, K.M (1987), "Thoughts on thinking: a critical human resource skill", *The Cornell Hotel and Restaurant Administrative Quarterly*, Vol. 28 No.2, pp. 51-5.

Hicks, H.G., Gullett, C.R. (1976), *The Management of Organisations*, 3rd International Studen Edition, McGraw-Hill Kogakusha Ltd, Tokyo, pp. 13.

Hicks, L (1990), "Excluded women: how can this happen in the hotel world?", *Service Industries Journal*, Vol. 10 No.2, pp. 348-63.

Hill, T. (1983), *Production / Operations Management*, Prentice-Hall, Englewood Cliffs, NJ.

Howard, B. (1992), *Operations Management*, Macmillan, Basingstoke, pp. 1.

Hsu, J.F, Gregory, S (1995), "Developing future hotel managers in Taiwan: from an industry viewpoint", *International Journal of Hospitality Management*, Vol. 14 No.3/4, pp. 261-9.

Ladkin, A, Riley, M (1996), "Mobility and structure in the career paths of UK hotel general managers: a labour market hybrid of the bureaucratic model?", *Tourism Management*, Vol. 17 No.6, pp. 443-52.

Lee, S.M., Schniederjans, M.J. (1994), *Operations Management*, Houghton Mifflin Company, Boston, MA, pp. 3.

Messenger, S. (1991), "The UK hospitality and tourism industry: an overview of the issues affecting the supply of education and training in the 1990s", *Progress in Tourism, Recreation and Hospitality Management*, Vol. 3 pp. 247-63.

Nebel, E.C.III, Braunlich, C.G, Zhang, Y (1994), "Career paths in American luxury hotels: hotel food and beverage directors", *International Journal of Contemporary Hospitality Management*, Vol. 6 No.6, pp. 3-9.

Nightingale, M. (1985), " The hospitality industry: defining quality for a quality assurance programme - a study in perceptions", *Service Industries Journal*, Vol. 5 No.1, pp. 9-22.

O'Driscoll, M.P, Humphries, M, Larsen, H.H (1991), "Managerial activities, competencies and effectiveness: manager and subordinate perceptions",

International Journal of Human Resources Management, Vol. 3 No.2, pp. 313-26.

Pavesic, D.V (1993), "Hospitality education 2005: curricular and programmatic trends", *Hospitality Research Journal*, Vol. 17 No.1, pp. 285-94.

Ruddy, J (1990), "Patterns of hotel management development in South East Asia", *Hospitality Research Journal*, Vol. 14 No.2, pp. 349-61.

Ruddy, J. (1989), "Career development of hotel managers in Hong Kong", *International Journal of Hospitality Management*, Vol. 8 No.3, pp. 215-25.

Slack, N. (1983), "Operations management and curriculum design", *Management Education and Development*, Vol. 14 No.1, pp. 19-32.

Tarpey, D (1991), "Mind your language", *Caterer and Hotelkeeper*, Vol. 184 No.3691, pp. 40-42.

Tas, R.E (1988), "Teaching future managers", *The Cornell Hotel and Restaurant Administration Quarterly*, Vol. 29 No.2, pp. 41-3.

Vollman, T.E. (1973), *Operations Management*, Addison-Wesley, Reading, MA.

Wild, R. (1984), *Production and Operations Management. Principles and Techniques*, 3rd, Holt, Rinehart and Winston, London, pp. 276.

Index